PRAISE FOR

"*Tomboyland* is everything I want an essay collection to be: beautiful, smart, difficult, honest, hopeful, and haunting, just like the experiences it depicts. It is a book that charts the history of a body against the land that defines it. It is a song for anyone who felt at once estranged and inextricably bound to a place. Melissa Faliveno has written a gorgeously complex ode to the Midwest that is destined to be passed urgently from hand to hand, an anthem sung by all the misfits in those vast places who have not yet seen themselves written."

—Melissa Febos, author of *Whip Smart* and *Abandon Me*

"*Tomboyland*, Melissa Faliveno's excellent collection of essays on growing up in Wisconsin and then beyond it, will give many people permission to be who they are and to write into and about where they're from. It will also show you how and when to leave that place, and how you can't ever leave it completely. Each essay carries Faliveno's Wisconsin inside it and made me want to lift weights in a dingy gym, welcome a moth infestation, kick ass at softball, rewatch *Twister*, and even visit Mount Horeb, the 'Troll Capital of the World.' If it can work on me this fast, I can only imagine what this book will do to you."

—Ander Monson, author of *I Will Take the Answer* and
Neck Deep and Other Predicaments

"These essays showcase, via hard-won displays, a twenty-first-century mind working to understand itself. Among the many treats of *Tomboyland* is how Melissa Faliveno's self-investigation doesn't just look inward to memory, experience, or feelings. Over the course of this book, she also looks externally in her quest for personal knowledge—turning to archives, interviews, and journalistic immersion. Such an extensive and dogged scope shows both how unique and how interconnected a single life can be. In Faliveno's deft hands, we experience all that builds a consciousness— food and sex and softball, dark bars and sprawling landscapes, roller derbies and deep conversations, and the F5 tornado that is human love."
      —Elena Passarello, author of *Animals Strike Curious Poses*

"In these smartly constructed, urgently delivered essays on class, gender, violence, rage, love, and sexuality—issues as entwined in these pages as they are in life—Melissa Faliveno brilliantly scrutinizes our most contemporary, most vital questions of self and culture. I didn't just read *Tomboyland*, I scribbled in its pages, photographed its passages, pressed it on friends, and felt an urgent need to talk about it. It will spark conversations that will become conflagrations. *Tomboyland* is a blaze of a book, as fiery and expansive as the Midwestern sky."
      —Alex Marzano-Lesnevich, author of *The Fact of a Body*

"I felt Melissa Faliveno's Midwest on a gut level—its F5 tornadoes, its rolling prairies, its bighearted people working their asses off. I grew up here, but it's okay if you didn't; *Tomboyland* will show you, tangling your body in place and the overwhelming need to both go back home and get the hell out. Faliveno's deeply felt and deeply researched essays— part personal narrative, part cultural criticism—feature softballs and guns, dresses and babies and bondage. They interrogate gender and expectations, what it means to be a family, to build a home in this beautiful mess of a world. My brain is still buzzing. So is my heart."
      —Megan Stielstra, author of *The Wrong Way to Save Your Life*

"In *Tomboyland*, Melissa Faliveno examines the spaces, selves, histories, and futures that live in the distance between binaries: between the bodies we have and the ones we claim, between the homes that have made us and those we have made for ourselves. This is a remarkable debut. I am grateful for the arrival of this bold new voice."

—Lacy M. Johnson, author of *The Reckonings*

"*Tomboyland* works through unlikely juxtaposition—tornadoes alongside God, vegetarianism alongside kink, guns alongside love. It is a coming-of-age story where everything is examined, everything is questioned, where the word *driftless* is both a region and a state of mind. At one point Faliveno's mother, while cooking meat, states, 'If I think about it, then I have to look at my whole life.' Faliveno takes this as a challenge, as she builds a life for us before our eyes. It is, in the end, about the nature of relationships, of love, of being alive."

—Nick Flynn, author of *Another Bullshit Night in Suck City* and *The Ticking Is the Bomb*

TOM
BOY
LAND

TOM

ESSAYS

BOY

MELISSA FALIVENO

LAND

TOPPLE
BOOKS

Little
a

Excerpt from *The Carrying* by Ada Limón used with permission from Milkweed Editions.

Excerpt from *Zami: A New Spelling of My Name* by Audre Lorde. Copyright © 1982 by Audre Lorde. Published by Crossing Press, Trumansburg, NY.

Published by Little A/TOPPLE Books, New York

www.apub.com

Amazon, the Amazon logo, Little A, and TOPPLE Books are trademarks of Amazon.com, Inc., or its affiliates.

ISBN-13: 9781542014199 (hardcover)
ISBN-10: 1542014190 (hardcover)

ISBN-13: 9781542014182 (paperback)
ISBN-10: 1542014182 (paperback)

Cover design by Micaela Alcaino

Printed in the United States of America

First edition

For my grandmothers: Mary Irene, original tomboy,
who gave me a love of the land, and Louise,
who gave me a name.

The way seemed shorter in the dark than in the day.

—Virginia Woolf, *The Voyage Out*

Table of Contents

A NOTE FROM TOPPLE BOOKS

What defines us? Is it our bodies? Or is it our *selves*? From the open fields of the American Midwest to the tight quarters of a Brooklyn metropolis, Melissa Faliveno's *Tomboyland* is a daring collection that confronts how both place and notions of gender shape us. Through devastating and deadly turns of weather, an F5 tornado, guns, and BDSM potlucks, Melissa explores the boundaries of land, safety, intimacy, and personhood, asking who we might all choose to be if we knew we'd be received with love and acceptance.

This is a book for those among us who can't be defined and those who don't want to be. A book that asks: What is family, and who can make one? Illuminating the intersections of class, desire, land, and how we make the bodies we've been given truly ours, *Tomboyland* strikes the heart of the TOPPLE ethos. With compassion and clarity, Melissa writes her readers into a landscape of belonging, courage, and visibility, and she does more than invite you into her world. Once there, she builds a home for you too.

—Jill Soloway, TOPPLE Books editor-at-large

AUTHOR'S NOTE

This is a work of nonfiction, which relies in no small part on memory—my own and others'—that most fallible and unreliable of narrators. With the help of extensive research, interviews, and fact-checking, I've attempted to tell the stories in this book—my own and others'—as honestly as possible, to tell the truth as far as I could find it. Some names and details have been changed to protect the people in these pages.

THE FINGER OF GOD

You have not come to a mountain that can be touched and
that is burning with fire; to darkness, gloom and storm.

—Hebrews 12:18

*I*t was a warm night in early June—the midwestern kind of warm specific to
spring, so humid it's hard to breathe—when a tornado struck and destroyed
a small Wisconsin town eight miles west of my own. I was just over a year old.
My mother, who was not yet thirty, younger than I am now and still figuring
out how to parent her only child, came into my bedroom as I slept. She stood at
the window, looking out into the darkness of the west. It was the same window
through which I would look for years to come, whenever the clouds began to
build—my face and fingers pressed to the glass, cranking it open to get a better
look at the sky. But that night, it was my mother who watched.

It was sometime after midnight.

Maybe the wind was howling. Maybe there was thunder. Maybe, more
likely, there was only silence—that still, strange calm Midwesterners know
so well, the kind that heralds the most violent of storms.

And then my mother saw them: fast, bright sparks of green, a second or
two apart—like flashbulbs in the distance against the dark. It took her a
few seconds to realize what she was seeing: a massive tornado, invisible in
the black of the night, striking each pole of the power lines that ran along
the highway—a road that connected a small doomed town and our own.

Soon she would pick me up, press my body to her chest, and hurry us down to the room beneath the stairs, where we would huddle together and wait out the storm. But for a second or two, she just stood in the dark, looking out into the night—struck still with fear, and maybe wonder, unsure if she was awake or dreaming—as a great, unstoppable force tore through a sleeping town, destroying everything in its path.

~

It was June 8, 1984. The town was called Barneveld, and the tornado—the largest in Wisconsin history—was an F5. On the Fujita Scale (since renamed the Enhanced Fujita Scale), which rates the intensity of a tornado from zero to five based on wind speeds and the severity of damage—from "minor" to "total destruction"—the F5 is the largest, rarest, and most powerful tornado. It carries winds of up to three hundred miles per hour and can stretch a mile in width. It has the power to rip entire houses off their foundations, crush steel-reinforced concrete like it's tin. It can pluck trees and livestock from the land and toss them into the sky; throw cars, trucks, tractors, and train cars a mile away. The F5 is dangerous, unpredictable, and unforgiving—a force of nature so destructive, so incomprehensibly powerful, that even the most scientifically minded among us can't help but think it biblical.

In the '90s action movie *Twister*, a group of storm chasers—led by Helen Hunt and the late Bill Paxton—pause around a dinner table in the Oklahoma stretch of Tornado Alley when someone asks what an F5 is like. Commotion at the table ceases; conversation comes to a halt; forks are placed gravely onto plates. One of the elder chasers on the team, a character nicknamed Preacher, stops in his tracks as he serves up a round of coffees. Stock still and serious, he says:

It's the finger of God.

I grew up in a small, God-fearing town in southern Wisconsin called Mount Horeb. A blue-collar place dealing in livestock feed and John Deere tractors, it was a farm town on its way to becoming a suburb, with a population back then of around three thousand. Mount Horeb is perched on a hill, surrounded on all sides by long, rolling fields of corn and wheat and soy. About eight miles to the west is Barneveld, a sister town; the two communities share feed mills, farmland, and a lumber co-op, congregations, families, and a high school football team. Between the two towns are the Blue Mounds, a stretch of low, tree-dotted mountains—a geological anomaly in that part of the state, in a region known as the Driftless Area—housing a network of caves beneath them. As kids, we were told that the mountains protected our little town like a castle's defensive wall: from storms, from spirits, from whatever dangers might come our way. We were told that there was something about the Blue Mounds—some inexplicable property of physics, maybe; something magical or even godlike—that kept Mount Horeb safe from tornadoes. If a tornado was moving in from the west, they said, the Mounds would stop it. The Mounds would protect us.

Mount Horeb takes its name from the Torah—specifically, from the book of Deuteronomy—as the mountain upon which God relayed the Ten Commandments to Moses. Though in the Christian Old Testament the mountain in question is Sinai, the pastor of our small Lutheran church returned to these biblical origins sometimes, reminding us during his sermons that the name of our little town meant "The Mountain of God."

My parents were both raised Catholic—my mother the oldest of eight, a fourth-generation Wisconsinite in an Irish-Catholic farm family, and my father the youngest of four, a second-generation Italian from New Jersey. There's a good chance some of my maternal relatives were Jewish, but because my great-grandmother was adopted—and because our family is so massive that the wires of shared history are constantly getting crossed, our stories told and retold like a generations-long game of telephone—no one knows for sure. (For years, above my grandparents' fireplace there hung a portrait of my great-great-aunt, a woman named Ida Feldman; my late grandfather, a GM line worker whose Swiss surname was Neuenschwander, famously insisted our family was neither German nor Jewish.) I was baptized Catholic, but when I was young my parents grew tired of fire and brimstone. They had both gone to Catholic school—had been put in coat closets, had their knuckles rapped with rulers by nuns, had been told too many times they were doomed to hell—and they wanted something different for me. So, like all good Midwesterners, we became Lutherans.

I went to church every Sunday, sang in the choir, and went to Sunday school until I left home at eighteen. I was confirmed at thirteen, which required two years of classes led by a young pastor and former UPS driver in the musty church basement on Wednesday nights—one particularly rigorous unit involved deconstructing Joan Osborne's chart-topping 1995 pop hit, "One of Us." I was in a youth group, part of a national organization I'd find out later had been sued at least once for employing cultlike recruiting tactics. In this club, or maybe cult, which was a signifier of both virtuousness and popularity in our small hometown, I sang songs about Jesus and the importance of abstinence. I listened to the older kids (called "leaders") give talks about avoiding temptations like drinking and drugs and sex. I eventually became a leader, too, and gave the same kind of talks about the same temptations—even as I, like so many kids in that group, was enthusiastically partaking in them.

I went to Christian camp every summer, where we assembled each night in August-hot theaters while well-groomed, white college kids paced around a stage with microphones spouting sermons disguised as personal stories of self-destruction and redemption. They played acoustic guitars and sang songs about Jesus, and invited us to stand up and commit ourselves to Christ. When I was sixteen, we went on a weeklong hiking trip in the Colorado Rockies. I carried a fifty-pound pack on my back, hip bones bloody from the pack digging into my skin, and was awoken one morning before dawn and instructed to find a large rock, carry it to the top of a nearby peak, and hurl it into the chasm below. This, they said, represented my sins, which I could cast off into the proverbial abyss only when I let the Lord and Savior into my heart. I climbed to the top of the mountain as the sun came up, raised my arms above my head, and launched the rock from that peak—casting off my teenage-girl sins, which back then seemed taller than the mountains. On the last night of the trip, I was led out into the forest and left there to spend the night alone. With only my sleeping bag, a Bible, and a flashlight, I was told to ponder the power of Jesus's protection. At some point, as I sat trembling in fear of bears, praying to God to make the morning come faster, my flashlight battery died.

I came home filled with Jesus's love. Using the green-screened IBM in our basement—still a few years away from that hallowed new treasure of dial-up internet, which I would eventually use to spelunk *X-Files* fansites and hunt-and-peck late-night messages in chat rooms to some nameless boy in Potosi—I typed up bible verses and printed them out, then taped them to my bedroom walls. But even as I proselytized to my bewildered family, even as I wore a sterling silver Jesus fish on my finger like an engagement ring, even as I listened to DC Talk and Jars of Clay, even as I prayed each night, I'm not sure I ever really believed. In a small town, the promises of religion are the language of protection, and I was being promised unconditional love—just as my body, and my very existence as a girl, had begun to betray me. Just as my desires had begun to consume me. Just as I was being taught to believe those desires were wrong, that they would mark me irreparably as both sinner and slut. So I swallowed the words that were taught to me at church, and at those Christian summer camps, like Communion. I tried my best to believe them. For a while, maybe I convinced myself I did.

What I believed in, through it all, was the weather. What I mean is I revered the weather, in all its volatility and power, as I knew I was supposed to revere God. In particular, I revered tornadoes. I could never really explain what it was about tornadoes that had a hold on me, but I knew it mirrored the fervor of faith they wanted us to adopt in church: an awe-inspired, fear-induced belief in something beyond my capacity to comprehend. I had never seen a tornado, but I knew one could strike at any time. I feared and exalted tornadoes. I worshipped them. I considered their ability to destroy—and in some cases to pardon—something holy.

I was nine or ten when the obsession began. This was the dawn of a strange and inexplicable few years in my small-girl life when I couldn't be interested in anything without becoming consumed by it. I was obsessed with the weather like I was obsessed with Pogs and pewter dragons fused to amethyst, with the Beatles and *The Kids in the Hall* and Andrew Lloyd Webber's *CATS* soundtrack. I tore through books about tornadoes, first at the public library and then at the Waldenbooks in the mall, thirty minutes away in Madison, where my mother and I drove on weekends. We spent hours in that tiny chain bookstore, where I snaked from the horror section to the nonfiction aisle, sitting on the floor with a stack of Christopher Pike and R. L. Stine and whatever slick new odes to destruction I could find.

I studied tornadoes. I learned how to prepare. I read about meteorology, weather patterns, the clashing of warm front and cold. I read about the jet stream, low-pressure systems, dew points, and super cells; about cumulous, cumulonimbus, and funnel clouds; about rotation, radars, and lead time—the number of minutes, or more often seconds, between warning and touchdown. I read about the static currents survivors said they could feel in their skin, about the green of the sky, the electric smell in the air—like a lightning-struck power line or a live wire. I read under the covers in bed with a flashlight. I read the words of scientists and storm chasers and meteorologists, who spoke, like prophets, of the warming of the earth, who warned of the coming years and the severity of storms that would only get worse.

A few years later, when my friends and I were buying *Teen Beat* and *Bop* from the grocery store and hanging centerfolds of the Backstreet Boys and Leonardo DiCaprio and Jonathan Taylor Thomas on our walls, I developed a crush on the local television meteorologist. His name was David George, and he was a pale middle-aged man with round cheeks and gray hair, thin lips and a Texas accent. I worshipped David and watched his forecasts religiously—sometimes, in the spring and summer during peak tornado season, all three nightly newscasts at five, six, and ten o'clock. When I was fourteen, my parents procured a glossy autographed headshot of the NBC 15 chief meteorologist himself and gave it to me as a Christmas present. I taped it up next to Leo and JTT, and each night before bed I admired their faces in the glow of my night-light—these androgynous boys and one cherubic middle-aged man. I wished them all good night and said a little prayer to David for keeping me safe.

If a tornado was the finger of God, then what did you call the man who predicted God's hand? David George was a prophet of severe weather. He offered not just protection but a sense of control just when I started becoming aware of my lack of it. Adolescence had become its own kind of storm system, volatile and unpredictable: My body's boyish build had begun to shift course, budding breasts and bleeding, and I began to realize that even the sturdiest structures, like family and home, could be blown away in an instant. I latched on to David as a strange kind of constant. Tornadoes were both childhood monster and wrath of God, and David told me when they would come. Standing against his green screen, hands following the invisible path of the jet stream, he told me when the humidity was rising, when the barometer was falling, when the low-pressure systems were careening toward the high. He told me when we were under a watch or a warning. He stayed up with me on summer nights, when the watches lasted well into the early-morning hours. He kept me updated on each cell's location, which direction it was heading, and what towns were in its path. A soothsayer, preparing us for who and what we might grieve, he told me the speed of straight-line winds, the diameter of hail, if a funnel had been spotted, and where it might touch down. He charted a path on the Doppler radar, a new technology then, to track the storm's trajectory. He said, "Get to the basement." He warned, "Find a windowless interior room." The way parents' nagging reminders hinted at their love, he said, "Take your flashlight, your radio, have extra batteries on hand." He sat with me, tie loosened, as long as the power stayed on and the station stayed on the air—even as the winds rippled waves across my twelve-inch TV screen. He stayed by my side while my parents slept, the two of them convinced the sirens would save us.

Twister was released in 1996, when I was thirteen. I saw the movie twice in theaters and owned a copy on VHS that I watched until the tape wore out and the picture on our tube TV began to wobble and wave like it did during a storm. I was fascinated by the idea of Oklahoma and Kansas, the dark heart of Tornado Alley. I dreamed of being a storm chaser, me and a crack team of scientists who might develop the ability to see inside a tornado—so we might better understand the storms and build better warning systems. So we might protect sleeping towns like Barneveld. It wasn't enough to be saved; I wanted to be the savior.

In its opening week, *Twister* brought in over $41 million, making it the number one blockbuster in North America (second only that summer to *Independence Day*). It went on to earn over $500 million, was played constantly on the USA Network, and was quickly dubbed a New American Classic. But Roger Ebert gave it just a startling two and a half stars, calling it "loud" and "dumb," and most other critics panned it, bemoaning the special effects taking a front seat in the proverbial storm-chasing pickup truck to character development and plot. On Rotten Tomatoes, the movie boasts a lousy 57 percent rating. When asked, meteorologists and storm chasers will still roll their eyes and tell you that, in terms of the movie's science, it's mostly bullshit.

I loved it. More than twenty years later, I still love it. On a recent rewatch (which I do at least once a year, typically at the height of tornado season), I discovered that even though I know the movie by heart, it still fills me with certain dread. I'm still terrified as Bill and Jo drive headlong into each storm, cows swooping by and oil tankers exploding in their path. It's a ridiculous movie, and of course I know every time how it will end: impossibly—with Bill and Jo strapped to a pipe in the middle of a pasture, swinging in the wind in the dead center of an F5 and miraculously surviving. But during those 113 ridiculous minutes, I'm still gripped by the possibilities the movie entertains. I'm still held fast by both the fear and the thrill of it. I'm still convinced that I, too, could survive an F5.

When I was a kid, I was enamored with Paxton's Bill Harding, who I perceived to be the hero of the film. He was stoic, like all good Midwesterners. He was serious, straitlaced, and smart, with no time for the hijinks of his fellow storm chasers, least of all his estranged wife, Jo, played by an obsessed and somewhat unhinged Helen Hunt. Jo was smart, but she was also unstable; she was wild and willful and reckless. Where Bill was solid, Jo was erratic. She was volatile. She was crazy, says Bill's new fiancée—the craziest one of them all. She was a woman who ran directly into the storm, despite the desperate protestations of the men in her crew, who banged her fists against the chest of a man who wanted to protect her—from harm, from nature, from herself. She is woman as fable, as harbinger: We're meant to be in awe of her, to marvel at her tenacity. But we're also meant to fear her. We watch, face in fists, as she screams into the wind and storms away; we watch in the end, with relief, as she is held at last in the arms of the man who loves her—who keeps her safe from the storm.

It wasn't until recently that I understood Jo had been the hero all along. With her unruly hair and dirt-stained clothes, her khakis that were almost certainly stuffed with pens and a small notebook and a compass and a knife and an assortment of tools I didn't even know about, her boyish mannerisms and short, androgynous name (unlike Bill's new fiancée, a nice proper woman named, horribly, Melissa), she was everything I wanted to be. Jo was a woman who carried both an all-encompassing fear and the obsession born of it, both desire and the pain from which it was created—a burden and a torch that burned in her and carried her forward, which a girl like me might have noticed had she only looked closely enough. Had she only possessed the tools to see.

I n the Midwest, people talk about the weather. It's the first topic to spring from our lips when we pick up the phone, when we step inside a friend's house for dinner, when we gather for a backyard barbecue. It's in the kitchen as we wash dishes, on living room couches as we "have a set" at the holidays. It's in talk of vacations and weekend plans, softball games and golf tournaments, the corn fest and the county fair. It's part of every conversation, a backdrop to everything we do. If it's going to rain, if it's calling for storms, the wind that split the birch in two. *Thank God it didn't hit the house,* we say. The lakes are low, the rivers high, the wheat is getting dry. *It's the humidity,* we say, *not the heat.* It's become something of a joke, but it has serious roots. For in the Midwest, the weather is volatile. It's unpredictable. A blue sky can change in a second to green. And so we look to the sky because the sky is the only reliable predictor of what might come. Perhaps especially for families like mine, whose livelihood was once tied directly to the crops, the weather is more influential than anything, more powerful than God himself. It can mean the difference between a good season and a bad one, having food on the table or not. For some farmers, it has literally meant life or death. So we keep thermometers and barometers and rain gauges nailed to our decks, stuck to the sides of our houses. We keep watch as those needles rise and fall, and we look to the sky with hope, with anticipation, with fear. We pray for rain, and we pray for it to stop. We pray to be spared from the wind.

"Going green," Bill says, his eyes to the sky, just before a tornado hits.

"Greenage," says Dusty, played by the late Philip Seymour Hoffman. Two ghosts waiting for a monster. He's giddy when he says it.

Tornado season changes depending on which part of the country you're in. In Wisconsin, the heart of the season stretches from March through July. Most tornadoes hit in the summer, between 3:00 p.m. and 9:00 p.m., but they can strike at any time, with little or no warning. The siren system works by county, and in Mount Horeb the tower is located near a softball field where I played summer games as a kid. It stands, a massive obelisk of cloud-gray steel, speakers on all sides—both beacon and warning, a promise of protection and a reminder of things to come.

In our small public school, we had tornado drills: A voice would crackle through speakers, telling us a warning had been issued, that we should leave our classrooms in an orderly fashion and follow our teachers to the designated shelter. It could be a hallway or the gym. It could be a bathroom or locker room. We sat on the floor against steel lockers, legs drawn to chests, told to take cover until the threat had expired. These drills were never frightening; they were thrilling. It was exciting to be crammed into a tight, dark space with your friends, with the boys and girls you had crushes on. There was something romantic about it. What if a tornado actually hit? We'd whisper, our small arms and legs brushing together, goose bumps rising up on flesh, huddled on the cold tile floor. What if the roof blew off the school, like it had in Barneveld, and we got sucked up into the sky? These wild fascinations of children, a fantasy of physics, like Dorothy spinning through the air on her bed, but never the possibility of death. We'd giggle and shiver in the windowless hallways, sure that the stone walls of the school would protect us.

The thing about tornadoes is they're still something of a mystery. What's funny is that, despite *Twister*'s tenuous science, its plot was inspired by actual meteorological experiments in the 1970s and 1980s— where DOROTHY was TOTO, an instrumented metal drum meant to be deposited in a tornado from the bed of a pickup truck. TOTO was never quite successful, but in recent years meteorologists have developed similar, and more effective, experiments to study twisters—all hinged on the idea of putting instruments of measurement directly in the path of a storm to better understand how it works and develop better warning systems. At the heart of it all, there's an obsession—the same one Jo and Bill had, that all storm chasers have—that's not unlike faith: the desire to know something unknowable, to understand this deadly miracle, this unpredictable and awe-inspiring act of nature, this mechanism of fate, this impossible act of God.

M y hometown has a thing for mythology. Settled mostly by Norwegians, Mount Horeb is known as the "Troll Capital of the World." We called it Mount Horrible when we were kids, but now, having lived far away for so long, I appreciate the strangeness of the town. If one were driving along Main Street, a single-stoplight stretch known as "the Trollway," one would behold more than a dozen statues of trolls carved out of tree stumps. Each troll is about four feet tall, and there's one on almost every block. The troll outside the telephone company plays an accordion; the troll outside an 1895 Queen Anne is a gardener. There's a tooth fairy troll, a carp fisher troll, a troll with a chicken on its head. There's a peddler troll, a tourist troll, a troll on a tricycle. They're ugly things, with large proboscises, straggly hair, and mischievous grins, that a local woodworker has carved from maples and oaks since the 1980s. His trolls were preceded by those of a Norwegian artist named Oljanna Cunneen, who started painting and installing plywood trolls around town in the 1960s. The relevance of the trolls to

Mount Horeb is a topic of local debate, but one theory suggests that the immigrants who settled the area believed the creatures—who, according to Scandinavian folklore, dwell in mountains and possess magical, prophetic powers—lived in the Blue Mounds and protected us from evil. Some of the tree-stump trolls have rotted, and some have been cut down. Others still stand, sentries for the town.

There's a murky line between story and myth. When I was a kid, my mother told me stories about tornadoes. She told me the story of the Barneveld tornado, the worst she'd ever known, and about tornadoes of her youth. She told these stories so often I felt like I had been there: watching those fast sparks of green through my bedroom window, watching a twister dance across a cornfield, scrambling for storm cellars, hacking at latches and hauling open heavy wooden doors, running down muddy stairs and hiding underground until the storm had passed. She told me decades-old tales that her mother and grandmother had told before her—of towns and trees and trailer parks demolished and others left untouched. She told me of the skies turning green, and she told me of the sound—like a freight train, she said, its low groan in the distance, growing louder and higher to a deafening teakettle whistle.

She told me of the tornado that hit her grandparents' farm, just outside Monroe, and of picking through the wreckage afterward: finding a potted plant that had been lifted from the porch, carried a few hundred feet, then set back down in a nearby field—upright, undamaged, the soil and leaves intact. And she told me the story that had gone down in family lore for generations, that would carry on with each new one—about a single blade of straw that had been lifted and tossed from a nearby barn and had somehow, impossibly, pierced the glass of a sliding glass door.

I wondered about this story—about the physics of it, if such a thing was even possible. I wondered if the story had been misremembered or made up entirely. If it began as a story to spook children around a campfire in the summer, and eventually, somewhere along the unreliable line of memory and time, had become the truth. I wondered about other stories too: if tornadoes actually sounded like freight trains, like everyone always said; if debris could be carried hundreds of miles away; if cars could end up on top of houses—or if these stories, like the blade of straw, were just tall tales that had become the truth over time. Or perhaps they had become something even more true than the truth, the way stories often do—when tales of fear and fragility, of warning and awe, function to protect or prepare us for danger.

I could have researched these stories, but I never did. I chose to let them live on, as my mother and my grandmother told them, as my family remembered them. I chose to believe them.

In the house where I grew up, a 1960s split-level ranch, we didn't have a storm cellar. No small stone fortress buried in the backyard, like young Jo had on her family farm in *Twister*, no fortified cavern like the one beneath my grandmother's house—a dirt-floored root cellar where she kept her canned goods next to the boiler. We had only a partial basement, halfway underground, with a dozen ground-level windows.

In a land so at risk of severe weather, it's strange that so many houses were built this way. It seems almost like defiance, as if saying to the weather, *I dare you.* Maybe it's willful ignorance. *It couldn't possibly happen to us.* Or maybe it has something to do with hope—that tragedy will keep its distance, that God will keep us safe.

There was a closet beneath the stairs. A small windowless passage packed with old luggage, tangled Christmas lights, piles of Sears shirt boxes, a curtain of musty coats on a rod, and a single bare light bulb on a chain. This was where we went, our small family of three—heads ducked low, backs bent at odd angles against sloping walls, the cat unwillingly clutched to my chest—when the sirens went off, when the watches turned to warnings. And this, back in 1984, long before my obsession with the weather began, was where my mother would take me after plucking me from my crib, when those green flashes in the distance got closer, when the wind began to bend the trees.

~

Technically, Barneveld was not a town. In 1984, with a population of only 580, it was designated, like Mount Horeb, a village. A speck, a spark, an almost indiscernible flash tucked away in the hills and valleys of southwestern Wisconsin. It was home to farmers, factory workers, waitresses and bartenders, hairdressers, mechanics, roofers and plumbers. It had a farm equipment dealership—referred to simply as "the implement." It had a feed mill, which was just about to hold its grand opening. Most of Barneveld's inhabitants had been born there, had grown up there, had families of their own there. Most of their parents and siblings lived there, too, sometimes in the same farmhouses that had been in their families for generations.

On the evening of June 7, the people of Barneveld might have walked back to their houses from their barns, having finished the evening chores. They might have closed up the implement or grocery store, the post office or bank, gotten into their trucks just as the clouds were beginning to build. They might have noticed the wind picking up; they might have noticed a stillness in the air. They probably all noticed it was humid—the air so thick they could slice it open. They might have turned the radio dial to get a better signal as they drove toward home. It might have been fuzzy out there, just over the western border of the Blue Mounds, where the signal was never great. They might have flipped on the TV when they got home to catch the forecast before dinner.

In 1984 there was no Doppler radar, no David George. There was a kindly old weatherman named Elmer who wore slick suits and patterned ties and talked about the weather the way most Wisconsinites did back then, and how many still do—in terms of how it might affect the crops. *You might hear some thunder tonight,* he might have said with a smile. *So batten down those hatches. But it'll mean good news for the corn!* After the ten o'clock newscast, there was no one at the station with their eyes toward the sky. And when the airwaves went dark, there was only silence—but for the black crackling fuzz of a deadened television screen.

It was a Thursday. Earlier that day, by midafternoon, severe storms had developed across Kansas, Missouri, Minnesota, and Iowa—part of a system that would go on to produce an outbreak of forty-six confirmed tornadoes in less than a day, including three F3s and one F4 that traveled over a hundred miles from northern Missouri into Iowa, killing three people. After dark, the storm shifted toward Wisconsin—and at around 11:00 p.m., the National Weather Service issued a tornado watch. This might have taken the form of a few long, loud tones on the radio had anyone been listening. It might have been a scrolling red ticker on the bottom of a television screen or a small cartoonish outline of a tornado in the bottom right-hand corner. But at that time of night, after Johnny Carson's monologue, most people had turned off their TVs and gone to bed.

The sirens never sounded.

Just before the tornado hit, there was a loud crack of thunder and a massive bolt of lightning. Power was cut to the town. Some people got out of bed, flipping light switches to find only darkness. But the sky, they said, was a strobe light, lightning striking more than two hundred times per minute. And then they heard the sound—like a freight train. For most people, it happened before they even had time to act, before they even knew what was happening. And in those early-morning hours, just before 1:00 a.m., an entire town was destroyed.

At its peak, the tornado was a quarter mile wide. Semitrucks and tractors were hurled into the sky; cars were tossed like pebbles. Trees were stripped bare of their leaves, and some were torn up from their roots. Walls and ceilings and stairways caved in; foundations were crushed to nothing. People were pinned beneath doors and drywall. Some rode their beds through a collapsing floor, all the way to the basement. Others were pulled straight out of their homes and flung into fields forty feet away. Barns, sheds, and silos were razed. Roads were ripped from the ground. The roof of the school was torn off, and a barn was deposited in the gym. More than ninety houses were leveled, and sixty more were badly damaged. Seventeen of Barneveld's eighteen businesses—including the grocery store, the municipal building, the bank, the library, the post office, the feed mill, the farm dealership, the American Legion Hall, the Village Bar and Restaurant, and the Thousand Curls Beauty Shop—and all three of the town's churches were demolished. Only the water tower, with the name BARNEVELD freshly painted in black against the white, and a brick bell tower in front of the Lutheran church stood standing.

Growing up, I'd heard that just before it struck, the tornado had hit transmission lines, cutting power to the town and silencing the sirens. Later, I read it was a bolt of lightning that did it. Recently, I was told there were no sirens at all in Barneveld at the time. In any case, emergency sirens were powered by electricity back then, so even if they had existed, they wouldn't have sounded. The town had no warning. It was an invisible monster that struck in the dead of night, another rarity when it comes to tornadoes, and no one saw it at all. And in the end, the Barneveld Tornado, as it came to be known—which a meteorologist at the National Weather Service in Madison called "the worst one I've ever seen"—wiped out 90 percent of the town. In a matter of seconds, it was responsible for nine deaths and left more than two hundred people seriously injured. It killed cows and horses and pets, and it caused an estimated $25 million in damage.

After carving a path through the center of town, the tornado traveled toward the Blue Mounds and ended in the nearby town of

Black Earth, where it ripped through cornfields, damaged houses, and destroyed several farms. It traveled for about thirty miles and was on the ground for nearly an hour before dissolving back into the clouds.

Growing up, I'd heard the story that after hitting Barneveld, the tornado had barreled directly toward Mount Horeb. That it had made a straight shot east to west, hit the Blue Mounds, and jumped back into the clouds before touching down again in Black Earth, barely missing us. And this was the story that would be told for years to come, that would become part of the mythology of Mount Horeb and its people—a legend as large as the trolls, as fateful as Moses on his mountain: that the Mounds, or maybe God himself, had protected us. A town just a few miles to the west was in ruins, but we on the Mountain of God were spared.

I'd find out later that the tornado was never actually headed toward Mount Horeb. It came close, missing us by a matter of miles. But like most storm systems, it didn't move west to east, the path that would have led to us. Aerial photographs and maps show a line traveling from the southwest to the northeast, an almost perfect forty-five-degree angle. Tornadoes do possess the ability to shift direction, but this one stayed on a pretty straight course. It didn't head our way and then skip us, miraculously diverting course, by the will of God or the magical properties of the Mounds. It's true that the town eight miles away—a community of our neighbors and family, our coworkers and friends—was destroyed and ours was not. But I'm not sure you could call us saved.

~

In the Barneveld Public Library, there are scrapbooks, photo albums, and newspaper clippings—items once kept and cataloged by residents—housed on the bottom shelves of a small back-room cabinet. It's spring 2019, in late May, just before the thirty-fifth anniversary of the tornado, and I find myself inside this library, which, like the rest of the town, was rebuilt after the storm. Later I walk along Main Street and see the houses and the businesses and the churches and the bars that were rebuilt too; their prefab siding still looks new. I drive along the back roads and see the houses that were never hit, then walk to the park and find a plaque dedicated to the nine people who died. But I spend most of my time in the library, in that small back room, blowing dust off photo albums. I turn their pages, the plastic sticking together, and pore over yellowed newspaper articles and Polaroids carefully pressed inside and captioned in fine cursive. *Sue and Charlie's place. The implement. The Lutheran Church.* Identifiers scrawled below photos of crumbled foundations, bed frames and lampshades and trailers, metal scraps wrapped around light posts, trees torn leafless and permanently bent, like they're still being blown by the wind. I spend hours in that room, thinking about the people who died. But what I have really come here to do is to find the people who lived.

We're sitting in Al Wright's feed mill, on the opposite end of town from his first property, which the tornado ripped away before it had even opened for business. Al is seventy-seven and wears a plaid collared shirt, wire-framed glasses, and a white baseball cap. His white sideburns peek out below the brim. He's fit, with a strong nose and chin, slate-blue eyes, and the skin of a man who spends his days outside, hauling bags of feed to the truck beds of farmers, chopping wood, and tending to the greenhouse he keeps in the summer. His smile lines and crow's-feet are deep. The shop is small, with wood-paneled walls, large windows, and a few shelves stuffed with tools and suet and farming supplies. Anchored to the wall in one corner of the room is a TV playing an afternoon soap opera, and we have to talk loudly over the sound of it. Al sits in a chair behind the counter while we talk, his hands folded on the desk in front of him. I stand, leaning over the counter to hear him.

Al has been running the mill for thirty-five years. It's the busy season, he told me over the phone before I arrived, but only one person comes into the shop while we talk. When I'd pulled up to the mill I'd spotted a younger man, tan and strong and shirtless, in the woodpile behind the mill. This, I find out later, is Al's son Jerry, who works with his father. He lived through the tornado too.

Before the tornado hit, Al was just a few days away from celebrating the grand opening of his feed mill. He was also an EMT. On the night of June 7, 1984, as the clock ticked over to midnight, he was out on call. What Al remembers most about that night, in the hours just before the storm, is that it was hot and muggy. He might have had the windows in the ambulance down. He had just dropped off a patient at a hospital in Madison and was on his way back home to Barneveld, the tiny town in which he had lived for his entire life, when the call radio clicked on.

The dispatcher asked for Al's location. He was on the west side of the city, he said, not far from Mount Horeb.

"Get back as fast as you can," the dispatcher said. "Your town has been destroyed by a tornado."

When he got back to Barneveld, fighting through police tape to enter, he was handed the body of a small boy. Everyone knew everyone in Barneveld back then, like they do today. Al knew the boy, and he knew the boy's parents.

"Protocol tells you that you decide who to transport," Al tells me. It takes a second to realize what he means: In a disaster situation, an EMT must make a call on who to take to the hospital and who to let go. He knew the boy was dead.

"But how do you say, 'He's gone'?" he asks me. He fights back tears as he says it, blotting his eyes with a handkerchief he's pulled from his pocket. It's not typical, out here, to see men cry, let alone men like Al—men who toil, men who work the land. I think of my grandfather, a man who was born on a farm and worked on the line at the GM plant in Janesville—a man I never once saw cry.

That night, Al took the dead boy to the hospital. He continued to transport bodies of the dead and wounded until morning and was only able to stop by his own house briefly to check on his family and assess the damage. He shined a flashlight on the wreckage and found a house without a roof, but his wife and children had been spared. He wouldn't gather with them until daylight, when the night's work was done.

On June 7, 1984, Jerry Wright was fifteen years old. School had just gotten out, and summer vacation had just begun. His skin was already tan from the sun, and the days were spread out before him in the way summer days do when you are young, the whole town and surrounding fields and farms and long hours of daylight seeming limitless, all yours.

Jerry was outside playing basketball with his friends. It was just a normal day, he says. It wasn't stormy, and it wasn't rainy. The sun was out, and there was just a little wind. But even so, like most people around town, young Jerry had a feeling.

"There's gonna be a storm tonight," he told his friends that day.

"Because you just felt it," he tells me now, nearly thirty-five years later. "But other than that, it was just a normal day."

Jerry is nearing fifty but looks much younger. He's tan and fit with light-brown hair, and he wears a T-shirt with a pair of faded jeans and work boots. You can tell just by looking at him that he's strong and spends most of his time outside. He reminds me of the boys I grew up with, and he has the same Wisconsin accent—nasal and long voweled, the ends of words clipped off—that so much of my own family has, that I once had too. He sits inside the shop on a plastic chair beneath the blaring TV, and I ask him what he remembers of that night.

"Well, a huge loud clap of thunder," he says. "It woke the whole town up. I remember the windows poppin' and a huge loud roar—so loud that you really couldn't hear anything. You couldn't even hear your voice, it was so loud. But just like that, it was over."

Afterward, he and his brothers grabbed flashlights and set off through town. They climbed through the rubble in the dark, heading to the houses of their extended family and friends.

"There was this sound in town," he says, then pauses for a beat, trying to find the right word. "There was a wail."

He looks at his father when he says it, asks if he remembers the sound. It was a gas leak, the sound, and it was heard that night and into the morning, casting an eerie soundtrack over the landscape of a demolished town.

"Were you scared?" I ask Jerry.

"Well, you know," he says, "when you're fifteen, it's like you're on an expedition. Every corner you turn, it's something different. You don't know what you're gonna find."

I can imagine him, that fifteen-year-old boy, giddy in the wreckage. Awestruck by the destruction. To see trucks wrapped around telephone poles, to find the buildings reduced to rubble. As bodies were pulled from beneath the piles of wood that were once his neighbors' houses, his heart might have been beating wildly in his chest. I imagine I might have felt the same.

After a while, a memory comes back to him. Around the site where the mill is now, which he says was a graveyard for cars back then, they'd found single blades of grass and small splinters of wood stuck into tires. His father's car, which had been parked at the fire station while he was on call that night, ended up on top of a fire truck.

Jerry shakes his head and is quiet for a few seconds.

"You don't really know the power of it," he says.

Joyce Aschliman was an EMT, too, but on the night of the tornado she was at home. Back then, she lived in a farmhouse just outside town.

"The day was pretty normal," she says. We're sitting in her small apartment in a retirement community in Mount Horeb, across the street from a park where I played as a kid. Joyce is in her eighties now; her husband is gone, and she lives alone. She has a full head of gray-white hair and wears glasses. She's calm and kind, and as we talk, she rocks back and forth in a plush pink chair that squeaks. There's a rhythm to the squeaking, and it seems to keep the beat of our conversation. She laughs and cries often while we talk, and sometimes I can't tell the difference.

"It was a very humid night," she says. "The air was pretty still."

Joyce's father had been in the hospital, and she'd been with her mother to see him that day. It was late when they got home, and her husband, Ernie, who owned and operated the implement with their two sons, Charlie and Bill, had already gone to bed. Their oldest daughter, Lori, who had just graduated from high school, was out with her friends.

"Old mother hens never go to bed till the chicks are home," Joyce says with a laugh. So she stayed up waiting. Then it started to storm. The wind picked up, and then the power went out. Way back before cell phones, the landline went dead too. Growing up on a cattle farm, Joyce had always been afraid of storms. When she was a girl, during a thunderstorm at suppertime just as her mother had come in from evening chores, the barn had been struck by lightning. It had taken her a long time to get over the fear. When the thunder started to roll that night, she thought it was just another storm.

"So it was nothing to do but wait," she says.

Soon she heard sirens—fire trucks or an ambulance—and saw flashing red lights. She assumed there'd been a barn fire nearby. Then a car pulled up to the house.

"And just like that, my son come flying to the door," she says, holding back tears and then letting them go, her voice sticking for a second, then rising in a sob. "And he told us the town was gone."

She woke her husband and told him they needed to go find Lori.

S ue Clerkin, whose last name back then was Aschliman, was Joyce's daughter-in-law. She was home that night too. During the day, she'd been building a fence in the yard to keep her two young boys safe.

"It was windy that day," she says. But, she adds, it's always windy in Barneveld.

Sue and I are sitting at a family restaurant in Mount Horeb. It's after lunch on a weekday, so the place is empty. We take a booth by the window. I order iced tea, and Sue gets a water. She's turning sixty soon—"too old to care what people think of me anymore"—and has close-cropped coppery hair and skin that's seen the sun. She has freckles, calloused hands, and a wry smile. She wears a striped T-shirt and slacks, having just come from work at the hospital in Madison. It's the same hospital where my father works, in the mailroom, and he and Sue regularly pass each other in the hallways as my father runs his deliveries. Such is the way of our small towns, unlikely intersections everywhere.

Having grown up on a farm, Sue reminds me of my grandmother and my mother and so many women in my family—tough in a way that feels specific to midwestern women: a little closed off, a little hard, a little suspicious of strangers like me, city slickers who ask a lot of questions. But when she opens up, which happens fast, she's friendly and funny and wears no pretense. Everything she is she puts right on the Formica table in front of us, for me to take or leave as I will. I can tell she's a woman who's wise to the world, who long ago stopped trying to live in the way other people expected her to. I like her immediately.

On the night of June 7, Sue put her kids to bed around 7:30 p.m. She stayed up late, as she often did when she was a young mother. When everyone else in the house was asleep, it was the time of night she liked to get things done. And then it started to storm.

"I remember watching the news," she says. "There was no storm warnings whatsoever. And when I was young, I grew up falling asleep to the rain and thunder and lightning outside, and it never scared me."

So she went to bed. It was around 12:30 a.m., and the wind had begun to howl.

"I didn't think anything of it, you know?" she says. "Just another thunderstorm. You never thought you'd have to run for your life."

Sue's two boys were seventeen months apart: Michael was four, and Matthew was just shy of his third birthday. They were both in their parents' bed that night, afraid of the storm. Sue got up to go to the bathroom, and then she heard the sound.

"It was like a freight train," she says. "It was just mammoth." She told Charlie to grab Michael and get to the basement. *A tornado's coming,* she yelled.

"You could tell," she says. "You could just hear it."

Charlie grabbed Michael and Sue grabbed Matthew, and they ran toward the root cellar. Charlie and Michael made it. But just as Sue was getting to the stairs, with Matthew pressed against her chest, the tornado struck the house.

Something hit her and Matthew from behind and sent them to the ground. Sue stayed crouched on her knees, holding her son beneath her, as the storm destroyed their house.

"Matthew never cried," Sue says.

When it was over, she rolled onto her back and heard Matthew take a single breath. She'd been taking EMT classes and recognized the breath as her son's last.

"I knew he was dead," she says. "I knew that was the end of life."

We sit for a few seconds in silence, her words hanging between us. She looks at me, and a small sad smile spreads across her face. I know this smile. It's one that's practiced across the passage of time, one meant to soothe a listener more than oneself.

Crouched around the body of her son, the crashing of wind and wood and glass settling to silence, Sue felt the rain: fat, quarter-size drops falling from the wide-open mouth of sky where the roof of her house had been. The temperature had dropped about thirty degrees, and it was cold.

"You couldn't hear anything," she says. "You couldn't see your hand in front of your face. It was pitch black."

In a great white flash of lightning, she noticed her finger was hanging by a small thread of skin. At the restaurant, she points to what remains of the finger, her middle left, cut down below the first knuckle. Too concerned with keeping her son safe, she had felt only a pinch.

She would find out later that a piece of flying debris from the house, likely part of a door, had struck Matthew in the head. The night of the Barneveld tornado, when Sue Clerkin lost her youngest son, she was just twenty-four years old.

~

In the early hours of morning, the sky dark and the power out, the residents of Barneveld walked around what was left of their town. They searched the foundations of their homes, crumbled to dust, calling out for family and friends, searching for lost pets and any clothes they might put on. They walked barefoot, in pajamas and T-shirts and underwear. Some wore black garbage bags to fend off the rain.

Sue's husband, Charlie, had glass in his feet and a hole in his shorts as they walked through the rubble to what was left of the fire station. Michael walked with them. They carried Matthew, and they handed his small body over to the EMTs. Al Wright sped him away to the hospital. Charlie's mother, Joyce, meanwhile, was looking for her daughter Lori. She searched the ruins of the town but couldn't find her anywhere. Sue was taken to another hospital, so Joyce and Charlie followed behind. Joyce wouldn't find out until the next morning that Lori was in the same hospital where Al had brought Matthew.

The tornado sucked Lori out of her car. She'd been hanging out with her friends at a restaurant in town and had run to her car when the wind picked up. A two-by-four crashed through the sunroof and tore through her arm. She was swept through the windshield and thrown a block away. Her nose was gone and her arm was badly injured; she had a dislocated shoulder, a broken collarbone, and two broken wrists. She was in the hospital for weeks and had nine surgeries over several months.

"We almost lost her," Joyce says, dabbing her eyes with a handkerchief.

Along with Matthew, eight other people died in the tornado, including a teacher, several farmers and military veterans, and an eight-year-old girl and her parents. Most of the people who died lived in the same area, a brand-new subdivision where Joyce's two sons had homes.

"We were very fortunate and very blessed," Joyce says. "We could have lost most of our family." She gets up at one point during our conversation and shows me a picture of Matthew. Like so many other photos that were lost in the storm, this one was found miles away. In the photo, the boy is blond and beaming.

"Our little towhead," Joyce says, smiling, and holds out the picture for me to see.

When Sue got out of the hospital, her mother drove her around town. For the first time, she was able to see the damage in the daylight.

"There was this *smell*," Sue says. "Some combination of dirt and gas. Like burnt dirt."

Back in Al's shop, we talk about his experiences in the days that followed the tornado.

"Well, you're kind of numb, you know?" he says. In the weeks after the storm, the EMT service stayed busy. They got a lot of stress-related calls, Al tells me. When I ask if he felt stress too, he hesitates.

"Well, I guess I did," he says eventually, repeating the words. "Our church uptown was destroyed. We had to tear that all down."

We talk about the debris that was found across the state—that people hiking in Blue Mounds had found photos, birth certificates, and other papers and objects they sent back to town. Al shows me an invoice pad, says he received invoices in the mail that were found fifty miles away. Checks, bills, letters, and a Barneveld State Bank pouch were found more than a hundred miles away, and heavier materials like plywood and aluminum siding were found along an eighty-five-mile path. A gas can from Randy Danz's Auto Service turned up in Green Bay, 175 miles from Barneveld.

This strange and sporadic path of belongings left in the wake of the storm spurred a landmark study on tornado debris led by a professor of meteorology at the University of Wisconsin. Even Ted Fujita himself, after whom the tornado scale is named, traveled to Barneveld from Chicago to tour the wreckage.

As we talk about this, Al remembers something. He walks over to a storage closet and pulls out a gray metal box.

"This was my time clock," he says, "of when the power went off." The box has a clockface on the front of it, stopped at 12:48. He'd kept it at the old mill, and he'd found it among the rubble. I tell him I've always wondered what time the tornado actually hit, that I'd read conflicting accounts. For a long time, I believed it was just after midnight.

"That's it," Al says, tapping a finger on the clock. "That's when it happened. And it'll never be plugged in again."

Barneveld began to rebuild. In the following days, with the threat of more storms not yet passed, residents and volunteers—including bands of Amish and Mennonite farmers from the area, who came in from across the state to help—worked from sunrise till dark. They picked through the town and nearby fields, salvaging what they could. Trucks hauled away heaps of rubble to be burned in a nearby rock quarry. The Red Cross sent in food and donated clothes. Barneveld was declared a federal disaster area by President Reagan, and FEMA sent mobile trailers in which homeless residents could live. The bank set up shop in a trailer too. While the post office had been destroyed, the postmistress, Marie Dimpfl, whose house had been spared, dug through the mail that was left, stuck an American flag in her yard, and kept the mail running out of her garage. A couple who was supposed to get married on the Friday after the tornado hit got married on Saturday instead; the wedding was held in a country church outside town rather than their own, which had been destroyed. Two days after the tornado, a pregnant woman whose house was gone gave birth to a baby girl. On the remains of a wall where the implement had been, someone had spray-painted the words WE'RE NOT GIVING UP, WE'RE GO ON. Someone had corrected it, spraying an *ing* above the word *go*. A farmwife named Betsy Thronson set up a soup kitchen in an industrial garage in town; she borrowed equipment from the school and cooked for days, then weeks, then months, often putting in twelve-hour days to feed the town. On breaks from cleanup, it was where people came to eat; it would eventually become a restaurant, where people continued to gather for years.

"That's where people would congregate," Sue tells me. "That's where the healing of everyone happened."

Joyce, who housed both her sons and their families while their homes were rebuilt, remembers pulling dirty clothes and bedsheets from the foundations of her sons' houses, taking them home, and washing them several times before they could be used.

"I remember we found Matthew's blanket," she says, not trying to hold back the tears now. "And I scrubbed that up."

The sound of chain saws buzzed through the thick late-spring air. Debris was bulldozed, and construction began on new houses and apartment buildings. The roof of the school was replaced. Damaged farmland was tilled again, and crops were replanted. Houses, businesses, barns, and bars were rebuilt. The churches rose again. On the following Arbor Day, nearly a year later, Jerry and his classmates planted trees.

"All the trees you see?" he says. "We planted them. So when some of them get really old, I can say, 'I planted those trees.'"

As I read old newspaper clippings about the tornado—along with a feature in *People* magazine from that summer—I see a particular narrative begin to emerge. Phrases and headlines like *A town is reborn* and *Barneveld rises from the ashes* appear again and again. The stories are often accompanied by an image that became iconic: the bell tower of the Lutheran church, standing solitary amid the rubble. At one point, I read an article in which a woman, whose farmhouse had been spared, is quoted as saying, "God was watching out for us."

How strange, it strikes me, to say such a thing: as if God had chosen to save her while allowing others to die, that her home and family were deliberately spared while others were destroyed. It reminds me of a line from *Twister*, when Jo explains her obsession with tornadoes to Bill, the root of which lies in her own childhood: *You've never seen it miss this house, miss that house, and come after you.* And it reminds me of the Mount Horeb narrative, this idea that we were the ones who were saved.

Like Mount Horeb, Barneveld is a God-fearing town. Most of the people I speak to mention their churches, and many of the articles I read focus on rebuilding the town's three chapels. Joyce tells me that in the wake of the storm, the town began holding ecumenical services—congregations from all three of the town's churches gathering together for services while the churches were rebuilt. Today, the town's congregations still gather for joint services for Easter and Thanksgiving.

Sue is the only one who doesn't talk about church. She speaks about the funeral services for her son, which were held in Mount Horeb, and the cemetery out in the country where they buried him. No one I speak with mentions God directly. Only Joyce makes a direct reference to her faith, when I asked if she still got scared when it storms.

"I don't," she says, rocking in her chair. "I just pray."

After Matthew's death, Sue drank. She stayed out late. In fine midwestern tradition, she played bar-league softball that summer and stayed out drinking with her friends. I tell her I've done this, too, the way so many Midwesterners do. Here, where we're never encouraged to talk about our problems, where we drink instead to deal with things like stress and death and grief—or, maybe more specifically, to numb it away. That summer, Sue would close down the country bar—the lights of the softball field gone dark behind it, nothing but corn beyond—and head home in the early hours of morning. She'd get a few hours of fitful sleep, then spend entire days at Matthew's grave.

"I was just trying to survive in my own little world," she says. Sue and Charlie eventually divorced. "They say the death of a child either makes or breaks a marriage," Sue says. "And it probably didn't break it, but it didn't help it either."

I wonder, when she says this, how the community responded—to the divorce, to the drinking, to the ways she wore her grief. I can't help but wonder about a woman who falls apart publicly, and about what a small Christian town—which by daylight speaks of the importance of faith, of loving your neighbor—might think of her when the night comes down, what they might say to their own behind closed doors. In so many ways, it seems true that the town came together in the wake of tragedy. That they stood hand in hand and grieved together, then rebuilt their town. But what of a woman who wears her tragedy aloud? Who doesn't hide it, like she's taught to, and bury it in the rubble she's meant to rebuild? Who, instead, holds the pain she's supposed to carry alone out in the open—like an offering, like a stone she can't cast off into the abyss—and asks for someone to take it? I ask her about this. After thinking about it for a while, Sue shrugs and smiles. It's not a bitter smile, but maybe a little sad. It's a smile that more than anything suggests acceptance, that a long time has passed, that in many ways she has moved on.

"I didn't get that love thing from Barneveld like everybody says they got," Sue says. "Maybe they did, but I never got that kind of love."

But her family did come together. Throughout our conversation, Sue returns frequently to Joyce—who took her family in, who cared for them, who supported Sue while she was grieving.

"She's like an angel," Sue says. "She was a godsend. She taught me how strong of a woman she really is."

Despite the divorce, the family is still close, and Sue and Joyce see each other often. They'll gather just a few days after we speak for the joint birthday party of Sue's two granddaughters—the daughters of her son from her second marriage.

Sue says she couldn't talk to her own mother about Matthew's death.

"My mother was a hard-core woman," she says. "And nobody talks about it. You know, it's like a sin to talk about it."

I tell her I think this is a cultural thing, a midwestern thing. And maybe what I mean is it's a class thing. It's something I think about often, having grown up in a small town—where you do your best to hide your pain, where if you let it go a whole town will know. Talking about your problems, I think, is something reserved for the upper classes, the educated classes, for families in which a life of the mind is more important than a life of work, and of the body, and of the land. Where Sue comes from, and where I come from—generations of farm families with little money and many mouths to feed—we don't have time for the kind of trouble that dwells in the brain or heart. We learn this from the stories of our forebears, who were more concerned with the kind of trouble a drought could bring or whether the crops would yield. We don't have the tools—the language, the education, the resources—to say some things aloud, to deal in the daylight with our problems. So we keep them to ourselves, and we carry them with us.

"You just didn't—" Sue stammers, trying to figure out how to say it. "You couldn't show your grief. You couldn't. They didn't want to talk about it. You didn't want to talk about it."

For so many midwestern families, that very silence—what we like to call *stoicism*—means strength.

"It's supposed to make you stronger," Sue says. Then she quickly adds, "And it does make you stronger." But in the end, she did talk about it—she went to counseling for eleven years. She can see the surprise on my face when she tells me this, even though I say nothing. She nods, an implicit understanding. Therapy is not only a rare thing where we come from but something that's still stigmatized; it's equated with narcissism, with frivolity, with weakness.

"You have to be able to talk about it," Sue says finally. "If you can't talk about it, you can't heal. You hold everything in, and it just kills you."

People in Barneveld don't talk about the storm much these days. They've moved on, Al says, and many have passed away. And those who are left, I ask, would they rather just forget it?

"I don't want to forget it," Joyce says, still holding the picture of Matthew in her hands. "Because it happened." She sets the picture down and settles back into her chair. I look at her hands as she rocks, resting on the arms of the chair while it squeaks. As a woman who spent years on a farm, taking care of children and animals, doing chores and keeping a household together, life has taken a toll on her hands. But even now, sitting in her carpeted apartment in Mount Horeb, years away from the farm she helped build, her hands still look strong. They remind me of my mother's hands, of my grandmother's hands.

"You know," she says—she's smiling a wistful smile, and her eyes are bright—"it was just part of life."

I don't know what I hoped to find when I went back to Barneveld. I suppose I went back, in some respect, to find the truth of a story that, over the past thirty-five years—a story nearly as old as me—had become more like a myth. In the restaurant in Mount Horeb, I talk with Sue Clerkin about stories. I talk about the ways in which a story, or maybe a myth, can carry on—how it can shape a memory or a place, how it can carry a family, or a town, for generations. She looks at me when I say this, and that tight-lipped smile spreads across her face.

"You know," she says, "they always said, 'The Mounds will protect you.'"

I sit for a second with this, hearing it for the first time from the mouth of someone from Barneveld, someone who survived the storm, someone who lost the very thing we never expect to lose. And I think of the way we all felt so protected, the Blue Mounds serving as some holy shoulder of God. I realize we were all told this story, on both sides of the mountain.

"That's what they told us too," I say. "It's the story I was told my whole life. It's the story I believed."

"Well," she says with a shrug, "the Mounds didn't protect us."

~

A few years ago, in August, my partner and I took a road trip out west. On the way home, we took Highway 70 across the middle of the country, which sent us for a full day across the length of Kansas. And that afternoon, the sky turned dark.

Kansas is situated in the heart of Tornado Alley, a portion of the Midwest and Great Plains that stretches from North Texas up through

South Dakota—an area whose particularly volatile climatological patterns make a perfect breeding ground for tornadoes. The United States accounts for nearly 75 percent of the world's tornadoes, and this is where most of them happen. In the past several years, as overall temperatures have increased and caused more extreme weather across the country, meteorologists have marked an eastward shift in that path. But the middle of the country still sees the most tornadoes each year.

All day I'd been watching the sky. Even in the morning, when the sun was out and the sky was still blue, the way the clouds were building—high and white and bulbous, great towers of clouds—had me on edge. The day was hot and humid. The sky got darker as we crossed the state line, heading toward what was to be our day's destination, a campsite near Lawrence. And the sky kept getting darker, the massive white wind turbines dotting a landscape of cornfields set in shocking contrast against the dark blue, then gray, then green of the sky.

"This isn't good," I said.

And then the sun went down. The wind picked up, and the rain came down hard, so heavy it was impossible to see. Traffic crawled. The wind roared. A low, constant rumble of thunder rolled through the black night, punctuated by deafening cracks that vibrated in the road beneath us. Lightning lit the sky like a strobe. I turned on the radio and tried to find a forecast.

"Tornado warnings across the state," a weatherman said. A funnel cloud had been spotted. "Wabaunsee, Osage, Shawnee Counties."

"What county are we in?" I asked aloud, then frantically checked my phone to find out. We were in Shawnee County.

"If you're in any of these areas," the voice on the radio said, "you should immediately take cover. If you're on the road, don't try to outrun it."

The rain was blinding, coming down in sheets. We pressed on for a while, crawling in the traffic, then took the next exit. We pulled over under the overpass, along with a few other cars and a semitruck, and sat in our rental car, terrified and helpless as the rain pounded and the wind howled. Thunder roared and cloud-to-ground lightning cracked every second. It was pitch black, out there in the middle of nowhere, but for the lightning. And every time the sky lit up, I expected to see it: the massive, unstoppable monster, barreling toward us across the plain, tearing through the corn. In those moments, I was certain this was the end. This was how we'd die, out here on the road, as the tornado pressed down upon us, then tossed us into the sky. And how fitting, I thought, to go this way. How inevitable. Almost as if it was fate.

When the rain let up, just briefly, we pulled back on the highway and sped toward Topeka. We pulled over once more under another overpass when the rain came back even heavier; then we pressed on again. We found the closest hotel, screamed into the parking lot, and ran for cover, then huddled in the lobby with the guests and staff until the storm passed.

In the end, we never saw it. But it had been there, somewhere, in the darkness—so close we could feel it. The next morning, there were reports of a tornado touching down less than a mile from the highway. I felt relief, of course, but in the light of day, there was also some part of me that was disappointed. As Jo says in *Twister*, scrambling out from under a bridge to get a better look at the tornado as it passes over, Bill struggling to restrain her: *I wanted to see it.*

Like God, like fear itself, like the darkest guts of grief—the cone of silence, the still and silent eye of the storm, the thing we cannot possibly know—it's something I've wanted to witness for as long as I can remember. It's something I've been trying my whole life to see.

~

Ever since the Barneveld tornado, Sue Clerkin has been afraid of storms.

"It's the wind that drives you nuts," she says. "The howling. You look out of the house, and you see the trees are half bent over and touching the ground."

It's a fear, she says, with some regret, that she has instilled in her children. Her oldest daughter sometimes calls her in a panic during storms. Sue calls her kids, too, whenever the clouds start to build. She asks them if they're watching the weather, if they're keeping their eyes to the sky.

Lori is scared of storms too. Joyce tells me her daughter once pulled over at a farmhouse as she was driving through a storm and asked the strangers who lived there if she could get in their basement.

Al doesn't have the same kind of fear, he says, because he didn't actually live through the storm. He's fortunate, he says, to not have heard the sound of the wind or watched the roof get torn from his house, like his wife and kids did.

"She said it was just like a freight train," Al says of his wife, repeating a line I've heard so often it sounds something like a prayer. And Jerry, who seemed so calm when we spoke, is vigilant during storms. He's always on watch, Al says, constantly monitoring the skies.

Sue lives in the country now, on a farm outside a small town not far from Barneveld, where she and her second husband raise Red and Black Angus cattle. Way out past the county centers, they can't always hear tornado sirens when they go off.

"It depends upon the way the wind is blowing," she says. I ask her if this scares her, and she says it does. But her husband, Pat, always says he'll protect her. She looks me in the eye when she tells me this, that familiar smile back on her face.

"And I say, 'You can't promise that, buddy.'"

When I left the Midwest and moved to New York, there was a thunderstorm in the spring. I called my landlord and asked if we could have access to the basement in case of tornadoes.

"Honey," he said with a laugh and a thick Irish accent, "we don't get tornadoes here." A tornado struck Queens the following summer.

When I first heard the Friday-night siren in Brooklyn signaling the start of Shabbat—the same siren that sounds in Wisconsin to signal a coming tornado—I ducked for cover. Once, while walking back from a park with friends as the sky turned dark, as the wind began to whip in such a way that the leaves were blown from their branches and spun, midair, in small cyclones, none of my companions listened when I said we should run.

It turns out, people who grow up on the coasts—those who don't call March through July tornado season—don't share the same thrilling fear that haunts me each spring. With coastal climates come hurricanes, but also an advanced warning system—with days or even weeks to prepare. By comparison, the average warning time for tornadoes is thirteen minutes. And sometimes, there's no warning at all. I've lived through two hurricanes in New York, and in both cases I watched people scramble in the days leading up to the storm, pillaging grocery-store shelves of every last loaf of bread, packing cars in a panic and hurrying out of town, their apartment windows taped in large blue Xs like a cross, like some desperate act of faith, like something already gone. Despite living in a mandatory evacuation zone, despite having family in New Orleans whose house was destroyed by Katrina, despite knowing that hurricanes can be just as deadly as tornadoes, I stayed. My decision wasn't wise, but I was never really afraid.

Fear, for me, is an unpredictable force—an unknowable, volatile thing that strikes suddenly, at any time. Fear, for me, is living in the annual path of destruction, where tree trunks are permanently twisted and silos wear cracks like reminders, where shallow ditches along empty rural highways are the only place to hide if you get caught on the road in a storm. Fear is the knowledge that you can be asleep one second, safe in your bed, and with a single clap of thunder your house can collapse around you. It's in the ghostly quiet that heralds sudden devastation. It's waiting for the wail of sirens, or worse—knowing they might never go off. It's a fear born in every Midwesterner, and no matter how far away you move, it never really leaves you.

I wonder, sometimes, if I believed in God, would I still feel so afraid?

On the first Wednesday of March, as winter turns to spring, the sirens in southern Wisconsin are tested for the first time of the year. Their wail starts out low, and then grows louder, each massive, oscillating horn creating a cyclical fade and roar, so loud at each peak it can be heard across county lines. They are tested this way every Wednesday at noon through November. But on that first day, when the season's first siren sounds, this is when people remember. They might remember the moments after a storm, pushing open cellar doors and climbing old stone steps to survey the damage on their farm. They might recall stepping among the ruins of their town, pulling up boards and unearthing belongings that once comprised a home, touching the twisted branches of trees, crouching to scratch crying cats. They might remember broken glass, a crumbled staircase, a roof caved in. They might remember a blanket. And they will remember this way every time a low growl of thunder rolls across the sky. They will remember when the clouds begin to build, when they billow and hum; when the leaves of maples start to whip and the branches of birches bend in the wind. They will remember when the air becomes so thick and electric they can feel it in their teeth, when the sky turns from blue to gray to green.

They don't test sirens where I live now, a thousand miles away from Mount Horeb, from Barneveld, from home. But sometimes, in early June, when the wind kicks up from the west, I think I can still hear them.

TOMBOY

I have always wanted to be both man and woman, to incorporate the strongest and richest parts of my mother and father within/into me—to share valleys and mountains upon my body the way the earth does in hills and peaks.

—Audre Lorde, *Zami: A New Spelling of My Name*

A few years ago, I went out for drinks with a new friend. We'd met at a mutual friend's birthday party, and this was our first time out alone. When I showed up to the bar, a dimly lit oyster spot in Brooklyn, I quickly realized she thought we were on a date. She wore a semitransparent white shirt and bright-red lipstick, her long hair falling in dark curls around her shoulders. She was attractive. We sat at the bar and talked; she flirted, and I tried not to. I downed a drink and some oysters, then ordered another round. The bar was packed and hot. I peeled off my sweater, and dabbing the sweat off my neck, worked up the nerve to say what I needed to.

"So," I started, "I should tell you." She leaned in closer. When we'd first arrived, she had pulled my chair, with me on top of it, closer to hers. It was a bold move, and one I couldn't help but admire. Our knees were almost touching.

"I'm in a relationship," I said with a grimace. "A committed one."

"Ah," she said, leaning back a little. A flash of disappointment in her eyes, her chin dipped in a slow nod of recognition. But she smiled. "Well, that's OK," she said.

"The thing is," I went on, procrastinating, searching the bottom of my glass for any sweet remnant of whiskey that might be hiding in the ice, "it's with a man."

To say I watched her face fall would be an understatement. It plummeted headlong off a cliff into a swamp of disbelief and despair.

"No," she said, stretching out the moan of the *oh* as she turned from me toward her drink, poured what was left of it down her throat, then planted her elbows on the bar and held her head in her hands. It was an inflated gesture, partly for comic effect—my new friend was funny—but her surprise was genuine.

"No way," she said, shaking her head.

I nodded, my stomach tight with regret—not for the fact itself but for the thought of disappointing this new person whom I liked so much, this funny queer woman who I hoped might be my friend. I felt an old, familiar fear: that she would no longer want anything to do with me now that she knew the truth.

She looked at me, shook her head, and said:

"I can't believe you're straight."

The night we first met, my partner, John, was sure I was gay. (And for what it's worth, I assumed the same of him, which makes for a pretty funny story to tell at parties.) I don't talk about my sexuality or gender identity much; I've never felt particularly connected to a certain identity, nor has any language ever quite seemed to fit. And where I come from, we're not raised to talk about ourselves—let alone our sexual proclivities or gender identities. I had never even heard the term *gender identity* until late in college, when I took a bold leap and enrolled in a women's studies class. It hadn't occurred to me a person *had* a gender identity, let alone that it might be in conflict with their biological sex.

I'm not straight. And my gender identity is complicated. I never really had a coming-out—in part because I never thought I had the right, and in part, as difficult as it is to admit, because I'm still terrified to say some things aloud. But it's also because I so often feel like I don't have the words. There are words I use sometimes: words like *bisexual*, which attempts to define who I am attracted to and who I seek intimacy from; words like *genderqueer* or simply *queer*, which attempts to define the ways my body doesn't conform to traditional notions of gender. I use these words because they're the best words I have. But sometimes they make me uneasy. And sometimes I feel like I'm still seeking the words that fit, that feel more right, that might help me feel like I belong.

My body is androgynous, both masculine and feminine. My gender expression fluctuates, depending on the day—what I'm wearing, what my hair is doing—but I typically look more traditionally masculine than feminine. The word *presentation* is sometimes used in this context, but I find the word problematic. It isn't just the choices I make about my appearance that make me androgynous but the body I was born with, the DNA that built me. Equal parts farm-family Midwesterner and swarthy Mediterranean, my body is a stovepipe, long and lean without much curve. My hips are narrow, my back and shoulders broad. My biceps are big and my breasts are small, my cheekbones sharp and my nose large. My body hair is dark and thick; it grows black and wild on my arms and legs, and with obnoxious consistency between my eyebrows and above my upper lip. My voice is deeper than that of many men I know.

I keep my hair short. In the summer, I cut it with clippers on the sides and a sharp edge at the neck; in the winter, I let it grow a little, and it curls around my ears in a style that's been called "the Tegan and

Sara," after the beloved Canadian lesbian-twin pop duo. My uniform is a T-shirt and jeans, unisex button-downs and utility boots. I keep my breasts tamped down with a sports bra or with something the fashion industry insists on calling a *bralette*. I haven't worn a dress in years and got rid of every skirt gathering dust in my wardrobe. At weddings and work events, I wear a suit. I don't wear makeup or jewelry, and I keep my fingernails short and unpainted. I rarely shave my legs and never my armpits. At this point in history, none of these things should sound radical. But you'd be surprised how they're still received in the world.

On average, I get misgendered at least twice a week. I get called *sir* far more often than *ma'am* or *miss*, a fact that makes itself most apparent in restaurants, where servers still insist on addressing their guests in these binary terms.

"For you, sir?" he will say, for the misgendering server is almost always a man. He might realize his mistake or second-guess his assumption. He'll stumble, flustered, stammer a bit.

"Oh," he might say. "Sorry."

"It's OK!" I'll say, my voice bright and cheery and pitched up a notch, an attempt to sound more like a woman. "No worries! Happens all the time!"

I hate myself when I do this. I feel complicit in the system that shames me, complicit in preserving my own shame. But I keep this collection of words and tones in my linguistic toolbox anyway, for just such an occasion, and use them to reassure the perpetrator that I'm not angry, that I'm friendly and unthreatening, that I won't punish him with a bad tip or a scene. That I will be the one to accommodate him. Sometimes, my dining companions remain oblivious to the small drama unfolding in front of them. But sometimes they notice, and this is even worse.

"What the hell?" they'll loud-whisper when he scurries away.

"Don't worry about it," I'll say, trying to change the subject.

"But *seriously*," they'll insist. "It's not like"—pause—"it's hard to tell."

In the silence that follows, my dining companions—be they friends or family or colleagues or strangers—will look down at their plates, their embarrassment palpable. I'll sip my drink or stuff calamari into my mouth and know that what lives in that silence, at least for a moment or two, are thoughts about my body. Sometimes, at least, I get a free dessert out of it.

Sometimes, I call myself a woman. But sometimes I avoid the word. At various points in my life I've wondered what exactly it means, and how I fit—or don't—into the shape of it. By default, I've always checked the "Female" box on applications and medical forms. But my body has never been a simple answer to any question. I don't look like a woman, and I don't always feel like one. Uncertainty is hardly unique among those of us born into female bodies, but as my own body moves through the world, it is marked by one common question: *What are you?* And the honest answer is—I don't really know.

Whenever I'm misgendered, I'm never sure how I feel. Sometimes I'm angry; sometimes I'm not. Sometimes it's shocking; sometimes it's not. Sometimes a *ma'am* or *miss* makes me flinch just as much as *sir*. (More than anything, I hate being called a *lady*; it makes me physically uncomfortable at best and like I want to punch things at worst. Other words used to address women—*girl, gal,* etc.—also make me twitchy, but slightly less gendered terms of endearment—*hon, babe, sweetie, darlin'*—I find far less offensive.) But what I always feel is embarrassment. It's a bodily feeling, a quick buzz in the back of my scalp, my guts lurching into my throat. When I walk into a women's bathroom and the person standing at the sink visibly starts at my presence, a flash of fear in her eyes, and whenever a man calls me *sir*, I feel like I'm standing naked in front of that bathroom mirror or bare-assed at that restaurant table while a stranger inspects my body. While they cock their heads and question, calculate, perform feats of mental gymnastics required to consider the categories, then place my body into one of them. While they figure out whether I might be some kind of threat. Sometimes I make a joke of it, because at this point in my life, and not least because of where I come from—where we're taught to avoid conflict, to keep the peace, to deflect attention by way of self-deprecation—a joke seems the only way out.

The truth, of course, is it's usually not funny. Sometimes it's frightening. In the past six months, I've been called *sir*, *mister*, *buddy*, *bro*, *fella*, and *man*. While buying shoelaces in a cobbler's shop, I got called *sir* three times by the same guy in a two-minute transaction, which I'm pretty sure was a record. On all but one of these occasions, it seemed like a genuine mistake. That one occasion, though, was different. It happened at night, at the bodega on my block in Brooklyn. As I was leaving, a man leaned against the ice cream cooler by the door, scratching a lottery ticket with a dime.

"Have a good night," I called out to the owner as I pulled open the door. The man with the lottery ticket stopped scratching.

"Good night—*mister*," he said, spitting out the word, the hiss of it hanging in the dusty air between us. I glanced over my shoulder at him as I left and watched his lips curl into a sneer. At first I thought I'd misheard him. Of all the things I've been called in my life, *mister* seemed like the furthest from a threat.

But everything I needed to know lived in that man's face. As I stepped out into the night, the streetlight on my block out as usual, I walked fast, not looking back, ready to run.

I know what it's like to be invisible. To be ignored or overlooked, to watch eyes avert, to have my identity denied. At the same time, I know what it's like to be visible: to be watched, to be stared at, to be the object of a glance, a gawk, a gaze, a frown, a furrowed brow, a rubberneck, a double take. I know what it's like to have a pair of eyes follow as I pass—locked on my body, questioning and scrutinizing and trying to decipher my code, to figure out what exactly I am. I've been called a *faggot*, a *dyke*, a *bitch*, a *cunt*, and countless creative combinations thereof. Once, when I was in graduate school in suburban New York, a car full of young men drove by as I walked home. They yelled "Fag!" and threw an entire uneaten taco at me through the window. (Imagine the level of hate it would take to waste a taco.) Once, in the same town, I was walking down the sidewalk and a middle-aged man and his young son approached. I smiled as they passed. The man looked me in the eye, scowled, and tucked his son into one wing of his suit coat—to hide me from view, to protect his small, impressionable progeny from the vile and blasphemous fact of my body.

It's no surprise that when I talk about harassment, I'm talking about men. When I talk about violence, I'm talking about men. Disproportionately, the people committing hate crimes are men. Those beating trans people to death are men. Because, in the end, men are taught to be threatened by those who disrupt their understanding of power. That threat becomes fear, which becomes rage, which becomes violence—and its main target is the very body that threatens them.

In *A Room of One's Own*, Virginia Woolf's famous treatise on the work of being a woman writer, she writes that men are bred with "the instinct for possession, the rage for acquisition." Such rage, Woolf writes, is "not merely the cry of wounded vanity; it [is] a protest against some infringement of his power to believe in himself."

If a man looks at my body and can't tell what I am—whether I am a woman or not, whether he is attracted to me or not, whether I might have sex with him or not, whether I might be some kind of deviant or the dirtiest word—a *feminist*—he might feel confused. He might feel angry. He might feel like everything he's been led to believe about himself and the world has been taken away. In the case of a serial rapist who stalked my neighborhood a few years ago, he might decide to start attacking women who look queer, because their bodies contradict his ideas of what women should be. Because their very existence defies his belief that their bodies should belong to him.

These days, I don't get catcalled when I walk down the street. I don't get whistled at on my way to the grocery store or standing on the subway platform. I don't get *Hey, baby* or *What's up, mama?* or *Give me a smile, sugar*, like I did when I looked more feminine. I don't fear the kind of daily unwanted attention that so many women and femme queer people get just for existing in public. But when I walk out of my apartment at night, when I round dark corners or pass beneath unlit scaffolding, I think of the man in the bodega. He is what I'm afraid of.

~

Growing up, I was a tomboy. It's what people called me and what I eventually started calling myself. At first, I resisted the word: I knew when people called me *tomboy* it was meant to call out my difference, that it set me apart from the other girls in my small midwestern town. And back then, I didn't want to be different. On more than one occasion I recall my small self, fists on hips, insisting, "I'm a tom*girl*," and campaigning to get the word to stick. But I also secretly loved the word *boy* attached to me. I played with the boys and acted like a boy. I fought and spat and swore and yelled, climbed trees and built forts and splashed in the mud. I played sports and rode bikes and banged up my knees. I hated anything deemed girly, rejected dresses and dolls and the color pink. When I was in second grade, I insisted my mother let me cut my hair short and spiky, like all the other boys. (After weeks of begging she relented, with the caveat that I leave it long in the back. She cut around my ears and I sculpted my spikes with gel, the rest of my hair cascading down my back, the first of several horrible mullets.)

On a deeper level, I often felt like a boy. I often wished I was a boy. Sometimes I even prayed to be a boy, pleading with a God I wasn't even sure I believed in that I might wake up the following day and everything would be different. Being a girl made me angry. It felt like a curse to be a girl, a cruel injustice that I had to be anything other than a boy. I fought with the boys who called me *girl* and with the girls who called me *boy*. On the school bus, when the older boys called me *beast* and spat in my hair, I spat back. I plucked the head off the only Barbie I owned, her impossibly proportioned and headless body serving as the one thing I understood a woman's body to be: the object of male desire. Alone in the bathtub, I smashed the green muscled bodies of my Teenage Mutant Ninja Turtles action figures against the smooth pale skin of my headless plastic woman. In my childhood fantasy, she fulfilled the role of girlfriend to Leonardo, the manliest hero of the sewer-dwelling mutant quartet. Their romance was always narrated from Leo's perspective, his repressed sexual energies expended deep below the surface of the water, among the bubbles, out of sight even from me.

One day, at the Montessori school I attended for preschool and kindergarten in my small Wisconsin town, my friends and I played outside in the sun. It was hot, and the boys ran around with their shirts off. So I took mine off too.

"Girls need to wear their shirts, Melissa," a teacher said.

Instead of putting my shirt back on, I climbed to the roof of the school. I have no idea how I got there, but in my memory there I stand, shirtless and defiant, bare feet on the hot slate shingles, waving my T-shirt triumphantly in the air and refusing to come down. In one version of the memory, I whip the shirt above my head like a lasso and launch it to the ground, laughing maniacally at my own dissidence. However it happened, what I know for sure is, at least for a little while, I stayed there—a veritable boy of summer, bare chested in the sun.

The word *tomboy* has a complicated past. First recorded in the mid-sixteenth century, it was used to describe a "rude and boisterous" boy. By the 1590s, it had become a slur used against "a wild, romping girl who acts like a boy" or, more commonly, a "strumpet, a bold or immodest woman." It was wielded, in particular, at girls of lower classes who behaved in ways deemed unladylike, classless, and vile. By the mid-1800s, *tomboy* became more than a word; it defined a code of conduct used as a way to encourage a more active lifestyle in young girls. While this might seem wholesome on the surface, the subtext was sinister. As Michelle Ann Abate writes in *Tomboys: A Literary and Cultural History*, when slavery was abolished in the United Kingdom, upper- and middle-class white families grew concerned that the white race would become the minority. The patriarchy encouraged girls to run and play and live more like boys, to eat a healthy diet, to exercise. Ultimately, to move away from the Victorian ideal of the "fair lady"—the frail, thin, pale, and inactive girl—and toward a robust, active one was a way to ensure that girls would be healthy enough to procreate, thus keeping the kingdom's white-majority status strong. This, too, was true in the antebellum United States: Combined with declining birth rates among upper- and middle-class whites and the decreasing vitality of the children they did produce, the abolition of slavery and an influx of immigrants led many white people to fear that a potential "race suicide" would soon be underway, and they would become the minority in the United States. Tomboyism among white American girls offered a solution. It was specifically encouraged so that girls would become vital, healthy, childbearing adults—so that, ultimately, they would become mothers. And what began as a word to deride those who bucked traditional expectations of femininity became, in essence, a way to perpetuate it.

Tomboy has, of course, adopted a less racist, less heteronormative, and more inclusive meaning since then. It is typically used to describe girls who act or dress in a masculine fashion and is often associated with early identity development among queer women. Androgynous clothing companies claim the word as a banner of pride, and queer communities have embraced it as a word to describe not just an appearance but an identity. Some research suggests a correlation between girls who identify as tomboys and those who grow up to identify as queer, trans, or nonbinary. Not every tomboy grows up to be queer, of course, but a lot of us do.

In rural spaces, girls grow up on the land. We play in the fields and the forest; we climb trees; we help our families garden and farm; we join the Future Farmers of America or the 4-H Club or the Girl Scouts, where outdoor skills are encouraged and honed. Where I come from, women are strong. We're built like barns, built to work. We might look more masculine, not least because we tend to do more traditionally masculine work.

This is true of many of the women in my family—including my late grandmother, my mother, and several of my aunts—almost all of whom have worked factory jobs or service jobs or both. I worked these kinds of jobs too. I started working when I was twelve, helping my parents take inventories of rural gas stations; crouched on our hands and knees in small dusty convenience stores across the state, we counted everything on the shelves by hand. My parents, who are now in their late sixties, still do this work. As a teenager, I worked on the floor of a discount clothing store— work both my parents did for much of their lives—and as a waitress and bartender at a pub in my hometown. I tended bar and waited tables in college too, and later worked as a barista, to pay my way through school.

I was the first in my immediate family to get a degree. Where I come from, we don't necessarily go to college. We might not have the money; we might not have the interest. We might have a family farm or business to take over; we might develop a skilled trade instead. We might join a union and stay in it for life. If we do go to college, we might go to technical and two-year programs for such trades. And we dress and present in a way that makes those jobs more efficient. Middle-aged and older women in particular tend toward the androgynous, with close-cropped hair and functional, less-than-fashionable clothing. (The slow cross-country crawl of fashion is a factor in this too. Not only do trends make their way to the flyover states at a snail's pace—a realization I made when I moved to New York, in 2009, and didn't own a single pair of skinny jeans—but sometimes they never make it at all. And if they do, few rural Midwesterners have the money or time to care.)

It's no wonder when people think of the tomboy, they often think of a Midwesterner, of a boyish little girl running around the prairies of Middle America like Laura Ingalls Wilder. They think of a farmer, of a woman in coveralls fixing a faucet. They think of a bartender, serving Miller Lite to construction workers at happy hour. Tomboys exist in other parts of the country, of course, in rural and urban spaces alike, as do women who work backbreaking jobs that keep them on their feet all day. But when I think of the rural Midwest, I think of it as a place where a girl's body is uniquely connected to the land in which she was born: where girls hunt and fish and fight and don't always shed their masculine characteristics as they get older. When I think of the Midwest, a place whose boundaries and borders are contentious, a place given so many different names—from the Great Plains to the Great Lakes states to the Upper Midwest—I think of a place that transcends boundaries, that defies definition, a body that holds within it a multitude of identities. When I think of my Midwest—the heartland, the hinterland, a place of farmland and factories, of forests and rivers and lakes—I think of it as Tomboyland.

~

In sixth grade, a new girl moved to town. We shared the same birth-day, and I swore to myself I would make her my best friend. I did, somehow, and for a few years we were inseparable. One night, I sat alone on my bedroom floor with my yearbook open and ran my finger over her photo. Without thinking, I bent down and kissed the page where her lips, in grainy black and white, were locked in a half smile, my little heart hammering in my chest.

In college, there was the girl in my poetry workshop who wrote an ode to new Chuck Taylors. There was the barista with a shaved head and a sleeve of tattoos. At the dawn of social media, when our MySpace pages became Facebook pages, we of the analog childhood discovered such platforms offered a new coded language to describe our sexual and romantic proclivities without actually having to name them. In 2005, during my fourth of a five-year college degree, I put together my first Facebook profile—carefully curating the songs and books and films that painted the best picture of my uniquely subversive and interesting self. With the fear and exhilaration that only the internet—with its new promise of anonymity and opportunity—could bring, I arrived at the "Interested In" section.

I had three options: "Men," "Women," or "Men and Women."

I hesitated. My heart raced. I felt dizzy, and my vision blurred at the edges. I clicked the third option. For a few minutes I panicked, my fingers hovering above the mouse, ready to change it. But eventually I moved my hand away. I sat at my desk, alone in my room, and considered the implications of this little virtual box. The options it offered seem limited now, but it was liberating then. It allowed me to say what I wanted to say—to call myself what I was pretty sure I might be—without having to use the word for it.

When you do a Google search of the word *bisexuality*, or at least when I last did, the fourth option on the auto dropdown was this: *Bisexuality doesn't exist.*

Bisexual erasure is a problem, and one I've experienced for years. I've gotten it from straight people, who say bisexuals are just deviants, just experimenting, just promiscuous (as if being attracted to multiple genders necessarily means you have more sex). But I've gotten it far more from queer people, many of whom have suggested, however subtly or not, that those who claim to be bisexual are repressed or pretending or both.

"That's not a real thing," a gay woman once told me.

"Girl, you're either one or the other," a gay man once said.

"Lesbians only!" the young girlfriend of a friend said once as a group of us planned a trip away for the weekend.

"The straight girls are stealing our signifiers," a friend once said of a queer-identified woman who was dating a man.

This isn't anything new. There is a long history of biphobia and erasure in the queer community. Bisexuality has been called antigay and antifeminist; it's been called a lie. More than once, Pride organizers have attempted to exclude bisexuals and trans people from marching in parades—the irony being that the very first Pride march was organized by a bisexual woman—as if those third and fourth letters in the acronym were just as imaginary as the people they represent.

For me, my body becomes the problem. My body, the lens through which people perceive not just my gender but also my sexuality. Because of how I look—the way I'm built and the signifiers I wear—people can't look at me and believe I could be anything other than a gay woman, or else a man. They certainly can't fathom that I might love a man. When I meet new people, queer or straight, I carry this anxiety with me—that as soon as I reveal I'm in a relationship with a man, I will be questioned or invalidated or both. Sometimes I don't offer this information. Sometimes I get outed. Sometimes I keep it like a secret.

Recently, a lesbian writer I follow on Twitter tweeted a scathing takedown of bisexuals, accusing us of functioning as tourists in the "queer community," of stealing words like *dyke* and trying on identities, of possessing the privilege of "passing as straight." (I wanted to respond, but of course I didn't, because the only place more terrifying than the real world is Twitter.) I haven't possessed the ability to "pass as straight" for nearly twenty years. When I walk down the street, alone or alongside my partner, I don't magically assimilate into the throngs of heterosexuals; if anything, I might stand out more. People can't figure out what I am, where my body exists in the context of this man. *Who and what are these bodies?* I can see people thinking. *And how do they fit together?*

I often hear the argument that, as a bisexual woman in a relationship with a man, I don't face the threat of a hate crime when I walk down the street holding hands with my partner. But while walking down the street with a man I've still been sneered at, spat at, and menaced, told I'm going to hell, and called any number of slurs. In one case, a man jumped at my partner and me as we passed him on the sidewalk. The man feinted like a boxer, fists bared for fighting, the white-knuckled threat of them swinging and stopping just short of my face.

I understand, to a certain extent, why gay people might respond negatively to bisexuals. We might be perceived as a threat to the work of gay rights, to the fight for equality they keep having to fight. We might be seen as participating in the system of heteronormativity—or at least having the option to—and thus not belonging in queer spaces. But it becomes, in essence, a kind of oppression Olympics—who is the more marginalized among us, who has more rights, and who belongs within our communities? Like so many of the systems in which we live, oppression is tricking the oppressed into oppressing each other.

It's a lonely place to be, excluded by the community to which I see myself belonging and existing outside the one in which they think I belong. Most of the time, when someone within the queer community tells me I don't belong there, I believe them.

I'm afraid I'm losing my identity," I tell my therapist. I'm talking about erasure, the process of making someone invisible, that cultural and political weapon used against entire populations—people of color, people with disabilities, queer and trans people, to name a few—that allows for the dehumanization of a body. If a body isn't real, then neither is the human who wears it.

"How do you lose your identity?" she asks, an eyebrow raised.

"I don't know," I tell her, because I'm not sure what I mean. I stumble through some half-baked ideas about the "queer community," about feeling separated from that community "because I'm bi—or whatever," because I've been in a relationship with a man for so long. That I've got a bunch of straight friends now; that my life feels so heteronormative. That, in some ways, it feels easier there, but with that comfort I feel a part of myself fading away. I say I don't feel queer enough to call myself queer. That maybe I don't have the right to. That when I look in the mirror, I'm not sure what I see. That I have no idea how I fit into the world, or how I'm perceived in it.

My therapist holds up a hand.

"Identity isn't what people think of you," she says. "It's how you think of yourself. It's how you live your life. It's how you carry yourself in the world."

~

As a species, we possess the indelible need to categorize, to classify, to contain. We want to look at a thing and know what it is. We want a race and a class and an age and a gender. We can't know or imagine what we can't define, so we've developed language to do this work for us—to give something a name, and in naming it give it an order, a meaning, a place in the world. But language—like gender, like sexuality—is fluid, not a static thing. And language provides a limited number of options. Beyond that, there is a vast expanse, a tunnel, a cave—a dim gray space without much light, if there's any light at all. Maybe it's the job of those of us who live in that liminal space, who live beyond what is already defined, to determine what might exist in the unnamed places between. To be the explorers. To set out into the darkness, strike a match, and get a good look around. To seek not answers, necessarily, but to stand still for a while and listen. And to know, at the very least, we tried. We faced the darkness of the unknown. We looked. We kept our eyes open, even when the match went out.

When I was a kid, I hated my name. I resented the very sound of it, the feel of it on my tongue: the kiss of those two *S*s, the *M* and the *E* and the *L* and the *I* flowing so fluidly together, the *A* like a sigh. A name so close to the word *mellifluous*, its loops and curls rolling together in one sweet, silky strand of honey—the Greek root of the name. *Melissa* was the name of not just a girl but a sweet girl, a girly girl. Picture Melissa: She is pretty and petite and probably blonde. She has a small ski-slope nose, is almost definitely a cheerleader. She goes by the name Missy. I wanted a name that was short and fast, sharp rather than sweet: Sam or Chris or Max or Jo. Something small but strong, landing like a punch or a jab, a *pow* or a *bam* like the fighting words in the comic books I read. Something masculine. *Melissa* was the twirl of a skirt, a lock of long hair. Soft and supple and feminine, the opposite of everything I was and wanted to be.

I've tried on several nicknames over the years: from M, the very first, given to me when I was four or five by my next-door neighbors— ambiguous and blessedly short, built of possibility, brevity, and ease. Many of my closest friends still call me M. I was Fali in high school, which was a pretty good fit for the time—sporty and precocious and a bit of a flirt. There was Harlot Brontë, my roller derby moniker, both a reclamation of a sexual slur and an invocation of a nineteenth-century literary feminist and revolutionary who wrote under a masculine pen name. A friend of mine named Melissa—a queer woman who has similar issues with her name—and I recently started calling one another Mitch; it started as a joke and then it stuck. Finally, there's Lou: short for my middle name and after my paternal grandmother, Louise, who also went by the shortened version. Lou is the Sam or Max I always wanted—strong and fast and androgynous—staked more firmly in the camp of male, a name that feels most like me. Still, I introduce myself as Melissa. I sign my name Melissa. It's the name my parents gave me— yes, after the Allman Brothers' song—and so it's the name I keep. But it still shocks me when I hear it. It feels strange on my tongue when I say it. After all these years, I still feel like I exist outside of it. It's a name that at once feels like mine but has never felt like me.

There are countless words one might use to describe their identity, categories and subcategories I can't even keep up with—each of which, in its creation, is an attempt to better define a body, a desire, a place in the world. To some, *bisexual* sounds problematic because it can be interpreted as perpetuating the gender binary. Like me, most people I know who identify as bisexual use the word to mean one who is oriented not toward persons of either sex, but to one's own gender and all others. For a hot second, more than a decade ago, I was drawn to the word *pansexual*, which was coined, in part, to expand upon this earlier binary understanding. I might have gotten behind it were it not for the evocation of Pan, Greek god of the wild, and his harem of nymphs—an image that doesn't do much for the nonmonosexual cause.

To describe my body, I've tried on the words *gender-fluid* and *non-binary*, but tend to land on *genderqueer* or *gender-nonconforming*. I let the words roll around in my mouth, whispering them to myself, saying them aloud only when I'm alone. Sometimes I think of myself a *soft butch*—in the lexicon, it means a lean toward the masculine with some feminine traits still apparent. This seems sort of right; I've never felt fully *butch*, but there's something about attaching the word *soft* to myself that also doesn't feel perfect. Part of what I like most about my body is its hardness. But sometimes, in the bathroom mirror, I look at the curve of my hip; I run a finger along the line of it, over its dip and bend, along the hard peak of the iliac crest. There have been times in my life when I looked at these hips with desperation, when I wished they were even more narrow than they are. But sometimes, I like that curve. There's something about it that feels elemental, something round and soft and open.

Of all the linguistic possibilities, *queer* is the word I return to most. It's a word I can use to describe both my gender and my sexuality without naming specifics. But in that broadness exists ambiguity, too, and when I call myself *queer* it's usually assumed I mean gay. The word also carries with it a whole other set of problems. Kids in my hometown used the word as a weapon, and a lot of people still do. And while I'm all about reclaiming language, there's still a part of me that flinches at the word. There's still a part of me that's scared of it. This is embarrassing to admit, in today's enlightened age. But it's a truth with which I'm still grappling.

The word *androgynous* comes from the Greek *andros*, "of man," and *gyne*, "of woman." Historically the word was used to describe an organism with both male and female sex characteristics (as a noun: *androgyne*), often used interchangeably with *hermaphrodite*. In botany: "having staminate and pistillate flowers in one fluorescence." More recent definitions, such as *Merriam-Webster's*, reflect a linguistic and cultural shift: "neither specifically feminine nor masculine." Or, from *Webster's New World Dictionary*: "not differentiated as to gender."

A few years ago, I was working at a literary conference when I saw someone I immediately recognized. I don't mean I'd met her before; it's more that I felt like I knew her. I saw myself in her. I introduced myself. Her handshake was firm and strong; she had a shaved head and an androgynous build. I found her attractive, but more than that I felt a sudden and certain kinship. She, I would find out, was bisexual, too, and in a long-term relationship with a man. And she, like me, has struggled with feelings of invisibility, especially within the queer community. Lately, she's been experimenting with the word *androgyne* to describe her body. I like this word, not least because of its linguistic roots, its tangible combination of both woman and man. It's hard enough, though, using words already ubiquitous in the LGBTQIA+ lexicon, so I'm not sure how I'd fare using this one. But then again, a new word, without any built-in implications, might be a kind of liberation. "What are the words," Audre Lorde wrote, "you do not yet have?"

~

There was the boy in the airport Hudson News who pointed at my body and laughed. There was the boy in the gas station in Kansas who tugged on his mother's skirt as they passed me in the candy aisle and asked, "Mama, is that a boy or a girl?" There was the man at a truck stop in Ohio, who stood in line for the men's room as I waited for the women's and said, "I think you're in the wrong line."

These are small things on the scale of harm a body can incur. I'm not being raped. I'm not being killed. I'm not being beaten or tortured or shot in the streets. But the small, everyday ways people question and threaten and mock—the way they try, in the end, to exert power over the bodies of others—this, too, is a kind of violence.

When I was twenty-two and still in college, I got a job as the editorial assistant to a well-known editor, a man who worked for a major New York publisher. We were throwing a party at an annual feminist literature convention at a hotel in Madison, Wisconsin. I had bought a new pair of dress pants and shiny black Oxfords, a dress shirt and blazer. I was broke, making below minimum wage, and had spent the better part of a paycheck on the outfit. As we set up for the party, I ran around the conference room stocking bottles of beer in a tub of ice and setting cocktail tables, as authors and editors I was excited to meet started trickling in. Then my boss found me.

"You're going to change, right?" he said.

"What?" I asked, unsure of what he was saying.

"You're going to put on a dress, right?"

"I was just going to wear this—" I stammered, looking down at my outfit, then around the room. It was what most of the men were wearing.

"You need to go home and put a skirt on or something," he said. "You look like a waiter."

I would like to tell you I told him to fuck off, that I stayed at the event in the outfit I had just drained my bank account to buy. But what really happened is I left the room, walked out to the parking garage, and drove back to my apartment on the other side of town. I put on a skirt. I put on nylons. I wiped the dust off an old pair of heels. I was twenty-two, it was my first job in an industry within which I hoped to build a career, and the editor I worked for—who would, years later, be fired from the publisher and banned from the convention; mine was not the only experience of its kind—was at the time a man who possessed a relative amount of power and influence in that industry. I didn't know what else to do but obey him. I drove back to the hotel, paid for parking a second time, and walked back into the party in my skirt and heels.

When I got there, my boss said, "That's better."

In the mid-nineteenth century, as tomboyism became more popular in the United States, so, too, did the tradition of what Abate calls "tomboy taming." Young girls were encouraged to be tomboys only until a certain age—namely, puberty—and were then trained out of it. This process might have taken the form of actual classes—such as tea-training and etiquette lessons, in which a young woman was taught how to set the table, to drink and serve tea, to keep a proper house for her husband and children—or was instilled in more implicit ways. It might have meant suggesting to a girl that it was time she traded her pants for a dress. That she should grow her hair out and start paying more attention to her grooming. That she was far too old to be playing outside with the boys.

Tomboyism, Abate writes, was specifically encouraged in childrearing manuals of the time, suggesting that girls who were tomboys would develop both the physical and mental constitution required for motherhood. Tomboyism was good for the health of the young girl and for bringing her up with a vital constitution, but when she came of breeding age, it was time to start thinking of attracting the boys, getting married, and having children. As Abate notes, one must look no further than Jo, the iconic gender-bending protagonist of Louisa May Alcott's *Little Women*, and her sister Meg, as an example of this. "You are old enough to leave off boyish tricks and to behave better, Josephine," Meg says to her younger sister. "You should remember that you are a young lady."

In tomboy taming, the hope was—and in many respects still is—that a girl might tame herself; that by nature, she'll simply grow out of it. For a time, this was what I did. On a recent trip home, I met up with two friends from high school. Both women have kids now, and we don't see each other very often. But we were close when we were kids, playing softball together and driving around town, hanging out in each other's basements, watching movies and music videos and talking about boys, parties, and college, dreaming of escape.

My friend Sarah still lives in our hometown, across the street from the park where we played softball in high school. We sat around her kitchen table on a Friday night, drinking wine and telling stories about the past, as her daughter ran around the living room. We talked about who had left town and who hadn't, who had changed and who was still the same.

"I think you've changed the most," Sarah said to me.

"Really?" I asked.

"You were such a girly girl," she said.

"A *girly* girl?" I repeated, stunned. "I was *girly*?"

"Well," she said, "you were always at your locker between class doing your hair. Wearing skirts, chasing boys."

I felt like I had been punched in the solar plexus. I felt like I was hearing someone else's story. And then I realized she was right. For so long, I'd thought of myself as a lifelong tomboy—that I was born this way, have always been this way. But the truth is that I built this narrative of myself, and my body, to align with how I inhabit it *now*—without realizing I'd done it. When I was a teenager, I did change. I traded in my baseball card collection and *GamePro* magazine and *Sonic the Hedgehog* comic books for *Seventeen*, *Bop*, and *Sassy*. I put away my hockey jerseys and Badgers Starter jacket and oversize Packers sweatshirts and started shopping at places like American Eagle Outfitters and Abercrombie & Fitch, attempting to fit my body into the tight clothes of the half-naked, elephant-riding, suntanned, hair-bleached teenagers on the walls of those stores.

I spent hours getting ready each morning before school, standing at the bathroom mirror, drawing on my eyeliner and penciling in over-plucked eyebrows with the fastidiousness that I had once used to draw my own comic books. I painted my mascara on just right, curled my bangs, and sprayed them with Aqua Net. I tried on multiple outfits each morning, and nothing ever felt right. I was never thin enough or sexy enough or fair enough. I was always self-conscious about my belly and arms, which always felt fat, and about my dark, frizzy hair, which was so unlike that of my school's popular girls, all tan and blonde and Nordic. When a flat iron proved useless in achieving the idyllic arrow-straight

Jennifer Aniston hair of the '90s, I started using a clothes iron instead. I laid my waist-length mane directly on the ironing board in the basement, pressing the steaming metal thing down upon my waves every day for months until they were burned to a crisp and smelled uncannily like a wet horse. (I'd read in *Sassy* that this was totally safe, as long as you used a towel, but my hair was stubborn, and I soon scrapped the towel for a more direct approach.) I hid this from my mother until I couldn't. I would emerge from the shower in the morning and the smell would follow me through the house and sit with me at the kitchen table as I ate my cereal.

"Have you been ironing your hair?" My mother, a child of the '60s, knew it when she smelled it. She picked up a charred clump of it and let it fall with a thud against my shoulders; then she turned away and gagged. This was the first time I would cut off all my hair.

I shaved my legs and sometimes my arms. For a while I used Nair, slicking my arms with the stinky stuff in the bathtub on a near-nightly basis; it never quite worked and left my arms dotted with thick, dark patches of hair. Once, before a summer vacation to Florida, my father gifted my mother and me a trip to a spa. Like a normal person, my mother selected items from the menu like a massage and a manicure. I, meanwhile, got my arms and legs waxed. On the white-sand beaches of Boca Raton, my fourteen-year-old body was red and swollen and sore, sick from the sun.

When I was in college, I eventually found my way back to tomboyhood. I cut off all my hair again, and didn't mind that it grew thick and dark on my arms and legs. I stopped wearing makeup. I still occasionally wore skirts to weddings, but it started to feel wrong, and I eventually got rid of them. I felt like I was waking up, like I was reinhabiting my body. But sometime between then and now, I had forgotten about all the years I had feminized myself, when someone might have considered me *girly*. If you had asked me a few years ago what that time was like for me, I probably would have compared it to dressing in drag against my will. Today, if I were told I had to wear a skirt to work or an event—a possibility that, as I write this, the Supreme Court is currently deciding—it would feel much worse than that. But when I think about that girl in high school, I'm not totally sure. Maybe there was part of her that felt powerful or at home in femininity. Or maybe femininity, insofar as what society expects it to look like, was just what I had learned it required for those of us born into female bodies to feel powerful, to feel at home.

Sometimes I think about growing my hair out. Sometimes I wonder if I might one day want to wear a dress again. Sometimes I feel committed to the shape my gender takes today, and sometimes I wonder how fluid that gender might be. Sometimes I miss being told I look nice, or pretty, or beautiful—things most people stopped telling me once I started looking more masculine. Sometimes I wonder what my life would look like if I started wearing makeup again, if I painted my nails and wore jewelry and donned the costume of signifiers expected of me—some of which would feel like a betrayal, like an act of violence against my body. I wonder what it would be like to once again reflect all that tells the world I am pretty, I am feminine, I am a normal human living in my body as I'm supposed to. That I am straight. That I am available to men. That I am a woman. I wonder if I might feel that power again.

And sometimes I wonder what it would be like to pass through the world as a man. Recently, in the woods of northern Wisconsin, the place where I often feel most at home and where I can live the butchest version of my self—think flannel shirts and baseball hats, hiking boots and fishing boats and fire building—I was mistaken for a man for an entire conversation. One woman repeatedly referred to me as *he* and *him* as we talked, until another woman took my name and quietly corrected her colleague. The experience was disconcerting. But it also left me with a thought I'd never had before. What if I did this all the time? What kind of power might I feel then?

I want to talk about the word *womanhood*, and what we mean when we say it. As I write this, I sit in a room alone. On my desk, I have an early edition of Virginia Woolf's *A Room of One's Own*, in addition to three books by Rebecca Solnit, both writers women, feminists, childless, and, in Woolf's case, queer.

In *A Room of One's Own*, originally a talk titled "Professions for Women," Woolf writes famously of killing the Angel in the House—the ideal woman, who cooks and cleans and cares for husband and children, who serves her family and never thinks of her own needs or desires.

"I did my best to kill her," Woolf writes. "My excuse, if I were to be had up in a court of law, would be that I acted in self-defence."

I have complicated feelings about marriage, and I'm pretty sure I don't want children. For many people, this makes me less of a woman.

I wonder sometimes why I feel attached to the word *woman* at all. I wonder why I can't separate myself from it like some people I know have been able to. Sometimes I'm sure I want to, and sometimes I'm sure I don't. I'd like to think of myself as someone who refuses to participate in the system of gender entirely, and yet I still seek its labels and identifiers to help give me meaning, to help me feel like I belong. I still prefer the pronouns *she* and *her*, in part because I like the sound of them attached to me, and in part because I feel connected to them. But I also understand that this is in great part a product of sociocultural learning—that from the second we are born (and in many cases long before, as in the obnoxious practice of gender-reveal parties), we are called *girl*. We are called *she*. Like my name, even though these words I was given don't always seem to fit, they still somehow feel like mine.

I suspect this feeling of connection has something to do with my forebears, my midwestern grandmother and great-grandmothers, strong women who worked the land. With my mother, a feminist and revolutionary in her own right, who burned her bra and protested the Vietnam War and argued with her father about his conservative politics and the evils of the patriarchy. My own identity as a woman, such as it is, was born of these women. When I think of myself as a woman, I think first of those who came before me.

Perhaps, as Solnit writes in the title essay of *The Mother of All Questions*, "There is no good answer to how to be a woman; the art may instead lie in how we refuse the question."

~

According to the Bisexual Resource Center, nearly half of bisexual women have considered or attempted suicide, compared to just over a quarter of lesbians and gay men. Bisexuals also report higher rates of depression and anxiety compared to lesbians and heterosexual women. One in two bisexual women has experienced violence by an intimate partner, as opposed to one in three lesbians and one in four heterosexual women. Bisexual women are less likely to be out to their doctors and families, and are more likely to have substance abuse issues.

I count myself among these statistics. I've suffered from clinical depression and anxiety, have been in violent relationships, have a history of self-harm, and have struggled with substance abuse. Luckily, I also have the privilege my whiteness affords: I have access to health care, therapy, and a network of people I can talk to. Many other people—especially trans people and queer people of color, and especially in this country, where health care is still considered a privilege rather than a right—aren't so lucky.

But the problem seems to be the same across race and socioeconomic status: If people—including and maybe especially those you count among your community, on whom you depend to lift you up and protect you—don't believe you exist, you might start to feel like you shouldn't.

A few years ago, I went to a doctor who told me to get off birth control. I'd been on the pill since I was eighteen, and it had started to cause what she described as prestroke symptoms.

"I guess I'll have to start using condoms," I said, half joking. She stopped typing up her notes and turned to look at me with a frown.

"Aren't you gay?" she asked.

I hesitated, a wave of panic rising up in my chest.

"I mean," I said, stammering, "I'm bisexual, I guess, but my partner is a man."

She rolled her eyes and sighed, then wagged a finger at me.

"See?" she said. "You people are the problem."

~

After years of waging a war against my body, I'm finally starting to feel more at home in it. I still wish it was stronger, leaner. I still find myself sizing up the more girlish parts of my body: my thighs, from which I can never seem to shed that extra layer of flesh; my stomach, which is never as hard as I want it to be; my breasts, which I wish were smaller than they are. I often wish I had no breasts at all, and sometimes think about getting top surgery. I wonder if, without breasts, I might feel more complete in my body, more aligned with who I imagine myself to be. Sometimes, I think, if I could only shed myself of these remaining traces of girl, I would be even more myself. And if I am a woman, maybe I would feel even more like the woman I imagine myself to be.

My partner and I are similar in shape and size. We look a little alike, wear each other's clothes, and have been mistaken on more than a few occasions for a gay couple. Sometimes I joke that I'm more of a gay man than a bisexual woman, but sometimes I wonder if there's more truth to that than I realize. And sometimes I feel like a fraud. Even though I don't pass as straight, and don't consider myself to be in a strictly heterosexual relationship, I still understand that I often benefit from the privileges of one. Sometimes I feel like my body has become a lie.

When John and I are together in public, sometimes I get uncomfortable. When I'm alone on the street, people can assume of me what they will, without the influence of another body next to mine. If they notice me at all, they'll almost certainly assume I'm queer—and this is the assumption I'd rather have people make, the read of me that feels right. Next to him, my body becomes more of a question.

I ask John how he feels when he walks next to me, how he felt the day we hopped into a cab and the driver asked us fellas where we were heading. I ask him how he sees me, and how it feels to be misread.

"Honestly, it doesn't bother me," he says, noting that he only gets angry on my behalf when I'm misgendered, because he knows how uncomfortable it makes me.

"But when I'm with you," he says, "I'm just with you—a beautiful, androgynous human. To me, you've only ever been you."

Sometimes I want to go home. I'm just not sure where that is anymore. I still call myself midwestern, and in many ways I think I still am. I feel like I belong to a landscape that made me: one of stillness and quiet, of trees and lakes and farmland, a place where I can hike in the woods and crunch through the snow and fill my lungs with fresh air. But does quiet necessitate more scrutiny? In small towns and rural spaces, like where I grew up, I feel more eyes on my body. With its androgynous shape and chosen childlessness, my body stands out. I am both a product of this place and a body that never quite fit in. In a city, where there are more bodies that look like mine, it's easier to pass unseen. And what freedom there is, in the annihilation of identity. In her 1930 essay "Street Haunting: A London Adventure," Virginia Woolf writes of the anonymity a city affords, where one can step out onto a city street in the evening and pass through throngs of people unnoticed. Solnit examines this idea further in her essay "Woolf's Darkness: Embracing the Inexplicable," noting that Woolf is describing "a form of society that doesn't enforce identity but liberates it, the society of strangers, the republic of the streets, the experience of being anonymous and free that big cities invented."

Now that I've lived in New York for more than a decade, I wonder if I'm more at home here than anywhere I've been. I wonder if, paradoxically, I'm safer here. As much as I long to leave this city—to return to the trees, to the land of my making, to the place I have always called home—I wonder if I might belong here instead.

In 2017, following the election, I attended several rallies in New York. Two were particularly powerful. The first was the Women's March, in January, which protested, among other things, gender inequity and the inauguration of a president who has harassed, disparaged, and assaulted women. As I marched with two million other New Yorkers, I felt unquestionably like a woman: one who was angry, frustrated, and fed up with the way women are still treated. A few months later, I went to the Dyke March. It's a protest march that began in Washington, DC, in the early '90s and is held every year in cities throughout the country. It's unsponsored, unpermitted, and unprotected, an activist-led, intersectional alternative to the increasingly corporate Pride parade. I was nervous about going. A quiet fear crawled around inside me, telling me

I wasn't queer enough to be there, that I certainly wasn't dyke enough. That if I met new people and told them I lived with a man, they'd kick me out of the parade. And wouldn't I deserve that? But several of my friends, all of them queer women, had encouraged me to go, insisting I belonged.

When I emerged from the subway, I stood outside the New York Public Library at Bryant Park, one of my favorite buildings in the city, and found myself among a massive crowd of bodies that looked a lot like mine. I spotted a friend, a lesbian, at the front of the line. She was serving as a marshal for the parade and was handing out signs and shirts to marchers. When she saw me, she smiled and called my name. Then she hugged me and handed me a shirt that said DYKE in big capital letters on the front.

"I'm so happy you're here," she said.

∼

I tell my therapist about my nondate with the new friend. I tell her that, despite our uncomfortable start at that oyster bar in Brooklyn, we've gone on to become close friends. I say it feels good to talk to this smart queer woman who likes to discuss books and writing and queerness.

"I'll bet that was confusing for you," my therapist says.

At first her words make me angry. I hear them as an accusation, a suggestion that I've heard from so many queer women in my life, that I'm repressed or closeted or both. Then she tells me she thinks it's time I start to confront the internalized homophobia I've been carrying around for so long. I sit there for a second, shocked and still and defensive. But as I leave her office that day and walk out into the sun, I begin to understand what she is asking of me—to interrogate this question about myself, which for most of my life has been much easier to avoid.

It turns out that when you spend your life surrounded by homophobia, and biphobia, it's pretty easy to turn it on yourself. To question your body, your identity, your very existence in the world. Something else my therapist reminds me often is this: To live well is to speak one's truth—even if that truth is just a question.

I write this on the property that once belonged to the poet Edna St. Vincent Millay, in the barn she built from a Sears and Roebuck kit with her own hands. Millay and her husband moved to this place, in the foothills of the Taconic Mountains in Upstate New York, when they grew tired of the city. They moved here for the quiet, for the trees and the mountains, for the creek that wanders through the property.

Millay preferred to go by the name Vincent. Her legacy over the years has been made into one of matronly nature sonnets, and it's true that her poetry was inspired by the walks she took in these mountains, under these trees. But what's also true, a story that rarely gets told, is that Vincent was a gender-nonconforming feminist and queer woman. She didn't necessarily use these labels, but she kept her hair short and wore suits and breeches and riding boots; she never had children, she and her husband had an open marriage, and she kept both women and men as lovers. Over the years, people have tried to define Edna St. Vincent Millay, but to the people who knew and loved her, she was, simply, Vincent.

I've stayed up here, on the land she called home, for the past two winters. It's a haven, a place where I can escape the city and return to the wilderness, where I can write and breathe in peace. I'm here now, in late February, staring out my window in the barn at a landscape of untouched snow, at the line of trees and the mountains beyond it as the sun sinks low over the horizon. Earlier today, I went for my daily hike in the woods. The crunch of my boots in the snow and the wind in the trees were the only sounds I heard. I peeked inside the window of Vincent's writing shack, then pressed on down a path and into the woods. I walked along a trail that's dotted with her poems, stopping to read each one aloud, talking to the trees, listening to the creak and groan of branches, the rustling of dead leaves. And I felt safe here, as I'm sure Vincent did. At home here. As if I belong in this place, to these trees, to this land that holds my body, sacred and holy and firm.

In her 2005 essay collection *A Field Guide to Getting Lost*, Rebecca Solnit writes, "to be lost is to be fully present, and to be fully present is to be capable of being in uncertainty and mystery."

I like this idea of willfully inhabiting a question, to dwell in the realm of the unknown, of the indefinite and indefinable, and to know you might never find an answer. I'm starting to think this might just be the key to survival.

So I'll take Solnit's advice and stop looking for answers. I'll keep trying to say things aloud, to use words even when I feel their limits. I'll remember that words—like us—are imperfect, are changing, are trying to do better. I'll remember that words can be resistance, that they can be a protest. That they can be used to liberate, to strengthen, to make visible those who have been unseen. That they can shed light on the darkness. That silence, as Audre Lorde wrote, is what kills us. I'll carry these words with me—not a burden but a beacon. I'll use this torch, and I'll travel down this dark path of unknowing. I'll stay awhile in this otherworld, this in-between, this mystery, this ephemeral space of body and language and identity—and just try to be alive here. I'll keep my eyes open and listen, as Sylvia Plath wrote, "to the old brag of my heart. I am, I am, I am."

OF A MOTH

But life is vigorous; the body lives.

—Virginia Woolf, *Night and Day*

For some months now, my apartment has been infested. Not with bedbugs or cockroaches or silverfish—those slick, sickly creatures that have plagued apartments of my past, and the apartments of so many in this huge, sprawling city by the sea—but with moths. Small, crawling, fluttering things, whose full-grown bodies look strikingly like butterflies, and whose larvae look devastatingly like maggots. The moths live not in my linen closets or dresser drawers, where one might expect them to live, nor in my curtains or clothes hamper; I do find them in these places sometimes, when I draw back my curtains on a rainy morning or when I pick through a pile of sweaters on my bedroom floor. In a billow of dust, they flutter out, frenetic and wild, their wings flapping frantically as they attempt to figure out where they are.

But the moths do not make their home in these places. Instead, they've built a settlement in my pantry—in the dark, narrow hallway connecting my bedroom and kitchen, its long row of cabinetry housing foods deemed nonperishable. The tile of the pantry floor is cracked; the old cupboard doors creak when they close and fall open on their own; some hang askew from rusted hinges. All are painted white but chipped down to wood. For months now, the moths have made this dark passage their home.

I tried everything I could to get rid of the pests. I cleaned obsessively with a cocktail of industrial-strength poisons; I purged opened food, months or years old. Upon discovering a commune of tiny, writhing larvae that had somehow made their way into a tin of almonds, I flung each of the eight pantry doors open, took every edible out of its cardboard or plastic packaging, dumped out and then sealed the contents up tightly in glass jars, cookie tins, and the few remaining Tupperware containers whose warped lids still fit snugly. Pasta in mason jars, cereal in large plastic bins, rows of new, shiny sarcophagus-like storage for my food. I was convinced that the moths, and the wormlike creatures that precede them, would be unable to chew through these tightly sealed tombs—that they would starve and die, and I would be left alone again.

When the moths first arrived, I had been living on my own for a little over a year, after having lived with a partner—by all accounts a man I would have eventually married—for five. We'd broken up, and I had moved across the country—leaving my family, my home, and the community I'd built for myself over the previous ten years. I gave away most of my things, packed a few boxes and bags into a car, and drove from my small midwestern home to New York, that hallowed, glittering metropolis on the coast, with the goal of starting over. The man drove with me—one last, long farewell. We spent two days together on the road, he got me settled in my new place, and then I watched him drive away. He would return to our small city, to our home, to our shared friends and community, and I would be left alone. I stood on the curb and waved, and he waved back. Then he turned a corner and was gone.

I'm someone who leaves quickly. And while I'd like to say I don't look back, the truth is that of course I do.

I moved into a crumbling little house, in a crumbling neighborhood, with a set of strangers. They were nice enough, my new roommates, but I kept mostly to myself: I worked, cooked, and ate alone. I shut myself inside my bedroom, eating bowls of canned soup on my bed, reading by lamplight, and eventually putting myself to sleep with a glass or two of whiskey each night. For the first time in years, I knew solitude—and I wanted nothing more. A year later, I moved into a second apartment with a new set of roommates, and we tried at first to be friends. But just a month or two after we'd moved in together, our interactions became increasingly diminished. It seemed in those days, by early fall, we existed only in one another's peripheries, living under the same roof, ostensibly together, but in reality floating in and out of an empty house, utterly alone. This was more my doing than theirs. Most days, I left the house, came home, made a quick dinner, then disappeared into my room with it. I'd emerge only when I had to, choosing times when I heard silence in the kitchen to sneak back out. Crusted bowls and mugs collected on my dresser and nightstand.

Anyone who has lived for a long time with a lover, and then suddenly does not, will understand what I mean by those crusted bowls, by those solo whiskeys, by the promise of solitude behind a closed door. That to be tethered, so intimately, for so long, and then to find yourself free, is both misery and miracle—a sudden and unlikely dream that brings both darkest despair and the euphoria of liberation. They'll understand the daily fixations on the ideas of togetherness and separateness; the idea that humans, or at least most of us, pair off and couple up and try as best as we can to stay with one mate for the rest of our lives, fueled in equal parts by love and connection and expectation, and at the root of it, the blind hope that we will never be alone again. And this, we're told, is what we should want most—a partner, children, family—those bound by sacrament or by state or by blood, who will, we believe with everything we have in our fragile human hearts, never leave us.

Those who have found themselves here will also understand what the transition from living with that lover to living with roommates, be they strangers or friends, is like. They will understand that, regardless of how much in common you may have with your new housemates— you're all artists, for instance, dancers or painters or poets—the solitude still finds you. No matter how closely you begin to coexist with them, or how genuinely you might want to be friends—no matter the number of people with whom a bathroom is shared or around whom you must dance to brew coffee in the mornings. Despite the dinner parties that are thrown and the spontaneous houseguests who arrive at the door to crash on the futon you found for cheap on Craigslist (crossing fingers and closing eyes and saying silent prayers for protection from bedbugs). Even when you come home after a long day of work to the warm smell of New Mexican red chiles simmering in the kitchen and your roommate—a woman with whom you share writing over wine and who will go on to become one of your closest friends—asks you to sit down and share a meal, even then you still feel entirely alone.

I felt this. Fully, inescapably, and nearly every day. The waves of loss surged and pitched and fell upon me like the swell of midwestern lakes during a summer storm, and I liked the weight. I just barely kept my head above the water, treading most days only enough to stay afloat but often letting my arms and legs go limp long enough to be pulled under. I liked the murky darkness under those waves, and I wanted to stay there. I realized, floating beneath the surface, that after years of being so intimately connected to one other human being, and after having that connection severed, I no longer had the desire to interact with anyone other than myself. These were dark days, the nights even darker. And in my darkest moments, typically accompanied by a third or fourth glass of whiskey in my unlit bedroom at night, I was convinced I would never want to form an intimate connection with anyone ever again. I was designed to be alone, and I wanted to stay that way.

The moths first arrived in late October, in the form of small whitish worms that had somehow, impossibly, made their blind and crawling way into one of my roommates' unopened bags of Japanese rice noodles. After much shrieking and waving of arms, fearing our apartment was infested with maggots, the first of many cleaning binges began. But it was too late: the worms—what we would shortly thereafter discover to be larvae—had hatched, and dozens of small winged creatures began crawling up the dark interior walls of the pantry, flying out and circling our heads every morning when we reached for a box of cereal, every evening when we pulled out the pasta. Like some kind of nightmare, the slick things were able to squeeze themselves inside even the most tightly sealed containers, unopened boxes and bags, the firmly twisted lids of mason jars. The moths and their larvae, it seemed, were unstoppable. And so, one dark Tuesday night, the brisk October wind setting bare branches of maples against the windows and bringing the promise of winter, the killing rampages began.

As I tore through the cabinets, I thought of Virginia Woolf's essay "The Death of the Moth." I thought of the author, sitting at her desk one warm afternoon in mid-September, watching a moth flutter and buzz and eventually fall to its death on the windowpane. And as I thought of that moth, slowing and struggling and finally succumbing, I felt my mind separate from my body, extracting itself from what was occurring on the ground and floating up into the dusty air above me. It drifted above the cabinets to a quiet corner where wall met ceiling, where a colony of larvae had spun a vast and intricate web. From my dissociated view, high in that corner—my mind wrapping itself inside that fragile white mesh, wanting to sleep for weeks inside the thick, sticky walls of my own homespun cocoon—I watched myself kill the moths below. I watched as my hands smashed bodies both winged and wormlike against the wood. I watched as I wiped the remains away, leaving streaks of brown and red on dirty white paint; I watched as my body moved, fast and frenetic, like the moths themselves. I thought of the pity Woolf had felt, watching the moth die before her. And as I watched myself crush one last small frantic body beneath the weight of my hand, leaving a bloom of blood upon the wall, I felt the same pity. A brief surge of despair. After all, I thought, these tiny, fluttering, struggling creatures were, as the author said, little or nothing but life.

The moths that live in my pantry are called *Plodia Interpunctella*, or, commonly, Indian meal moths. They are also known as the pantry moth, the flour moth, and the North American High-flyer. Their larvae, sometimes referred to as waxworms, are grain-feeding pests found worldwide that feast on various foods of grain origin. They are most commonly found in breads, cereals, rice, spices, dried fruits and nuts, coffee, chocolate, and flour. The food they infest, I discovered when pulling out a box of crackers one day and nearly throwing a handful of larvae into my mouth, often becomes webbed together, the worms having spun cocoons for themselves inside their new, grainy homes.

Despite their name, the moths in my apartment do not actually originate in India. The common name for the species was coined in the mid-nineteenth century by New York entomologist Asa Fitch, who, in a report published in 1856, noted that the larvae primarily infested cornmeal, which was first produced in North America by indigenous people and was often referred to by colonists as "Indian meal." Meal moths look from a distance like most moths: They are small, about the size of a pinky fingernail, and light brown in color. On close inspection, though, the tiny fluttering things are nothing short of extraordinary. A fully grown adult meal moth is approximately eight to ten millimeters in length, with a sixteen- to twenty-millimeter wingspan. Its forewings are sturdy and brilliant in color, speckled with various shades of brown, bronze, and copper; the lower wings are thin, fragile, and light, an almost pale yellow in parts and gray in others, with small dark lines like veins running along their perimeters. When the wings are open, stretched wide, the intricate pattern on each appears to be perfectly symmetrical.

One day, while sweeping up the remains of a dead moth carcass from beneath the hem of my bedroom curtain, I picked up the body and held it in the light of the window. I studied his body—his angles, his shape, his design. He was compact and smooth. A light layer of fur covered his wings. He had six legs, long and sinewy and tucked tightly beneath him. On either side of his head were the dark circles of his eyes, and from above them shot two short antennae. As I turned him over in the warm glow of the afternoon sun, I ran the tip of my pinky over the length of his wings. When a moth is at rest, one cannot actually see its body. One can see only its wings, which come together upon the moth's back and encase its small frame. If you were to pry open a moth's closed wings, you would see its torso beneath, lean and narrow, built for flight, light brown with thin black bands running horizontally down its length. But with the wings closed tightly together, covering and protecting the body like a sheath, the pattern of each separate wing comes together to create a pattern entirely different than its individual design—something complete, something whole. These insects, I realized, these pests, were carefully and beautifully built. They were strong, lithe, and lovely. That day in my bedroom, my dead moth—the colors of his body burning bright in the sun—seemed to me nothing short of perfect.

I set my dead moth on the windowsill, the late-afternoon light filtering in through the glass and pooling around his body. I looked at his wings—which were stiff by then with death. How long my small friend had been dead—days, weeks?—I didn't know, but as I picked him up again, his body resting weightlessly in my hand, it was as if his once-resilient frame had become a fragile shell overnight. One frail and paper-thin wing, once strong enough to hold his body in the air, began to crumble in my fingers. This tiny creature, this once robust little thing, who had been busy proliferating in my pantry just days before, was gone now, and quite literally falling apart in my hand. But in that bright afternoon sunlight, the browns and coppers of his wings looked golden.

Unsurprisingly, I deemed my moth *he*. I did what it is we always do when we speak of creatures whose sex is uncertain—of insects, birds, and animals; of dark figures behind tinted windows, driving cars that cut us off. Of humans like me, for whom it's simply hard to tell: creatures who may be one thing or another, who may be both; whose bodies, regardless, we assume the power to name—like we know them, like they're ours to possess.

M oths and butterflies belong to the order Lepidoptera. Moths make up the majority of this order, with around two hundred thousand different species—about ten times the number of butterfly species—with thousands more having yet to be named. Etymologically, the word *moth* comes from the Old English *moððe*, a word that shares a root with the word for *maggot*. The word in English and other Germanic languages—*motti* in Old Norse, *Mot* in Dutch, and *Motte* in German— all share the same root as the word *mother*. While the scientific study of moths and butterflies is known as lepidopterology, the common name for a moth enthusiast or watcher is a *mother*.

The entire life cycle of the moth may take anywhere from thirty to three hundred days. Female moths lay between sixty and four hundred eggs on the surface of food, which will hatch and spawn larvae in up to two weeks' time. Up close, the moth larvae are a creamy white in color with small brown heads; from afar, and in certain lights, they sometimes appear reddish brown. Usually, though, they just resemble the vague color of grain, which makes them difficult to identify among granules of rice or bowls of cereal. When moth larvae mature, they are typically about twelve millimeters long. Depending on the temperature, the larval stage can last from two to forty-one weeks. A moth larva will then build a cocoon, most often in the darkest place it can find, out of which will emerge a fully grown and winged moth. Rather than spin a cocoon, some moth larvae will instead burrow holes in the ground, where they will live in darkness until their metamorphosis.

Most moths are nocturnal, but those in my house seem, for the most part, to follow a pattern far more human. They fly by day and sleep at night; they buzz around my bedroom as long as the lights are on, and fall silent almost as soon as I turn them off. But when I can't sleep at night—as happens often, particularly when I am alone—and I turn on my bedside lamp to read, the moths wake up with me and resume their overhead flight for as long as I lie awake in the light. Despite their nocturnal tendencies, moths are attracted to light, particularly the artificial kind, though the reason for this remains mysterious. One hypothesis deals with a concept called celestial navigation, an idea involving moths' use of the moon to navigate their way through the world, substituting artificial light when their celestial guide is lost in the clouds. Another theory deals with darkness, suggesting that, paradoxically, while a moth is instinctually attracted to darkness, it seeks out the light for protection from predators.

The theory I like, though, is one that addresses male moths' attraction to candlelight. The hypothesis asserts that the infrared spectra of a candle's flame gives off emissions similar to the vibrational frequencies of female moths' pheromones. The male moth senses the fire and is powerfully and uncontrollably attracted to—sometimes, it would seem, as if possessed by—the flame. One night in the dark of mid-November, while lying alone in bed, I witnessed this. I noticed a moth fluttering wildly from across the room toward my bedside table, upon which a single candle burned. His flight seemed erratic, alight with madness, as he rushed toward the flame. When he reached the candle, he spun in fast, wild circles above the glowing light for just a few seconds, then quickly and simply plummeted headlong into the fire. His body crackled like newspaper; his wings sizzled instantly into nothing. And within seconds, what remained of his small wingless torso was belly-up, floating in the pool of wax below the still-burning flame.

A few months after the moths first arrived, I started sleeping with someone new. Being alone, of course, does not necessarily mean celibacy—and sleeping with strangers can be the loneliest act of all. For that first lonely year in New York, I found myself in the beds and atop the crusty futons of several strangers: some women, some men, some who identified as neither. People I mostly met at bars and went home with for a night, some who wanted more from me than I could give them. They would ask me to stay, and I always said no, slipping back into the night—or in some cases, into the brilliant glow of morning—to make my way back home, on my own.

But this new body, the first I'd allowed into my own bed, came as something of a surprise. I'd grown so accustomed to—and fond of—being alone, of my room and my bed serving as sanctuaries. I was convinced that a life of interiority and solitude was the path I was on, and I certainly wasn't looking for romance. And then there he was, this body in my bed, and I wanted him to stay there. He was young and lean and healthy, his angles sharp, his muscles sinewy and defined. Our bodies were similar in shape and size; they shared the same eye color, similar hair, and freckles. Sometimes, limbs tangled together, I lost sight of which arm or leg belonged to which body. And without warning, I began to remember how to share my bed and my body with someone else. We spent hours in bed, and sometimes days, and I turned toward his warm and buzzing skin as it slept next to mine instead of away from it. In the mornings, I didn't want him to leave. We ate breakfast in bed and dinner, too, crumbs from the crusts of frozen pizza under the sheets, pressing into my skin. This was at times disconcerting, but also—surprisingly, bewilderingly—welcome. I moved hesitantly at first, afraid and protective of both my body and my space, but I soon began to forget about my plight to be alone. And while those old familiar feelings of darkness continued to creep in every so often, I started to think again about sharing my life with another human being.

By the time John came into my life, in late November, I had grown so accustomed to the company of the moths that I often forgot they were there. The cleaning frenzies of my roommates and I had, by then, proven useless, and the killing sprees had ended altogether. My skin no longer crawled when I opened a pantry door to find one there, crouched in the dark corner of the cupboard, then dashing out toward the ceiling light above my head. I'd stopped checking my cereal for larvae; I'd stopped repackaging my food when I brought it home from the store. I'd begun leaving my bedroom door open more often, allowing them to fly outside their pantry den and inside the room where I slept and worked. In the mornings, they would perch next to me on my desk while I wrote. At night, while I read in bed, I could hear their clamor inside the glowing yellow shade of my bedside lamp. I'd gotten used to their fluttering about my head, their darting into the small bathroom connected to my room, their squeezing in through the crack beneath the door to join me while I brushed my teeth. I'd started keeping the bedside lamp on at night while I slept, letting the hum of their buzzing harmonize with the dull bulb, lulling me to sleep. One might even say that, by then, I had begun to enjoy the low din they produced in the soft light of my room. I suppose the moths, in some strange way, had become my companions. They were almost always around, buzzing about the room and occupying my space, lingering, circling, eating my food, and keeping me up at night. But over time, I not only got used to these annoyances; I came to expect them—when I went to bed at night, and when I woke up in the morning. Somehow, at some point over the course of that month, the moths had begun to feel like home.

When John began spending the nights with me, I realized the presence of the moths—or, perhaps more specifically, my assimilation to their presence—might be disturbing to my new bedfellow. Despite this, I did not renew my efforts to kill them. I considered it, made half-hearted attempts when he was around, but only briefly. I began lighting more candles, but this was more toward the effort of mood setting rather than moth extermination. Sometimes, as those candles flickered at my bedside, I would hear that quick, familiar zap and the long, slow sizzle to follow, and I would once again feel pity—maybe even regret. And sometimes, when the moon was full and its light illuminated my room at night, I would catch John swatting at the moths in his sleep as they circled his head. I found myself, on those nights, watching his sleepy hands in the darkness, half waving in the air above his gently rising and falling chest, uncertain as to where my regret belonged.

When I turned eighteen and left home, I got a butterfly tattoo. It's on my right hip, and the blacks and reds of the ink have long since faded. It's embarrassing now, but I'm sure it meant something important to me then. I got it my first semester in college, a spontaneous decision I made with a friend. We were drunk and giddy, buzzing with the thrill of being on our own for the first time. We drove to the tattoo parlor in the middle of the city, two clichés, and I picked an image from the wall. I still remember the feeling of the ink as the man pressed it into my skin: a pressure, a tickle, then pain—a bright jolt of it that hummed through my skin and made my teeth buzz. I liked the pain of it and would soon seek it again. When the man was finished, wiping the blood clean with a cloth, the ghost of the pain still humming, there it was: a little butterfly in flight, just above my hip bone.

In common lore that spans cultures and centuries, the butterfly has most often represented things like beauty, freedom, growth, and eternal life. In ancient Greek, the word *psyche*, like the goddess so named, was often used to mean both "butterfly" and "soul." The moth, however, despite its similarities to the butterfly, has historically represented the grotesque, its symbolism given to ideas of darkness and death—consider the old Japanese horror film *Mothra* or the iconic death's-head moth from *Silence of the Lambs*—and, perhaps most commonly, destruction:

"How much less in them that dwell in houses of clay," asks the book of Job, 4:19, "whose foundation is in the dust, which are crushed before the moth?"

In the world of lepidopterology, the actual difference between butterflies and moths is somewhat uncertain. The only biological distinction concerns the shape of their antennae: While the butterfly belongs to the suborder Rhopalocera, or "clubbed horn," the moth, who lacks the club, belongs to Heterocera, or "varied horn." Other than that, most lepidopterists contend, the differences remain uncertain. What is indisputable, though, is this: Both butterflies and moths begin as eggs and hatch to larvae—a stage during which they are young and thriving, eating their way through life. They then enter a period of darkness, weaving thick cocoons around themselves, sleeping in the dark for days or weeks or even months. And eventually, whenever they or perhaps other external forces determine it's time—when the afternoon sun of a late-fall day shines a certain way, maybe, or when the moon hangs in the night sky at just the right degree—they break forth from the darkness they created and back out into the light, as intricate, winged creatures.

Sometimes, in the pale light of early morning, our bodies pressed together upon the bed in which I slept alone for so long, John runs his finger along the faded edges of my tattoo. I told him, as I've told all my lovers, that I regret having gotten it. But sometimes, when his fingers run along those lines, causing tiny follicles beneath the ink to stand on end, making the wings seem almost to break forth from my skin, I think maybe the thing I regret no longer exists. That perhaps, instead, there's been a metamorphosis, and the small winged thing on my hip is no longer a butterfly—that it disappeared for a time into darkness and emerged again as a moth.

The moths in my house are still around. It seemed, for a while, in the depths of winter, as though they'd begun to diminish. But now, as winter has pressed on into spring and the warm rains of April are just around the corner, they seem to have returned. Their presence comes in waves—at times they are many; at others, I rarely see them. But even when they seem at their weakest, I will still see a stray, brown and blurred in flight, sail out from behind a cabinet door. I'll still see one, solitarily perched—sometimes so still that I can't tell whether it's alive or dead—atop a box of oats. One might still flutter out from behind my bedroom curtains when I pull them open in the morning to let in the light. And sometimes, at night, one fated, frantic thing will still spiral headlong into the candle I keep burning by my bed. I'm sure eventually they'll be gone for good; their time under the warmth of my roof will have passed, and they will pick up and move on. Or perhaps they'll stay here in this house, and I'll be the one who goes first. Either way, when their constant fluttering around my head has ceased, when the buzz of their flight has gone, I'm sure I'll remember again how much I loved the quiet. But sometimes, mostly on the rare nights when I'm alone, I still hear that old familiar hum of wings beating fast inside the soft-yellow lampshade by my bed. On those nights, I'll leave the light on.

SWITCH-HITTER

A few summers ago, in early June, while visiting my hometown, I drove to the softball field at night. This occurred as if at the hands of some invisible force rather than my own—someone else's hands shifting my mother's 1995 Saturn coupe into fifth gear on backcountry roads, past the turn to our house, through the town's single stoplight, blinking red, and down the dim-yellow dark of Main Street. I drove to the edge of town, out where the houses turn to cornfields, and cut the engine. Stepping out into the cool summer night, I heard nothing but crickets—a silence so loud it's deafening to ears now trained to the din of a city. I stood outside the chain-link fence behind home plate, reached my arms up high, and snaked my fingers through the small diamonds of wire. I hung on to them like I did when I was a teenage girl, chewing sunflower seeds and spitting their shells through the fence and onto the field. Then I took off my shoes, stepped with bare feet into cold sand, and walked out to home plate.

In the house where I grew up, where my parents still live, there are photos on the wall. A huge ceiling-high collage, the first thing you see when you walk in the front door, serves as something of a shrine: documenting, among other things, each year of my life—my parents' only child—until I left home at eighteen. For decades, the same photos have hung on that wall. But on this particular trip home, they had been rearranged.

"A change of pace," my mother said.

Some of the frames were empty. Others had new photos inside. Replacing glossy school shots—eight-by-tens of an awkward sixteen-year-old girl in a tight shirt and too much mascara with penciled-in eyebrows, big bangs, and straightened hair—were smaller shots of a younger girl. No makeup and hair wild, in a volleyball jersey and shorts, with a ball on one knee. In ice hockey pads and newly sharpened skates, stick in hand. And a black-and-white shot from the softball field, a girl in knee socks and cleats, crouched low, glove hovering just above the dirt. Head down, eyes narrow, waiting.

I had forgotten about the photo. I had forgotten what it felt like to be on the field. I had forgotten what it felt like to be so young, called up to varsity when all the starters had been busted for drinking. I had forgotten what it felt like to live in a place where sports meant every-thing, where to be good at sports meant you were everything too—the marker by which success was measured and small-town heroes were made. I had forgotten what it felt like to be a girl who believed it, to be a girl crouched in the sand, ready for anything, who felt like she had all the power in the world.

As a kid, I was on the first and only girls' ice hockey team in Wisconsin. Because of our singular position in the state, we played against boys' teams. We were not, however, allowed to check—for those unfamiliar with hockey, this is the ubiquitous and glorious act of smash-ing one's opponents into the plexiglass boards, arguably the most sat-isfying part of the sport—our prepubescent girl bodies having been deemed too fragile for such violence. I lasted a few years on the ice, during which time I was penalized and ejected more than once—for hurling the weight of my small body into the bodies of boys, for crushing them against the boards, and on one occasion, for slashing a boy with my stick. I played center, and on the face-off line just before the puck dropped, the boy had spat the word *bitch* through the slick grimace of his mouth guard, his small, sharp teeth grinning beneath the rubber. The word rang in my head as he grabbed the puck and sprinted down the ice. I chased him, skating as fast as I could, and when I caught him I raised my stick over my head and brought it down across his back as hard as I could. He fell to his knees as the whistle blew.

I could have told the ref why I did it, as he skated me to the exit. But I never did. I kept quiet and took my punishment, the way I was taught to. I kept the boy's secret, and I kept the shame of it.

I hung up my skates and played volleyball, ran track, spent a summer on the swim team. But my truest love—the game I'd played since my hand could support a glove, my father and I playing catch in the backyard—was softball. From the tender age of five, perched at a wobbly rubber tee, a team T-shirt hanging past my thighs with a local car dealership logo across the chest, to coach pitch, summer league, and eventually high school ball, the game was my life. I played tournaments in June and July, the heat of a Wisconsin summer frying transformers at country parks. I rearranged schedules at the restaurant where I worked to play on weekends. I traveled all over the state with my teammates, the same girls I'd been playing with since we were small.

Today, I'm a closet jock. When I talk about softball I mention it as a passing phase, a surprising fact I can throw out at parties to delight writers and artists and musicians, the nerdy nonathlete types I mostly surround myself with these days. But the truth is I lived for the sport: my cleats in the dirt, digging out a spot at home plate; the windmill pitch, watching the ball rise up from the pitcher's hip, coming fast at sixty miles an hour; the fast snap of a swing and the sharp crack of aluminum; the jolt in my fingers and down the length of my arms like an electrical surge with a hard hit on a cold spring day; watching the ball sail high and long to the left field fence. Sand swirling up in small cyclones when the wind kicked up, watching the dust settle over the mound. The smell of an approaching April rain and playing through the drizzle, then running for cover when the sky opened up. Waiting for lightning and thunder to pass while we huddled together in the dugout. Team bus rides and envoys of parents in cars, a parade home from away games, stopping in fast-food restaurants for dinner as a team. And sprinting and sliding and stealing bases, my arms and legs covered in dirt. Running and diving to catch a ball, feeling my body stretch and fire and hurtle and fly.

~

Softball is something of an anomaly in that it's one of the few gendered sports in the world: a girl version of a boy's sport. While there were several baseball teams for women in the mid-nineteenth century—mostly at progressive women's colleges like Vassar and Smith—organized baseball at every level is played almost entirely by men and boys. Softball, meanwhile, is a sport assigned to girls, with schools and recreational departments segregating the two sports from the earliest age. Most softball careers can go only so far as college; since the late 1970s, there have been a few fledgling professional women's outfits in the United States, most recently the four-team National Pro Fastpitch league, but so far nothing has garnered enough attention or funding to last. Men, of course, can and do play softball. Recreational and coed leagues are popular across the country and are particularly prominent in the Midwest, where those high-arching tosses of bar-league slow-pitch and pitchers of beer on the bleachers are a ubiquitous part of summer nights. But for girls who want to play baseball, the options are limited, where they exist at all.

In his 1911 book *America's National Game*, sporting-goods magnate A. G. Spalding proclaimed the game of baseball to be not just all

American but also all male. A woman "may take part in the grandstand, with applause for the brilliant play, with waving kerchief to the hero," he wrote. But "Base Ball is too strenuous for womankind."

Since 1974, after a string of lawsuits, Little League of America has technically allowed girls on its baseball teams, but it strongly encourages them to join its softball division instead. In defense of this position, Little League officials have been quoted as arguing that baseball is a contact sport, that girls' bones are weaker than boys', that facial injuries could ruin girls' prospects later in life, that being struck in the chest by a ball could cause breast cancer. In a 1974 *Sports Illustrated* article by Frank Deford covering the lawsuits, the Little League president at the time voiced horror that coaches would not be able to "pat girls on the rear end the way they naturally do boys."

Perhaps unsurprisingly, softball was actually invented for men, by men, in 1887 in Chicago, as a shorter version of baseball to play indoors during the cold midwestern winters. Also born in Chicago was the All-American Girls Professional Baseball League (AAGPBL), its fifteen teams housed in small cities throughout the upper Midwest— several of them, such as the Kenosha Comets, the Racine Belles, and the Milwaukee Chicks, were based in Wisconsin. Anyone who has seen *A League of Their Own* knows the league was established during World War II, in 1943, when American men were drafted and baseball executives like Philip K. Wrigley were forced to scheme up a way to save the sport from bankruptcy as its stars were deployed. Cue the short-skirted uniforms and the movie's iconic montage of lumbering, scrappy, sometimes sexy farmers' daughters and tough city girls portrayed by Rosie O'Donnell and Madonna and Geena Davis being subjected to charm school, taking tea and ballet, being turned into ladies.

The league's motto was "Play like a man, look like a lady." The players, many of whom were called up from country softball leagues, not only had to wear skirts—which were in no way conducive to sliding and often left players with huge raspberries on their asses and thighs or open cuts filled with sand—they also had to wear lipstick and keep their hair long. No bobs, they were told, and some players were even released from their contracts for sporting short cuts. The reason for this, said the men in charge, was so the players would always look like ladies, even as they were engaging in such rough-and-tumble play, and so be more pleasing to the men in the stands. The unspoken reason was to ensure no one would suspect there might be lesbians on the league. There were, of course. As sportswriter Britni de la Cretaz reports in her article "The Hidden Queer History Behind *A League of Their Own*," several AAGPBL players were closeted, because at the time everyone was, and because they would have lost their roster spots if they came out. So they lived in secret, in some cases forming romantic partnerships with teammates that would last for the rest of their lives.

After the war, the All-American Girls Professional Baseball League was kept alive for nearly a decade. But the league held its last season in 1954, and for the most part, America's favorite pastime returned to its so-called natural order: Men would again play baseball, and women, should they possess such boyish proclivities, would play softball—the softer, gentler sport, for the softer, gentler sex.

When I was a kid, I loved baseball. The walls of the elementary school cafeteria were plastered with posters: Paul Molitor crushing one out of County Stadium; Robin Yount and his big red mustache crouched at shortstop or frozen midleap about to snatch a hard high fly to center. These were the heroes. I had a baseball card collection and picked up packs of Topps on weekend grocery store trips with my mother. My Molitor rookie card was my most prized possession. I watched games on TV with my father, who grew up in New Jersey and told me stories about the Yankees of the '50s and '60s, about Joe DiMaggio and Lou Gehrig, about heading into the Bronx to catch a cheap daytime game with his brothers. My mother's father, a diehard

Cubs fan who rarely left home without his Cubs jacket and cap, always had a game on the radio, regardless of who was playing. Whenever I visited my grandparents, Harry Caray and Bob Uecker narrated games through crackling speakers as if they were epic radio dramas. Once in a while, on a school field trip, we took a bus to Milwaukee to catch a Brewers game. I brought my glove with me, a brown leather Mizuno, well-oiled and stretched to form a perfect pocket, hoping I might catch a long fly out to the stands, imagining myself on the field beneath the lights.

The boys said *dyke*. The boys said *queer*. As they rode by the softball field on their bikes, the boys shouted it from the road, laughing as they pedaled. They said *butch, lesbo, lezzie*. They said *rug-muncher, pussy-puncher*. They said *muff-diver, carpetbagger, beaver-eater*. They said *cherry-picker, fur-trader, fuzz-bumper*. They said *scissor-sister, sister-fister, bean-flicker*. They said switch-hitter. They said, *She bats for the other team*. They said, *She plays softball, if you know what I mean*.

In the Midwest, softball is something of a hallowed thing for girls. Here in America's heartland, where so many girls are born and raised by generations of farm families, their bodies built for bailing hay, their shoulders broad, their backs and hands strong, their muscles long and lean. Like they were born to play ball. Like they came out of the womb with gloves on their hands, cleats already digging into the dirt. With the preternatural ability—God given, their parents might say—to crush a ball over the fence, to dig into a swing with their wide, sturdy hips. Like they were made for it.

But such reverence didn't extend to the boys. Growing up in a small town, where boys were boys and girls were girls, playing softball also meant being called a lesbian. This was the worst possible insult, one we worked hard to combat. This meant overcompensating. When we were young, it meant screaming, *"You're gay!"* as the boys rode by. Later, it meant applying too much makeup, even and perhaps especially before games. Making sure our hair was just right, straightened and sprayed at lockers between class. Wearing short skirts and high heels and low-cut shirts on game days. All this to assure the boys, and the men, that even though we played softball, we were still girls; that we were sexy, available, and straight. That our bodies were objects for them to desire.

I went to college fewer than thirty miles away from my hometown, at the University of Wisconsin in Madison, an NCAA Division I public school where sports are considered holy, where football players are gods, are given scooters to get around campus, fed steak dinners, and provided with private tutors. On campus, and in that college town, when I'd tell people I had played softball, a common response—one that always came from men, including but not limited to friends, roommates, boyfriends, dates, one-night stands, classmates, and strangers—was this: "Is that a euphemism?"

I'd laugh along with the joke, roll with the punches, throw some vaguely homophobic ribbing back, always doing my best to be the kind of girl such men held on a pedestal—a chill girl, a funny girl, the kind of girl who's never uptight, who prefers sports to shopping, who drinks beer and can hold her liquor and still looks good in a skirt when she needs to. Both one of the guys and the kind of girl those guys wanted.

I'd forgotten so many things. The smell of the field, the feel of cleats in the sand. That I'd won scholarships and awards. MVP, First-Team All-Conference, All-State Honorable Mention, Female Athlete of the Year. I'd forgotten I was good.

I was reminded of this while looking through a series of scrapbooks my mother had made for me while I was growing up. Four fat volumes in all, they'd been collecting dust in the closet for years. Certificates and medals taped to the pages, honor roll lists, concert programs, poems, and photos of friends, newspaper clippings with her handwritten notes in the margins. She had kept everything.

I sat on the floor of my childhood bedroom—which had since been renovated into part guest room, part shrine to my youth, complete with trophies and melodramatic self-portraits from sophomore photography class, stuffed animals and a somewhat-alarming collection of *The Lion King* action figures and porcelain cats—and looked through all four binders, whose spines were bursting. As I sat there, the silence of night buzzing in my ears, I remembered what it had felt like to be a girl inside that room. The boredom, the longing, the hatred of my body, the desire to be what I was told was the ideal—smaller, thinner, fairer, prettier, better. And the crickets outside my open windows, the summer wind in the leaves, bending the branches of the birch tree in the front yard, where as a kid I'd climbed so high.

In high school, softball became an obsession. My goal wasn't just to be good; it was to be perfect. I was the team captain and lead-off hitter. I was fast—I broke records for stolen bases and eventually broke my own. I was never once thrown out on a steal. My coach called me *the gazelle*. I played center field, where my speed was put to use. I sprinted to catch pop flies and line drives, diving to catch anything that came my way. I jumped, I leaped, I soared.

I trained twice a day, even in the summer. Three hours in the morning and three hours at night, in the high school weight room and batting cage, running sprints on the football field, ladder drills in the gym. During the school year, I was one of only two or three girls in a weight room full of boys. One was a girl who grew up in the country and had a landscaping job in the summer. She had blonde hair and freckles, and when we spotted each other on the bench press I watched her biceps strain against the weight. One winter, she and I joined the power-lifting team—two girls on a roster of football players, traveling to other towns to compete in the squat, bench press, and dead lift. We wore cut-off T-shirts and mesh basketball shorts, just like the boys. We trained with the boys, screaming at each other to do one more rep. We sweated and grunted. We squatted, curled, and rowed. We jumped and sprinted, Grapevined and Ickey Shuffled. We made weight, sometimes fasting for days in order to slip into the lower weight class on the morning of a match. I went on a strict diet of peanut butter, tuna fish, and high-protein, low-sugar energy powder—supplied by the football coach—much to the dismay of my mother, whose beef casseroles and pasta, potatoes, and gravy I began to pick at, then skip altogether. I never considered this behavior a problem; it was simply what was required in order to be the best. I was willing to do whatever it took.

~

In a small midwestern town, darkness gets buried like a secret. I came from a place that kept silence like a curse, a people who stuck to their silence like work. In a place where the land is both fertile and hard, lush and alive then brutally cold—a land we work with our hands until they're hard, a land that decides our fate no matter the toil—we are silent about our hopes. We are silent about our fears. We are silent about money, unless we think someone has too much. We are silent, most of all, about our bodies, our desires, and our pain. In my family, we sat in our silence; we steeped and stewed in it; we kept it packed inside until, inevitably, the pressure became too much to bear. Historically, this took the form of fights, infrequent but ferocious bursts of built-up rage, which more than once became epic grudges that lasted for decades— that in some cases were taken to the grave. My grandmother—Irish, a drinker, who took afternoon tea that was brandy on ice, who was generous and funny but with a temper that could blow the roof off a farmhouse like an F5—fought famously with her only sister at the funeral of one of their seven brothers. They never spoke again, a silence that lasted more than forty years. When my grandmother died, her sister didn't come to the funeral. My mother wrote to her aunt—her godmother, with whom she'd been close as a kid—but my great-aunt, who I never met, never responded. My mother and grandmother also went for a year or so without speaking; my mother and I once did the same. I learned early that conflict could lead to a lifetime of silence—so I did my best to keep quiet, even when the silence itself became the problem.

Like most teenagers, I was moody. This was what we called it anyway. What's perhaps more accurate is that I was an erratic and sometimes volatile force. I vacillated between brooding, sullen silence and fits of rage—the kind of rage that living in silence only ensures. But what lived between those poles, hiding out of sight, was sadness. I carried it around with me all the time, a darkness and desperation that lived in my chest and my stomach, that buried itself in my thighs, in my belly, in my small budding breasts. It was something I carried, like a good midwestern girl, in secret. I smiled in the daylight, laughed and joked with my friends, did well in school, and did my best to project an image of a well-adjusted kid. But at night, I sat on my bedroom floor and dreamed of death. I thought of a friend who had once swallowed a bunch of pills and wondered if I might do the same. I thought of a boy who had slit his wrists in the high school bathroom, how he'd left a trail of blood behind him as he'd walked down the newly carpeted hallway. I thought about how, afterward, the entire student body of our small public high school had to disinfect our shoes. How we'd formed a line through the cafeteria, snaking single file past the vending machines and into the janitor's closet, where we stepped one by one into buckets of bleach. Beyond the stringent sting of it was the smell of spaghetti and meat sauce cooking for lunch. I thought about the din that hung in the hallways then, and wondered if my absence would leave such a sound.

Back then, I didn't know the word *depression*. Or if I knew it, I never thought it was meant for me. The concept was abstract, something reserved for Lifetime movies and bad young-adult novels. It wasn't something for normal kids like me. Back then, I thought of sadness like some horror-movie monster, a corporeal darkness, a shadow that lurked at the end of an unlit hallway—something that could catch you only if you glimpsed it. If you listened for it closely enough on some quiet night in bed, when the locusts and crickets and cicadas of summer were silent. That if you closed your eyes and plugged your ears and held your breath beneath the covers, if you kept all the lights on, it might never find you. I didn't know then that it lived not just inside the walls of our homes but in the bloodlines that built them—that both the monster itself and the ways we try to fight it could be carried on. I watched it come and go in my family, in those nearest to me, never able to fully comprehend it. I was terrified to come home from school each day, never knowing what I might find. The monster, I knew, was hiding in that dark hallway; it hovered over the kitchen table and circled my parents like a storm, and I knew it would eventually find me too—the lights above me starting to flicker and dim, until one day there would be no light at all. Like the boy who slit his wrists in the high school bathroom, who did not die but eventually disappeared from school and then from town, until he was nothing but a whisper, a vague and hazy memory. Until years later, when I would discover he had tried again, and this time he had succeeded.

For Midwesterners like me, rather than talking about our problems we seek power over them. For some, this might mean an obsessive focus on work. For others, it might mean school or family or faith. For others still, like many in my own family, it means drinking. For me, as a girl—one who never felt at home in her body, who fought to fit inside it—I sought that power in sports. I found it in pushing my body to its limits. In a small town like mine, sports were the pinnacle of success. To be good at sports was to be accomplished, successful, and respected. To be good at sports was to be a good kid. To be a girl who's good at sports was to be a good girl. And this, I think, is what I most wanted to be.

When I discovered the weight room, it felt how I imagine some people feel in church, sitting in a quiet chapel on a Sunday, feeling the hum of some holy energy inside their body. I grew up going to church, but the only place I ever felt that kind of peace—the pull of some energy far beyond me, holding me aloft, keeping me safe from the outside world—was in the weight room. It was the closest I'd ever come to meditation—a veil of stillness falling down around me, living in the rhythm of my breath, lulling me into a trance of calm. It was a small sticky room that smelled of teenage boy: body odor and dirty socks, old rubber mats and the sharp smell of disinfectant. But it was my strange, smelly little home. There were a couple of bench presses and a squat rack, a treadmill and a row of free weights below a wall-length mirror. I pushed out sets of ten and twelve, my muscles contracting and pressing against themselves. Between each set, I stood in front of the mirror and let my mind fall away, caught in the steady driving beat of the bad '90s music that poured through the speakers: Metallica and Rage Against the Machine, Jay-Z and Korn, Eminem and Limp Bizkit. And our favorite terrible soundtrack at the turn of the century, when I was seventeen: Linkin Park's 2000 nu-metal masterpiece *Hybrid Theory*. I hefted and roared along with the boys as the late Chester Bennington—whose suicide two decades later came as a surprise to no one—screamed about betrayal and pain and sadness and all-consuming rage. We felt it, too, like we felt everything else: deeply, acutely, as if we were the only people on the planet to feel it, the pain of teenage love and desire and loss, the desperate need to break free from our town, from our whole lives. We screamed along with those sad, angry lyrics as we thrust literal weight off our chests, lost in our own thoughts together, a quiet communion of adolescent testosterone and angst.

I loved being in that small room of boys, and men, the lot of us pushing ourselves to be stronger. In the weight room, I wasn't just some girl. Maybe I wasn't a girl at all. I wasn't an object of desire. I was a friend, an athlete, and a teammate. We spotted each other, held our hands out, hovering under the bar of the bench press, our bodies so close beneath the squat rack, poised and ready to carry the weight. Prepared to save each other.

In the summers when I was seventeen and eighteen, I went to the weight room in the early morning, before my shifts at the local pub. I was often the only one there at 6:00 a.m.; I'd press "Play" on the CD player, and the music blared for me alone. Sometimes I'd go back after work, doing two-a-days with the preseason football team. But as much as I loved to be there with the boys, it was when I was alone on those summer mornings—when I wasn't performing for anyone but me, when the only eyes on me were my own—that I felt the strongest, the safest, the most at home. I watched my muscles contract with each curl, watched them shake beneath the weight of the bench. My thighs trembled beneath the squat bar; my triceps flexed with each military press. I watched my arms and shoulders and chest get stronger. My thighs and calves and waist more defined. Getting harder, faster, leaner. Feeling the rush of fighting through pain, of pushing my body to exhaustion. And driving it, the feeling that I had the ability to build my body into something perfect, a tool that could combat darkness, a vessel to hold not sadness but strength. I made my body a weapon; I made my body a war.

On the weight room wall, there were red letters hand-painted on white stone: PAIN IS WEAKNESS LEAVING THE BODY. It was the motto of our power-lifting team; the phrase was printed on the backs of our T-shirts. I repeated it to myself with every set, every rep, every lap, as my body burned. I chanted it like a mantra, repeated it like a prayer.

~

The thing about memory is it's transient. It moves through you as you move through the world. It degrades with the passing of time. Sometimes it sticks, and sometimes it vanishes. Traces will come back to you now and again—with a faded photo, the smell of newly cut grass or spring rain, the way a certain summer light hits the midwestern sky just right. But much of it will leave you. Some of it will break down naturally, and some of it will be buried for a reason. We can work on digging such memories up, but these things have a way of working themselves to the surface all on their own.

~

I imagine yourself a teenage girl. You are fourteen, fifteen, then sixteen and seventeen, then teetering on that hallowed edge of eighteen—when you will be legal, when you will be free, when you will be an adult. When, you believe, you will have control over your life. Across the distance of those four years, your body will have gone from straight as an arrow to subtly curved: still long and lean but with the suggestion of hips and breasts, barely A cups but irrefutable—this proof of girl becoming woman. Though, of course, you are not a woman, as much as you believe yourself to be.

Now imagine a man—an adult man, more than twice your age. He is your teacher. He is also your coach. He is married with several children. You are in love with him. At least this is what you think it is. More than love, of course, it is infatuation: the desperate and reckless longing of a child, an inconsolable need to obtain something unattainable. It is an obsession. But you don't know this, not yet; you won't know it for years to come. For now, this thing you feel is a love so consuming it keeps you awake at night; it's the star-crossed kind, fated and dramatic, the kind you see in the movies and read about in Shakespeare plays, which you recite aloud in English class, the slow bloom of a blush spreading across your neck as you say such words of love aloud, imagining yourself the doomed heroine and this man the hero. You are a teenage girl, after all, and this is all you know about love.

He is your coach, and you are his captain. His right-hand man, his Number One. You live for softball season. You live for practice in the spring, when the two of you are partners for warm-up games of catch, when he will stand close and evaluate your swing, remind you to drive your hips forward and not to drop your shoulder. You live for bus rides to games, when you will sit together in the front seat, far away from the team, to put together the lineup. You live for games, when you sprint and leap to catch a fly, when you steal second, when you hit a triple, when he will smile and cheer and give you a high five; when you know he's proud of you.

He knows how you feel. You flirt mercilessly, make innuendoes and mixtapes, give him wildly inappropriate gifts like a tight-fitting sweater from the Old Navy where you work at sixteen, wrapping the package carefully and slipping a note inside. Sometimes, when you pass him in the hallways, you swing your hips in such a way that you hope he'll notice. You wear short skirts and tight shirts, high '90s platform heels that you know accentuate your legs, long and lean and muscular, shaved and lotioned to a shine.

He will not act on your advances. You interpret this as nobility, as strength in the face of your sinful attempts to seduce him. Because this is how you see yourself sometimes: a sinner, an instigator, a bad girl. But he doesn't dissuade your advances either. He doesn't shut them down or tell you it's inappropriate. He laughs at your flirtations and holds your gaze. You send him late-night emails and he responds. And there will be other moments: on the bus to a game, your legs hitched up on the seat in front of you, when your knee will fall against his and he doesn't move away. A ride home, after practice, when the silence fills up his car, fills up the whole Wisconsin night, and all you can hear is your pulse, thrumming in your throat. There will be a day in his classroom, when you will stand too close—because you always stand too close, just like that song by The Police, which you play on repeat and imagine is your anthem—when you feel the heat of his bare arm next to yours, the hum of his skin so close. And sometimes you will revel in this feeling of being a bad girl. Sometimes it makes you feel so strong. You will begin to understand that your body can be another kind of tool: the kind that might get you what you want. And what you want is to be wanted. What you want is to be loved. What you want is approval. What you want, perhaps most of all, is to feel like you're in control of something.

The day you turn eighteen, in April of your senior year, you will spend hours getting ready in the morning. You will wear your four-inch heels and a short black skirt and a tight blue shirt whose neckline plunges just far enough to expose your small chest. You will apply more eyeliner than usual and spray your neck and wrists with ck one. When you get to school, you will walk to his classroom, where you sometimes meet to talk about practice or an upcoming game. Where you talk strategy, review notes about the teams you'll be playing—if the pitcher is throwing heat, who's out this game with an injury or suspension, who's having a bad season, and who's on fire. On this morning you will walk toward him, your heels clicking against the tile. He will look up at you from his desk, and his face will tell you everything you need to know about your body and the kind of power it possesses. You do not yet know about the power it lacks—or how your youth and naiveté can be weapons used against you. You will find this out, in time. Soon, you will know it more clearly than you know anything. But on this day, you feel so powerful.

~

I kept my love a secret. In an attempt to seem normal, I went out with boys my age. When I was a sophomore, my first boyfriend broke up with me because I wouldn't sleep with him. It flipped on a switch of understanding: to make boys, and men, like me, I had to put out. I lost my virginity when I was seventeen, with a twenty-one-year-old guy I worked with at Old Navy who stopped returning my calls as soon as we slept together. In between, I made out with boys at parties, in pickup trucks and Trans Ams, parked out on the shoulders of country roads, in cornfields, on the street outside my house. I made out with them even when I didn't really want to and rarely felt anything like pleasure. I often let them go further—to first base, second, then third, and on a few occasions all the way home. At a house party one Friday night, I sat on a generator in someone's backyard and made out with boy a year younger than me. I left a hickey on his neck so huge, my friends said it had its own area code. A close friend of my parents—a sweet older man who came to my softball games—had nicknamed me "The Vacuum Cleaner" because of my prowess in center field, much to the delight of my teammates. After the hickey incident, they started calling me "Hoover," and when they toilet-papered my house, they scrawled the word on the driveway in shaving cream. I didn't tell my parents about this version of the nickname. It was embarrassing at first, but over time I started to wear it less with humiliation and something more like pride. Even as the girls in my school—sometimes even those who I thought were my friends—whispered to each other and called me a slut, I knew I had what boys wanted: a female body and a willingness to give it to them. I knew—because I'd spent my whole life having learned it, having seen it on TV, in magazines, and in movies, watching it unfold in the hierarchies of popularity in my small-town school—that this was the most important thing. That this was what all girls and women should strive to attain. That to be wanted by boys, by men, meant the same thing as being loved.

The summer after my senior year, I was invited to train at the home of the best softball coach in the state. My coach had arranged the visit, and we drove there together on a Saturday morning in June. The best coach in the state lived about an hour north of my hometown, in another small town just like it, where sports, and especially girls' softball, carried a long and storied tradition. The coach lived out in the country and had built his own ball field and batting cage in his backyard in a clearing among a dense circle of tall pine trees. He invited only a few girls to train privately with him there.

In the fall, I was going to play softball at the University of Wisconsin, the top program in the state and one of the best in the country. This was the plan. I had interest from other schools, smaller programs in the state and across the Midwest, but I was holding out for UW. After national recruits were made, a handful of girls from throughout Wisconsin were formally invited to try out as walk-on freshmen. I was one of them. Only two or three players would get a spot.

In the backyard of the best coach in the state, I took swings. *Cuts*, they called them. The two men watched me from behind. I was calm in the cage, my fingers wrapped loosely around the black-tape grip of the bat. I dug my feet into the ground, pivoting into the pitch, finding the sweet spot, and connecting with the ball. I watched it fly up and away, then get swallowed in the black netting of the cage.

I felt their eyes on me. No matter how focused on the task at hand, I was always aware of my body, hoping my coach was watching. That he noticed the muscles in my arms as they twitched and flexed, my hips as they rotated left—as they drove forward, hard and quick, into the swing.

Each time I connected, the two men said, *Atta girl.* Or *That's it.* Or *There it is.* Each time I missed, they said, *You got this, kid. You got this.* Or *Follow through.* Or *Eyes on the ball, babe, eyes on the ball.* On the infield, at shortstop, I crouched low, my glove just above the dirt. The best coach in the state stood at home plate with a five-gallon bucket of balls and a bat. He drove each ball up the middle, down the pipe, shot line drives at chest height. I stopped them all, scooping the balls from the dirt and firing them to first, where my coach stood to catch them. I launched each ball directly into the pocket of his glove with a loud snap that echoed through the trees around us.

"Thatta *girl*," he shouted with each snap, grinning with pride, and I radiated with joy.

When they sent me to center field, the two men took turns taking hits from home plate. Bucket after bucket of balls, their big bodies grunting and sweating as they swung. I sprinted. I dove. I worked harder than I ever had. I caught every ball. I pushed my body to perform each task at the highest possible level. I was the strongest and the fastest and the best I'd ever been. From home plate, a hundred feet away, the men watched me. They shouted and yelled and cheered, their big deep voices like shots of adrenaline, filling up my throat and chest, keeping my body going.

Nothing about that day seemed strange to me then. I'm sure nothing about it seemed strange to my parents or my teammates or anyone else in the community. There's nothing strange at all, particularly in a small town, about girl athletes and the men who coach them. It's simply a way of life. I was simply an athlete, training with two coaches out in the country. I was a teenage girl, performing for two adult men in a circle of trees. I was a girl who would have done anything for their approval, to make them believe I was good. So that I might believe it too.

Afterward, soaked in sweat and slick with sand, my shirt and shorts stuck to my skin, my body hot from the high summer sun, I walked in from the field toward the men standing at home plate. The best coach in the state nodded and smiled.

"You'll make it if you want it," he said.

I didn't make it. On the day of tryouts, a cool September morning on the University of Wisconsin field—where I'd arrived at sunrise, the huge silent beauty of the stadium like a chapel—I choked. The semester had yet to begin, but I'd moved into the dorms by then, continuing my training on campus—running the bike paths at dawn, sprinting up stadium stairs, lifting weights during the day, and hitting the cages at night. I was at the top of my game. But that morning, I missed balls in the outfield; I fumbled grounders in the dirt. At batting practice, I don't remember if I hit a single ball. I ran the bases as hard as I could, but my legs felt like rubber, disconnected from my body. I didn't make the cut. I still had an offer from a reputable Division III school a few hours north, but I turned it down. It was either the best or it was nothing at all.

For a long time, the words of the best high school coach in the state would haunt me: *You'll make it if you want it.* I thought I had wanted nothing else. I couldn't understand what could have possibly happened. I couldn't believe what I had lost and couldn't imagine my life without it. It took me years to understand that maybe, in the end, I hadn't wanted it after all. So much of what I did—the training, the lifting, the practicing—had been about my coach. Maybe, I started to wonder, it had all been about him, more than it had ever been about the sport. This was the story I began to tell myself, and the one I eventually believed. At some point along the way, I forgot that I had once loved the game.

~

When I stopped playing softball, I started to drink. I had done my fair share of partying in high school, but in college I drank like it was my job. I drank cheap beer and whiskey, Jell-O shots and Jäger bombs and UV Blue vodka, even more atrocious things like Rumple Minze and Goldschläger, flaming shots of Everclear, shots of Kahlúa with whipped cream, which we called "blow jobs" and drank without using our hands. I drank whatever was poured from dirty taps into cloudy pint glasses at the sports bars I'd snuck into, still underage with a fake ID; I drank red Solo cups of Milwaukee's Best—"the Beast"— poured from kegs at house parties. On a college campus where binge-drinking is cheerfully referred to as a major, where football tailgate parties start at 8:00 a.m. on game days, where it isn't uncommon for a 130-pound person to put away a case of beer on a Friday night and "three-beer queer" is the highest order of insult, it was easy, at first, to pass relatively unnoticed. My roommates and I had season tickets to the football games, and on Saturday mornings we started partying early, beer pong in backyards at breakfast and still going strong at bar time, the lot of us swaying and stumbling home together from State Street at 2:00 a.m., after-parties till dawn. We wore our ability to drink all day like a badge.

I played some slow-pitch in coed bar leagues, which were more about drinking than competition. We'd close down those dive bars after each game, putting away pitchers of Miller Lite and singing karaoke and drunkenly dancing the electric slide with a bunch of townies in mesh shorts until the lights went up. I drove home drunk, swerving down country roads and keeping my eyes on the lines, and would wake up in the morning with no recollection of getting home.

My roommates staged an intervention, but I wasn't interested in hearing it. I wasn't interested in stopping. Once, in late fall, I drove home after a night out and sat in the yard behind my house so my roommates wouldn't hear me puke. I woke at dawn, upright against the garage, my fingers gray with frostbite. I started going to parties alone and drank until I blacked out, doing beer bongs and keg stands, much to the delight of the college boys around me, who wrapped their thick hands around my ankles as I chugged. I bought cheap bags of pot from sketchy dealers and smoked myself to sleep. I did lines of coke off dining room tables and passed out on the floor. I went to sports bars alone, the kind frequented by older men. I started having sex, and a lot of it, without much consideration for who I was bringing home or going home with—or, more often than not, fucking in bathrooms, in alleys and kitchens and back seats of cars. Such sex was mostly anonymous, often unprotected, and I was so drunk I rarely remembered what I'd done the night before or who I'd been with. Something might trigger a recollection the next day—a bruise on my thigh, a bloody tampon on my bedroom floor. I spent most mornings curled into a ball on the bath mat, sick and ashamed and retching, fragments of memory from the night before flashing through my brain.

These men were often older, often married, sometimes guys I played slow-pitch with: meaty midwestern guys who reminded me of my coach, who liked sports and wore polo shirts and drank cheap beer at college bars. I don't remember most of them. I don't remember how many there were, but I know there were many. I don't remember their names. All I know is I looked for them. I walked into bars and found them. I targeted them, and I wanted to conquer them. I wanted to have power over the thing I was told all my life had more power than me.

I gained twenty pounds, and it wasn't muscle. I moved out of one house and into another, a crumbling place that should have been condemned, its rotting walls housing at least one family of dead squirrels. I moved in with a new set of roommates, three friends from high school who usually spent the night at their boyfriends' houses. I sat in my bedroom most nights, drinking alone and inflicting injuries on myself. I cut myself, slapped myself, punched myself, stood in front of the mirror and watched big purple bruises bloom on my body, bright beads of blood and then small rivers on my skin, on the soft parts of myself that once were strong.

"Pain is weakness leaving the body," I said aloud one night, drunk and laughing, as I ran the blade of a kitchen knife along the main artery of my left arm and watched it open.

One night, I cut too deep. In the emergency room, a doctor put eleven stitches in my arm. When he asked for my ID, he looked down at it and then up at me.

"Well," he said, "happy birthday."

"Thanks," I said. "Never liked them."

I was twenty-three. When he finished stitching me up, he asked if I had tried to kill myself. I didn't say yes, but I also didn't say no. The truth was I wasn't sure. What I knew was I had gotten so drunk that everything went dark, that there was nothing but despair buzzing in my ears and behind my eyes. That I had wanted the buzzing to stop for good. That as I watched the bright lines of blood run down my arm, it had felt like release. Like a purging, like catharsis. Like sacrifice.

"I think I just wanted to feel myself again," I said. The words hung in the sweet, sterile air of the hospital room, the night's whiskey beginning to wear off, the sun through the windows beginning to rise.

I'm not sure when it started, but one day I was struck by a strange sensation—sudden, out of nowhere—like my brain was separating from my body. Then it started happening every day. I was in my fifth year of college, a degree I almost didn't finish. I'd dropped down to part-time and was working two jobs to pay for school, tending bar at a pub across from the football stadium at night and working at a coffee shop in the mornings, sometimes clocking only three or four hours of drunken sleep. One morning, as I pulled shots of espresso, I felt like I was being lifted out of my body and pulled toward the ceiling. I watched from that suspended state while, below me, my hand passed a drink to a customer. The sounds of the café—the grind of the beans in the hopper, my own voice and the voices of regulars, chairs scraping against linoleum floors, porcelain cups clinking against saucers—were muffled, muted, miles away.

One day I was driving to class from work, and my vision began to blur at the edges. I started to sweat, my hands clammy on the wheel. My heart hammered inside my throat, in my fingers, behind my eyes. The blur turned to darkness, closing in over my sight line like the shutter on a camera lens. I pulled over on the side of the road and waited until my vision returned, until the sweating stopped and my heart slowed down, until it felt less like I was about to die.

I went to a psychiatrist, who diagnosed me with major depression, generalized anxiety disorder, and panic disorder. Hearing these words attached to me was like a dream, like I was watching the doctor scribble prescriptions on a pad for someone else. He gave me a cocktail of drugs—Prozac and Klonopin, then Lexapro and Xanax—and I moved through life in a stumbling haze, taking the benzos like candy and washing them down with whiskey. I blacked out and forgot whole days—which became weeks, then months, and then whole years of my life.

After cycling through a few more doctors and drugs, none of which did much but thicken that fog, a friend recommended I talk to her therapist. A gay woman who had studied literature, she seemed to see me in a way the others hadn't. We talked about books and writing. We talked about things I'd never said aloud. She helped me understand that the behaviors in which I'd been engaging—the drinking, the cutting, the sex—were all forms of self-harm, of self-destruction, an attempt to release feelings of powerlessness and the rage that powerlessness can create. She helped me understand that words like *depression* and *anxiety* and *panic* were real, that they could be attached to me. She explained that the out-of-body episodes I'd been experiencing—a phenomenon called depersonalization, a state in which one loses all sense of identity—are a form of dissociation, a defense mechanism born of post-traumatic stress, often from repressing that trauma. Sometimes, she told me, we get so good at repressing it, we bury it so deeply, that we forget it ever happened. But the memory is still there somewhere, hiding somewhere deep. Like all things we bury, it's bound to surface.

On a midwestern college campus, on a night in early fall, a college girl is drunk. She is nineteen or twenty, and she finds herself alone at a party thrown by football players. She is in a backyard with a keg, surrounded by boys who are not yet men but think they are, and she is being hoisted upside down and held at the ankles while she wraps her lips around the spigot and drinks. The boys are chanting *Go, Go, Go* in deep-voiced unison, and she likes the sound of it. She likes to think these boys are cheering for her. She believes they are. She believes she is liked, she is wanted, and she thinks this is power.

And then she is inside a house with one of the football players, in an unlit room, the party raging on just outside the window. She is on an old, sagging couch, and this boy who is not yet a man, a stranger, is on top of her. He is a lineman, or something like it, and his big, fleshy body pushes into her. At first she lets him. At first she wants him to. And then she doesn't. She tells him she wants to stop. He keeps going anyway, heavy and sweating on top of her and saying nothing. And she says it again, *I want to stop*. And he says, his hot breath on her face, *It's too late now*, and keeps going, the weight of his big body pressing into her stomach. She lies still, drunk and dizzy and watching small beads of sweat form on his forehead, matting his dark hair, as the room starts to spin, and waits for him to finish. After all, she thinks, she allowed it to begin. He does finish, after an eternity, with a slow, shuddering wave, then rolls off her body and pulls up a pair of sagging white briefs over thick white legs, while she sits up on the dirty couch and puts her jeans back on. He walks her to the door and offers to give her a ride home on his Vespa. She says, *No, thank you*, and walks home alone through the empty streets, her whole body beating, thrumming along to the noise of the night. And just like the memory of this night, the sound will fade a little at a time, a little more each day, until there is only darkness where it used to be, a loud buzzing in her ears.

The college girl could be anyone. But of course the college girl was me. Nearly twenty years later, I still have a hard time accepting this truth. It's a story I don't talk about, a story I never tell. I've spent so many years pretending it didn't happen, using all my power to repress it that, for a while, I forgot it had. Today, when hazy flashes of the memory emerge, I still see it like a dream. I see someone else's body in that yard doing keg stands. I see someone else's body on that couch. It's a body without a face, just the anonymous figure of a young woman; I put her, instead of me, beneath that stranger's big body, in the path of danger.

On the rare occasions I do talk about it, behind only the safest doors, I only ever use the word *assault*. I've never actually called it what it was. I still can't bring myself to say the word, *rape*, aloud.

Forgive me this product of my past. Forgive me this nature of mine. Forgive me the power of the cultural hand, which still has its grip on my body, which tells me that all that is bad, and all that I've battled— all the shame I carry, all the invisible damage that still lives inside my body—was brought on by me. Forgive me for being unable, after all these years, to pry those fingers, finally and fully, from myself. Forgive me for not knowing how to be free. Forgive me for all of it—because I haven't yet forgiven myself.

~

Just after I graduated college, I started playing roller derby. It was a new sport, made by women for women, a community that would eventually expand its language to include trans, nonbinary, and gender-queer skaters. Madison's league was one of the first among the modern resurgence of the sport, and a friend encouraged me to join. I had to try out, an intensive two-day session that required hours of skating and skills assessments. After the first day of tryouts, while I anxiously awaited a callback for the next day, I realized I wanted it. I did get called back, and after another day of tryouts, I made the team. It was only the league's third year of existence, and I was excited to be a part of something new, something I would be helping to build from the ground up.

Roller derby was a sport unlike any other I had been a part of: It was weird and funny and subversive—halftime shows and after-parties featured drag performances, punk bands, fire throwers, and circus acts; mascots in spandex and gorilla costumes ran around the track. For the first few years, rather than a penalty box, there was something called "spank alley." Roller derby's mission was a feminist one, and it was a sport made for people on the fringes. But it was also athletic. It was strong, fast, and competitive. It required hours of training each week, both on the track and at the gym. It was slamming my body into other bodies and, instead of being ejected for it, being told to do it again, and harder. It was aggressive and violent without being harmful. It was sprinting again. It was crossovers and body checks and hockey stops. It was jumping into the air and sailing over a line of skaters. It was flying again. It was being strong again.

I cut off all my hair. I watched muscles replace fat on my arms and shoulders and stomach. We did a lot of drinking, but I stopped drinking alone. I stopped cutting myself. I showed off the bruises and blood on my shoulders and thighs rather than trying to hide them. I felt like I was shedding a skin, like I was reemerging into the world after a long period of sleep. I felt, for perhaps the first time in my life, like my body was my own. I lived in it without shame, without being motivated by a male desire for it. I felt like I had been set free.

I was also good. I was named rookie of the year my first season, MVP my second, and became a cocaptain my third. I made the all-star team and traveled around the country competing against other teams. I was an athlete again. I felt joy playing a sport again. I felt confident and powerful.

You could say I found myself in roller derby, but I think what's more true is that I found a tribe—a community of women and gender benders who had never quite fit inside the boxes that society prescribes—who helped me inhabit my body more consciously, who showed me it was possible to move through the world in a way that was both strong and safe, who woke me up. I fell in love with roller derby like I had once loved softball, but it was different: for the first time in my life, I felt truly at home—with a team and a community of women who saw me fully, who understood and identified with me, from whom I had nothing to hide. It was the first time I'd told some secrets aloud. It was also the first time I'd heard the word *queer* in a positive light and understood it might apply to me.

It was also the first time I fell in love with a woman. She was androgynous like me, with short hair and toned muscles—the small, powerful body of an athlete. I had slept with women before, but almost always in secret, and always when I was drunk. It was the first time I kissed a woman in public, held her hand in the street. It was the first time I knew I had the capacity to love men and women and people whose bodies walked the line somewhere between or beyond them. Perhaps more important, it was the first time I understood that love wasn't synonymous with the subjugation of my body—that one's body can exist on an equal plane with the body it loves, rather than be in service to it. Our bodies—pressed together on a Saturday morning in the springtime, the sun coming in through orange curtains; our bodies—so close in shape and size and strength; our bodies—laid bare, open and vulnerable and alive.

I started playing softball again. Some fellow skaters recruited me for their women's fast-pitch league. I was back in center field and the lead-off hitter. I stole bases. I caught long flies. I sent a few hard hits rocketing toward the clouds. (I got ejected once, for screaming at an umpire over a bad call, much to the delight of my teammates. I screamed at him some more after he threw me out, and he made it a two-game suspension.) But it was summer in Wisconsin, and I was back on the field: the sun setting behind us in the seventh inning, the lights flickering on above us, the breeze kicking up clouds of dust. This time, though, my team was composed of many openly queer women. We made jokes about softball and queerness, told stories about playing ball as kids, budding butches trying to look femme, squeezing ourselves into skirts and heels. We played one game each season in drag, wearing pastel prom dresses as we stepped to the plate. I laughed over stories that once brought me shame, and they didn't feel quite so powerful.

A few years later, when I moved to New York, I joined a new roller derby league. One night, after a game, I was at a sports bar with my teammates. I stood at the bar and ordered a drink, watching a Mets game on TV while I waited for my beer. A group of men sat at the bar, and one of them pulled his chair closer to where I stood.

"You a baseball fan?" he asked.

"Sure," I said, keeping my eyes on the game.

"Too bad ladies can't play," he said. "You look like you'd be good."

"I played softball," I said.

"Oh, OK," he said, raising both hands in the air. "I get it." Then he laughed and slapped his hands back down on the bar. "So you bat for the other team?"

He said it loud enough for his friends to hear, and they laughed along with him.

In a past life, I might have laughed too. I might have looked at this man and winked and said something like, "Don't you worry. I play for the home team." I might have traded a joke with him and his friends, using their own misogynistic and homophobic language. I might have flirted, might have touched his arm, might have even taken him home. I might have engaged in any number of behaviors that at some point I had learned were expected of me, were desired of me, would make men like me.

But this time, I took a long drink from my beer, then looked the man in the eyes.

"I'm a switch-hitter," I said. "But I'm not swinging for you."

Lately I've been thinking about the word *reclaim*. From the Latin *reclamare*: to cry out or protest. To recall from wrong or improper conduct. To rescue from an undesirable state. To demand or obtain the return of. To restore to use. To reform. To regain possession. Its definitions make it seem like a finite thing, something mastered or achieved. I think what's more true, at least for me, is that reclamation is a continuous process. It's one I've been engaged in for most of my adult life, this ongoing attempt to reclaim my body from the systems to which I once worked so hard to belong. To uncover the secrets and silences I've kept, these truths I once worked so hard to bury.

Maybe this process isn't a reclamation at all. Maybe, instead, it's a claiming, for the very first time, of my body and my stories as my own. Of my body as the crying out. Of my body as the protest. Of my body as a weapon that I build for me.

Not long ago, I returned to the weight room. My gym in Brooklyn is a spare place, inhabited mostly by men and a small number of women. When I stand in front of the mirror, watching myself do bicep curls and military presses, I try to remember what the girl inside this body looked like back then, in the mirror of the high school weight room. But the memory is old, and the image is blurry. Sometimes I catch a glimpse of her. I can see her long dark hair pulled back into a ponytail. I can see flashes of her body, softer then, baby fat on her face, her arms, her thighs—still such a girl, trying so hard to be a woman. Maybe it's because I've cut the sleeves off a few more T-shirts these days. Maybe it's because I've downloaded the records we used to listen to in that high school weight room. It's terrible music, the kind I'd never admit to listening to in mixed company. But I blast *Hybrid Theory* in my earbuds anyway, a secret summoning of my past, listening to the late Chester Bennington howl about the wounds that crawl in his skin and will not heal, about being so close to the edge that he's about to break, about forfeiting the game. I sing along in my head as I lift, laughing at the lyrics but inhabiting the music anyway, in all its perfect melodrama, all those overwrought high school hymns. And I remember, for a little while, what it felt like to live inside the body of that girl—to be fueled by both desperation and desire, to push her body to its limits in an attempt to create something good.

Today, as I stand in front of this wall of mirrors, I feel the ache of muscle tissue being broken down and rebuilt, again and again, coming back each day a little stronger. And maybe it feels something like rebirth. Maybe more so it feels like forgiveness. Today, my body takes the shape not of that teenage girl nor what she imagined she would become—so far beyond the fantasies of her youth, the picture of what her life might be—but something more alive, something more powerful, something so much better.

~

When I went home, it was the first time in years I'd been back in the summer. Something about it—the smell of a Wisconsin June, the symphony of crickets at night, the wind like water in the trees—unearthed memories of the past, things I had forgotten. They returned to me in flashes, in an instant, in the distance between a pitch and a hit. I remembered the faces of my friends, the girls I'd played ball with since we were five. I remembered my white pinstripe pants, stained with grass and sand, and one of my closest friends, a girl who usually rode the bench, who traded her pants with me when I bled through mine. Who wore my bloody pants so I wouldn't have to, even when she got sent in to play in the seventh inning. I remembered never having felt so loved. I remembered bus rides back from games, Sir Mix-a-Lot through shitty boom box speakers, hanging out the windows of that hot yellow Blue Bird bus, our bare legs sticking to brown vinyl seats. I remembered spaghetti dinners and car washes in gas station parking lots, wearing our jerseys at school on game days and walking through the halls in packs. I remembered our parents in the stands, eating peanuts and laughing at their own inside jokes, our number one fans. I remembered taking a line drive to the face, bleeding from my eye, refusing to go to the emergency room until the game was over, and the first boy I ever kissed, who was training to be an EMT, wiping blood from my face. I remembered my sixteenth birthday, my parents and team gathering around me as I blew out the candles of my cake after a game. I remembered my well-oiled Mizuno glove and the number 6 on my jersey. I remembered the game I once loved—a love that had, over time, become synonymous with guilt and shame and failure—and the game I love still.

That summer night, when I drove to the softball field, sometime around midnight—the floodlights above me dark and my hometown asleep—I dug my bare feet in the sand. And then I ran the bases. Once, twice, three and four and five times around the diamond I ran, springing off the inside corner of each base, sprinting the curve of the field as fast as I could. I kicked up dirt as I ran, my legs covered in sand. Hands on knees, breathing hard, I caught my breath and did it again. Standing in an invisible batter's box, the white chalk long washed away by rain, I let my hips settle in for a swing. I looked at the empty stands and heard the sound of a crowd rising up around me. I walked out to center field and stood in the grass, long and wild in the off-season, cool and damp with dew. I looked at the yellow streetlights of the town where I grew up, then back toward home plate—the view with which I was once so familiar, a battlefield that once felt like mine. And I lay down in the grass, crickets springing out around me, and stared up at the sky like I did when I was a kid, the night air on my arms and legs, the cool earth of early summer settling into my skin. And in the darkness of that night, I remembered the sun setting in the seventh inning, the floodlights of the field turning on at dusk—flickering first and then bursting, filling the field with light—making my whole body hum.

MEAT AND POTATOES

When I moved from Wisconsin to New York, more than ten years ago now, my new roommate analyzed my handshake. Kacey was a lesbian, a few years older than me. We were in graduate school together, and she quickly became known for this particular party trick. It was a way for her to flirt with women, to break the ice and talk about sex at house parties and bars filled with awkward writer types who were prone to standing against walls, clutching their sweating bottles of beer, and talking to no one. It worked a little like palm reading. Kacey would shake a person's hand, then begin a careful analysis: deciphering the firmness of the shake, the grip of the fingers, the stretch of the arm—the various movements of the shaker's hand and body, her eye contact, and a host of other bodily cues—and what it all meant about her personality, her sexuality, and ultimately, what kind of lover she'd be.

A few weeks into the semester, in late September, Kacey and I sat in our living room on a Saturday night, drinking beers, still getting to know one another. She was smart, gregarious, and very funny. She had a magnetic charm, and when she walked into a room, she commanded it. She was from the East Coast and had gone to an Ivy League school, and when I told her, shortly after we moved in together, that I'd gone to college at the University of Wisconsin—a fact about which I'd only ever been proud, it being the best school in my home state and having been the first in my family to finish college—she asked: "Is that a state school?"

She didn't mean anything by it, I don't think. But it was the first time I'd ever felt self-conscious about where I'd come from, a feeling that would become common in my new life on the coast. I was a small-town Midwesterner from a working-class family whose parents didn't have college degrees, let alone master's or PhDs, like so many people I would meet. Back home, I had felt smart, driven, and accomplished; in New York, I felt unremarkable at best and backwoods at worst. For the first time in my life, I felt the parameters of class and where I fit within them.

That night in our living room, after spending the first few weeks of school curiously watching Kacey do the handshake trick to other women in our program, I asked her to do it to me. I extended my arm and shook her hand. It was a midwestern handshake, a masculine handshake, firm and strong and succinct—the kind I had learned from my father. In the Midwest, you learn early to never trust anyone with a weak handshake.

Kacey held on to my hand for a few seconds, looking at me. Then she nodded, one side of her lips curling up into a grin.

"Meat and potatoes," she said.

Kacey had an arsenal of words and phrases she returned to often in this game—titillating ones like *dominant*, *submissive*, *versatile*, or *tops from the bottom*—but I'd never heard this one before. It felt like an insult.

"What does that mean?" I said, snatching my hand away.

"Nothing bad," she said with a laugh. "Just that there's no pretense. You put it all out there."

"So, what?" I said, unconvinced. "I'm like, vanilla or something?"

"No, no, no," she said. "You're a straight shooter, salt of the earth."

This made some sense. This I'd been called before. But I still wasn't satisfied. I couldn't help but think Kacey was calling me the furthest thing from what I believed myself, and my sex life, to be: basic, boring, utterly normal.

"What you see," she said, looking me in the eyes, "is what you get."

The first time I got whipped, it didn't feel euphoric. People who find pleasure in pain often liken it to a runner's high: that late burst of endorphins, and then ecstasy, that carries you to the end of a long, painful act—when something that hurts suddenly becomes a swell of exhilaration, a full-body buzzing of joy.

It wasn't like that for me. Not at first, anyway. At first, the pain was just pain. It hurt and kept hurting. It didn't feel anything like pleasure. I gritted my teeth, tensed my muscles, flinched with every stroke of a whip, every smack of a cane, every dull thwack of a flog. My whole body braced itself against the electric shock of the violet wand. I resisted the pain. It didn't turn me on. But I never used my safe word. I kept saying *Yes*.

I was still in college when I discovered BDSM. At the time, I'd been inflicting pain on myself for several years. Cutting was a ritual that, at its peak, I practiced nightly, typically while very drunk, alone in my bedroom, melodramatically listening to Johnny Cash's cover of Nine Inch Nails' "Hurt" on repeat by candlelight. It was a methodical practice, controlled and ritualistic and highly emo, until it got worse. I sat in lecture halls and classrooms bleeding through my shirt and eventually put myself in the hospital. But for a while, cutting was a release. Sometimes it was even euphoric. And then I found a different way to experience pain.

It started with Connor, a regular at the coffee shop where I worked. I was twenty-one, and he was thirty-four. He was originally from rural Illinois and had come to Madison to work on his PhD. He was roguish and handsome in an unconventional way, with freckles and shaggy brown hair that fell in his eyes. He was divorced, had a six-year-old daughter, and was an environmentalist, a writer, and a rare-book dealer. I fell in love fast.

Connor came in every morning before work. He'd order a cappuccino, and we'd talk politics or art or books; I'd listen, bleary-eyed and usually hungover—from a shift at the bar the night before or a house party I had helped close down—as he told me about the novel he was working on or the first edition of *The Bluest Eye* he'd found while scouting a used bookstore over the weekend. Then he'd settle in by the window with the *New York Times* and ignore me. I gave him my number and he eventually called.

In the coffee shop parking lot on the day of our first date—we went to a bookstore—he told me he didn't believe in monogamy. I wasn't sure if I did either.

"I'm too old for you anyway," he said. I joked that the last guy I loved was nearly twenty years older than me, so he was doing fine.

"No, really," he said. "You're too young. Don't you dare fall in love with me."

This, of course, only made me want him more.

The age difference was never a problem for me—you could say, back then, I had a type—but it was for some of my friends. I found their concerns obnoxious and insulting then, but I can see now, at thirty-six, what this disparity might have looked like from the outside. While I don't consider such an age difference between a woman and man to be an inherent problem—among my closest friends, both heterosexual and not, several are in marriages and partnerships with at least ten years' difference between them—I understand that in many such cases there exists an imbalance of power. And in a culture that oversexualizes women and girls, it's a dynamic in which many young women find themselves without choosing it, and without a way out. But it was a dynamic I was actively seeking.

What was even more of a problem for my friends was the idea of nonmonogamy. They told me it was a terrible idea, that an open relationship was just an excuse for a man to sleep with a lot of women. They told me I deserved better. I interpreted this perspective as antiquated, closed-minded, and square, rather than a genuine concern for me. I'm sure now that their concern was real, but it's also true that my friends back then were pretty traditional, very midwestern, and very heteronormative. This was also 2004, well before real sexual freedom was at the front of our national conversations, not least in the middle of the country; nonmonogamy was at best a joke and at worst a sign of serious delinquency. My friends saw Connor only as an older divorced man with a kid, who was taking advantage of a younger girl. But what I saw was unlike anyone I'd ever met. Connor spoke four languages and had lived abroad. He had a massive library of rare books in his apartment, which he collected and sold on the side. He taught me how to scout, how to identify a true first edition, and how to determine its value; we became partners in bookselling and built a library together. He'd had a rough past—he was adopted, his father had committed suicide, and he, like me, had struggled with depression and self-harm. We spent our first few weeks together comparing scars and trading stories. He struggled with anxiety but was working on it, like I was trying to do too. He was something of a misanthrope, but he was also generous, sweet, and very funny. He loved his daughter, foreign movies, travel, and weird European electronica I'd never heard. More than pretty much anything else, he loved to cook for the people he loved.

Had Connor wanted to be exclusive, I probably would have said yes. But I had always been suspicious of monogamy. I'd said since I was a kid that I would never get married. I'd seen so many divorces and bad marriages, people staying together in terrible dynamics because of religion, or because of the kids, and it all seemed like a scam. I wondered if humans were really cut out for it at all. I was pretty sure I wasn't. I'd been in a few relationships, but each time I'd known from the beginning it wouldn't last. I never stuck around long enough to find out; I usually ended up cheating and leaving, sure to be the one to blow it up before it could explode on its own. I believed the whole system was rigged—that it was a construct and an expectation and a trap, especially for women. The idea of an open relationship was exciting, an experiment for which I was ready.

Not long after we started dating, Connor introduced me to kink. I was still cutting, but I was curious about the idea of both accepting and inflicting pain in a safe and positive space—a way to enact pain without shame and maybe transform it into pleasure. We went slowly at first, practicing only in private—gentle things like spanking, handcuffs, my wrists tied to bedposts with silk ties. Connor bought me a custom silver-and-black catsuit handmade in Austria, and we frequented the few fetish shops in Madison, where he bought me other outfits and an assortment of toys and accessories: a leather whip, a collar and leash and harness, knee-high PVC boots, a bright-pink wig, and a strap-on. I read *The Ethical Slut* and *The Story of O* and the diaries of Anaïs Nin. We watched *Secretary* and role-played some of the scenes.

Sometimes called *S&M*, sometimes *SM*, sometimes *the fetish scene*, and sometimes simply *kink*, the BDSM scene in Madison, Wisconsin, in the early 2000s was not a massive one, but it was a scene. The main event in town was a monthly theme night called Leather and Lace, held at an industrial goth club called the Inferno on the east side of town, just down the road from the Oscar Mayer plant where my father had once worked. Leather and Lace was more a costume party than an actual fetish event, a space for bondage-inspired outfits, drinking, and dancing to '80s goth music like The Cure and Bauhaus and Siouxsie and the Banshees. Connor and I went often, and met a crew of other like-minded kinksters—people who were alternative, weird, and had liberated ideas about the shapes that love and relationships could take. Some became lovers, some became friends, and some became both. We were also among the first regulars at a new event called Kink(ed), held at another club near campus. It was a so-called play night, which meant a bevy of kinky activities at various stations throughout the club. There was a pommel horse, over which one could be bent and whipped; a large wooden X-shaped structure called a Saint Andrew's Cross, to which one could be tied and flogged; and a table in the back where one could check out any number of wicked-looking implements to administer such acts of torture. There was a piercing station, where I watched a woman have her lips sewn shut. A local dominatrix led her sub-boy around the dance floor on a leash. There was a practitioner of Shibari, or Japanese rope bondage, whom I allowed to tie me up so tightly I could barely breathe, the thick rope cutting into my bare chest and arms. There were stage shows, including latex body painting, fire play, and a pony parade—in which people dressed up in pony suits and were corralled around the stage in harnesses—and, most notably, flesh-hook suspension: a practice in which people were hoisted into the air by a system of pulleys attached to metal hooks pierced into their shoulder blades.

On a few occasions, we invited couples from such events—and on some more misguided occasions, from Craigslist—to our apartment or met them at a hotel for a nightlong round of debauchery until sunrise. Once, we ate a continental breakfast in the lobby of a Motel 6, just outside town, with a young, clean-shaven, conservative military man and his wife, with whom we had spent the previous night. A NASCAR race booming out of the television, our heads heavy with hangovers, we picked at our toast as the man talked about his support of the war in Iraq. We didn't talk about all the things we'd done the night before.

We went to house parties in the suburbs, and far out in the country, where people my parents' age and older had built dungeons in their basements and hosted play parties on Saturday nights. At these parties, I was tied to a crucifix and whipped, and I did some whipping myself. I tried my hand at fisting—I was shown by a man how to do it, my fingers and then my wrist and then a few inches of my forearm disappearing into a woman for the first time. I tried (and hated) tickle play, and I was strapped to a handmade swing in a barn loft and tortured by a man in leather who went by the name Sir Keith. It was a strange subset of the scene—or maybe it was just a suburban midwestern one—made up mostly of older hetero couples and a handful of bisexuals. Some applied dominance and submission to every facet of their lives—women who needed permission from their masters to leave the house; men who needed permission from their mistresses to eat or bathe or speak. There were dominatrices who kept their subs in cages or left them tied up on a chain in the yard like dogs. Some were just older married couples whose kids had left home and who faced the empty nest in a different way than most people I knew.

Connor and I also spent much of our five years together traveling across Europe. I had never been abroad, had never even considered the need for a passport, but we bought cheap tickets in the fall and spring, jetting off to Berlin and Prague, Dublin and Belfast, Zurich and Milan and Paris, and spent two summers in a medieval bastide town in the south of France. In some of these cities, we explored the fetish scene. In Berlin, we found a place called the Darkside Club, an unmarked basement-level dungeon that housed tunnels and dark rooms in which one might be strapped to a doctor's table and cut with scalpels, where trans doms in rubber dresses bound and flogged subs onstage, where people had sex in open stables and voyeurs could watch. We spent two nights there, stumbling out into the back alley exit at sunrise and back to our hostel to get a few hours of sleep before doing some sightseeing, then heading back to the dungeon.

We talked about moving to Berlin, where Connor had lived before and would live again, where we might live such a lifestyle more openly, in a country where such behaviors aren't seen as deviant, where one doesn't have to hide the fact that they're into kink. We both saw the United States as prudish and puritanical, and we fancied ourselves sexual revolutionaries. For a time, considering where we came from,

I suppose we were. A nonmonogamous bisexual kinkster with a penchant for leather and gender fuckery, I was as far away from "meat and potatoes" as I would ever be.

~

When you grow up in the Midwest—or at least where I did, in the rural, mostly white, working-class Christian part—you grow up eating meat. In my house, and in most of the houses I knew, dinner consisted of two main ingredients: meat and potatoes. Dinner was pot roast and potatoes, pork chops and potatoes; it was chicken or turkey and mashed potatoes; it was barbecued ribs, hamburgers, hot dogs, and brats with potato salad. It was Friday-night fish fry—with fries or a baked potato. On take-out night, it was a burger and fries from A&W or Hardee's, fried chicken and mashed potatoes from KFC. On special occasions, it was steak and a foil-wrapped potato on the grill.

Inside the six-foot freezer in our garage was a quarter cow—which we bought from my second cousin each Christmas—grown and slaughtered and sliced into various cuts, grounds, and rounds on the family farm just over the Illinois border. Every roast, rib eye, T-bone, and strip, each package of hamburger and chuck, was wrapped tightly in thick white paper, stacked neatly on each snowy shelf for my mother to linger over, select, extract, and eventually cook, for as far back as I can remember. And this is what fed our family.

The thing is, I hated meat. Unless it was slathered in gravy and buried beneath mashed potatoes, stirred into a thick sauce and poured over pasta, squashed thin between bready buns and smothered in ketchup, or folded inside the creamy contents of a casserole, slow-cooked chili, or stew, so tender that it was merely a suggestion—a conduit for whatever carbohydrate-loaded carriage, whatever glorious, gluttonous medleys of salt and starch I really enjoyed consuming—a big chunk of meat on my plate was enough to make my hungry heart sink. I rarely objected, though. Where I come from, you eat what you're given and clean your plate. My parents had both been beaten for not finishing food—my father with a barber's strap and my mother with a hairbrush—and while I wasn't at risk of a beating, I had absorbed this understanding like salt to starch. So I chewed the proverbial fat, tearing into the flesh and choking down the gristle, pressing my fork into the tender flank of a bloody steak and trying my best not to think about the animal I was eating.

Until I left home, the possibility of not eating meat never entered my mind. No one in my family, or my school, none of my friends or their families—no one that I knew, literally anywhere—was a *vegetarian*. It was a word I'd heard but only as one hears a ghost story: It might be something that exists, but no empirical evidence has ever shown you such a thing. I might have heard the word mentioned in a snarky Sunday op-ed decrying the liberal capital city of Madison and its crunchy hippie inhabitants, those who dwelled in communal houses and composted, who celebrated the solstice and lived off dandelions and pine needles and kelp from the lakes. These were creatures of myth, these crunchy, crusty plant-eaters, and it was a picture that seemed absurd. The vegetarian was a joke, a parody, a ridiculous piece of lore, a strange foreign being who might as well have lived a continent away. And in America's Dairyland, the term *vegan* was a slur, was blasphemy, was an atrocity unto man.

The closest anyone in my family came to vegetarianism was an aunt, my mother's youngest sister, who was closer in age to me than my mother. She had gone to college in the vast metropolis of Milwaukee, played piano, and was the most cultured person I'd ever met when I was a kid. She didn't eat red meat, requiring chicken sausages or turkey burgers at cookouts. This is what my family called a vegetarian. I never asked why she didn't eat red meat. It might have been because she grew up around cows, which were closer to horses and dogs and cats—those animals we arbitrarily deem to be pets rather than food—than fowl. Or maybe it was the fact that to bite into red meat means to confront something; specifically, the blood of the animal it once was. And in a midwestern family like mine, confronting things has never been our strong suit.

Both of my mother's parents grew up on farms. Their parents were multigenerational Irish and Swiss-German farm families in southern Wisconsin. My grandfather's surname comes from the German word meaning "farmer" or one who occupies newly cleared forest or land. My mother and her oldest siblings lived in a farmhouse in the same area, and even after they moved to the "city"—a nearby town of roughly two thousand people—the kids spent summers and weekends at their grandparents' farm, milking cows and butchering chickens and harvesting vegetables. On more than one occasion, my mother watched in horror as the headless bodies of chickens ran around the barnyard, spinning in fast frenzied circles as their necks spurted blood, until after what seemed like a lifetime they collapsed in a heap of feather and dust. If that doesn't turn you into a vegetarian, I'm not sure anything will.

My grandfather worked the line at the General Motors plant in Janesville; my grandmother worked on various lines, too, including a cheese factory in Monroe, where she tested the melting points of cheddar and Swiss, marble and American. It was a job that turned her into a rare breed of Wisconsinite: one who didn't like cheese. Providing for a family of eleven meant buying and cooking the cheapest and easiest foods available. Even in the golden age of the motor industry—long before GM eventually collapsed and my grandfather lost nearly fifty years of pension—things were tight. My grandfather worked third shift, so he was rarely home for dinner, but he did shoot squirrels and turkeys and deer, which would often feed the family in his absence. He made venison jerky and kept it on hand, as my uncles still do. Sometimes, when he came home late at night, my mother would wake to the smell of cow tongue frying in butter, onto which my grandfather would stack a slab of Limburger cheese and eat as his favorite sandwich. My grandmother, meanwhile, stocked her pantry with food that could keep through the interminable Wisconsin winters—food that could be stored, that could stretch. The family canned the vegetables they harvested from the farm and from my grandmother's own garden, then blanched and froze the rest. Like my parents, they kept a side of beef from the farm, packaged in its various cuts, in their freezer. Dinner was often a one-pot meal like goulash, a staple composed almost entirely of food they grew or raised—ground beef from the farm, vegetables from the garden like onions, tomatoes, and green peppers—mixed with elbow macaroni. They rarely had dessert, as my grandmother, having grown up during the Depression, considered butter and sugar precious commodities.

My grandmother did most of the cooking, but the older girls always had to help. "Never the boys," my mother said. On Fridays, because they were Catholic, they ate frozen fish sticks. Any fresh fish they ate they caught themselves from nearby rivers and lakes.

"Meals had to be fast, and they had to be a lot," my mother said. "Nothing fancy, meat and potatoes."

My father, meanwhile, grew up in Orange, New Jersey. His parents were first-generation Italians from Naples raised in Newark, which meant they spoke a curious Neapolitan-English pidgin they passed on to my father and his brothers—a strange dialect that involves the omission of some letters and the insertion of others—most commonly dropping the last letter from a word, substituting any hard *C* sound for *G*, a stray *R* for a *D*, so that *ricotta* becomes "rigott," *manicotti* becomes "manigott," *mozzarella* becomes "moozadell," *capicola* becomes "gabbagool," and so forth. It's the reason that, in the United States, we have "Parmesan" rather than *Parmigiano*. Anyone who has seen *The Sopranos* knows what I'm talking about.

My grandfather owned a barbershop in Orange, cutting hair and giving straight-razor shaves for a nickel to the neighborhood Italians. He worked late, keeping the shop open for the second-shifters to come in after work, so he, too, was rarely home for dinner. My father's mother worked only in the kitchen, making three meals a day for her husband and kids.

"It was her domain," my father said.

My father's family ate mostly lentils and pasta ("bast") or "Minest," short for *Minestra*—a stew made of savoy cabbage, cannellini beans, and large chunks of fresh pepperoni. On Fridays it was fish, fresh from the market, and during Lent it was that most hallowed dish: *baccalà*—a giant white fish, typically cod, soaked in salted water in the bathtub for several nights. On Christmas Eve, it was the Feast of the Seven Fishes. When my father, the youngest of four, started working nights in high school, doing inventories of grocery stores and bodegas in Manhattan and Brooklyn and Queens, he'd get home at one or two o'clock in the morning. His mother would be waiting up.

"Want me to make you something to eat?" she'd say.

At least once a week, typically on Sundays, Grandma Fal made red sauce. To many Italian Americans, the word is *gravy*, a word that possesses a much different meaning in the Midwest. *Gravy* to Italian Americans means marinara, Bolognese, ragù, alla vodka—it's all gravy. On the hot lunch menu at my Wisconsin public school, it was "meat sauce." My family's red sauce, from southern Italy to my grandmother's kitchen and eventually to my mother's, means a magical combination of ground beef and sweet Italian sausage thrown into a large stockpot and browned with garlic and onions. It means stewed tomatoes, from a garden if possible, and thick slices of button mushrooms. It means fresh basil and oregano, a generous amount of sugar, and some secret ingredients I'm not allowed to reveal. It means meatballs, made of the same combination of beef and pork, an egg to congeal them, milk to soften them, and a hearty amount of bread crumbs, oregano, and Parm.

It means meat so tender it quite literally melts on your tongue, the smell of the sauce filling up the house as it simmers for a whole day on the stove. It means spaghetti cooked al dente, just a quick dip in boiling water for truly fresh pasta—which my grandmother often made from scratch—the tooth of a fork-twirled mouthful the perfect vehicle for the sauce. It means crusty bread—ideally *banel*—and salted butter, sopping up the sauce at the bottom of a bowl.

Of the recipes that were carried down to my midwestern family, the one that stuck was the sauce. It's the recipe that my father's mother passed on to my mother, who eventually passed it on to me. It's the recipe that connects me to the side of my family I never really knew growing up—both of my paternal grandparents were dead by the time I was twelve, and I met them only a handful of times. It's the recipe that all families with even a sliver of Italian descent do not just hold dear but protect with a kind of vehement secrecy and pride that is rarely, if ever, attributed to anything else. In a cookbook my mother made for me when I left home, she calls it "Spaghetti à la Mama Fal." It's what I make when I want to feed my friends. It's what I make when I want to seduce someone I'm dating. It's what I make when I feel alone or homesick. And no matter how many times I've attempted to make it without the meat—or worse, with imitation meat—it's a certain failure. Not that such variations taste bad, necessarily; it's just not the same meal. It's not even close to what I want.

Because the thing is this: What I want is irreplaceable. What I want comes from a feeling so intimate, and so increasingly elusive, that to obtain it is like a kind of nirvana. What I want is home. It's the garlic and onions popping in olive oil; the thick, plump tomatoes as their skins start to shrivel and peel away in the heat; the sweet smell of basil and oregano that fills the house on a Sunday. It's the first taste test, standing over the stove and burning the roof of your mouth. It's the slick strings of pasta slopping hot specks of sauce onto your chin. It's the tenderness of the meatballs as they dissolve on your tongue, it's the oil on your lips. It's being transported to a place and a time that exists with each day a little more hazily in the dark pockets of the mind. It's the taste and the smell and the feeling of a place, and a time, shards and slivers and pale ghosts of which you can conjure sometimes, but to which, in the end, you can never really return.

~

After a while, the pain began to transform. Lost in the rhythm of a whip, I felt the sting subside—first a sharpness and then a smoothing out. It melted into a kind of deep, corporeal buzzing, like the first sip of a strong beer on a summer day and an empty stomach, or the first few bites of a very good meal. Endorphins rushed to my brain. I got lost in the fog of it. As I watched my skin turn red, as the welts from the cat-o'-nine-tails blossomed on my arms and shoulders and thighs, as a heavy leather flog beat my flesh like a meat tenderizer, a tingle would rise up in my skin, the hairs on my arms and neck standing up until my whole body was humming. It began to feel euphoric. Like cutting, being beaten was like falling into a fugue and at the same time waking up—a catharsis, a swell of feeling, then release, and then calm. But in BDSM, I knew that I would emerge on the other side of the pain in the hands of someone who would take care of me. I knew that I was safe.

At first, masochism seemed at odds with my budding identification as a feminist. Being hurt at the hands of men, in particular, seemed like the opposite of everything I wanted to be. I'm not sure if I've ever been able to fully reconcile this. It was consensual, and it was something that I was choosing, but it still felt, at times, like a betrayal. At the most basic level, I wanted to be dominated—by men, specifically, but also by women. Before getting involved in the BDSM scene, I always thought of myself as more dominant than submissive. So often, though, the things we hope to be true about ourselves and the things we really want are incongruous.

I started to think of myself as a sub. I liked pain. I liked, in particular, to watch the hand of a dom as they whipped or flogged me: to watch their steady, calculated strength, beneath which there seemed to boil a slow sea of desire, or rage, or their own euphoria—expressed in a methodical, rhythmic kind of violence. In each crack of a whip against my skin, there was a need I was satisfying. There was a hunger, and I was feeding it.

But my experience as a sub slowly became about more than just the receipt of pain. I wanted to have decisions made for me. I wanted to be told what to do. I wanted to be bossed around, given orders that I could follow perfectly. I wanted to be rewarded for being a good girl. I wanted to be hurt and then held—tender hands addressing my wounds, tucking me into bed. I wanted to be taken care of.

~

When I left home for college, I ate like shit. Alone on my own for the first time with unfettered access to a university cafeteria, I gained not just the freshman fifteen but twenty, eating nothing but cheeseburgers and fries, pepperoni pizzas, and fried chicken sandwiches slathered in mayo nearly every day. Food—like booze, like sex, like cutting—became another way to hurt myself. But then I moved off campus and lost my access to the cafeteria. What I discovered in its stead was a whole new world of food.

I discovered sushi. I discovered Thai and Indian and Laotian curry. I discovered jerk chicken and lentil stew. I discovered the food carts on State Street, which introduced me to Filipino and West African food. I discovered real Mexican food (Ortega being not just a factory where my aunt worked but as close to Mexican as we ever got). I discovered arepas and corn tortillas. I discovered kale and watercress and yellow beets; tabbouleh, falafel, and hummus; tofu, tempeh, and seitan. I discovered feta. I discovered foods that are culinary staples in my life now, but that back then I had never encountered. The first time I said *quinoa* aloud, at a dinner party, I pronounced it "quinn-oh-ah." I didn't learn how to use chopsticks until I was in my midtwenties, and I'm still not very good at them. (And let me tell you, it's embarrassing, to live in New York City and be bad at chopsticks. Nothing gives a yokel away faster.) I reveled in this new terrain of food, in this new way of eating. It felt different, exciting, and further away from home than I could have possibly imagined.

W here I come from, when we talk about midwestern food, we're talking about casseroles and hot dish, beef stew and pot roast. We're talking about cookouts with burgers and brats, potlucks in the park. We're talking about Sunday-night chicken dinner and Friday-night fish fry. We're talking about the food that has fed midwestern families for generations.

But there's a problem: When we imagine those families, sitting around their tables to eat this food, more often than not, the families we imagine are white. And when we imagine the food atop those tables, we think of it as white food too. We think of it as all American. We think of it as normal.

"Can't we just have something normal?" a Wisconsin friend once said, when we suggested ordering Thai for dinner.

"Nothing too spicy," people say.

"Nothing too weird," others have said.

"Well that's different," every white midwestern mother has said about any food deemed foreign, exotic, or strange.

In the grocery store in my hometown, there's an aisle labeled "Ethnic Food." All foods considered not normal, and as such un-American, are packed into this one aisle: hard taco shells, mostly; hot sauce and beans; rice, soy sauce, and hoisin. There's instant Indian curry in a box, pad thai and peanut and Sichuan sauce, row upon row of ramen.

There's chickpeas and lentils, a small corner of kosher food. There are cans of water chestnuts and crunchy chow mein noodles. This is where "foreign" foods are found, which suggests that the rest of the store is "American"—filled with the foods that so many people would have you believe are American too: burgers and frozen pizza and fries, steak and sausages and potatoes and pasta. All of which came from immigrants, of course, but the ones that today would be considered white, perpetuating the false idea that there is any kind of food that's actually American. That there's any kind of person who can claim to be all American.

But sometimes my family surprises me. At certain potlucks and parties in Wisconsin, I'm still called "city girl" like it's a sickness. But two summers ago, my mother came to New York with three of her sisters and my teenage cousin. Against my advice they stayed in Times Square, which, as one might imagine, was a nightmare for people accustomed to the country—people who never encounter such a crowd, let alone have to walk for several long blocks through it. For one of my aunts, it was her first time in New York, and she swore it would be her last. But one afternoon, I took them out to lunch at a Japanese restaurant in Manhattan. It was a gamble—and an attempt to steer the group away from the burgers and pizza and hot dogs that had been on the menu thus far. Neither my mother nor her sisters were accustomed to Japanese food, or with using chopsticks, and I assumed they'd ask for forks. But they fumbled with their chopsticks like champs—and I fumbled right along with them—and they ate things they could not identify and had never encountered. And they loved it.

Connor taught me how to cook. My mother taught me the basics, a few staples, and how to bake. But in our small Madison kitchen, Connor taught me how to use and sharpen a chef's knife. While garlic powder had been a common ingredient in my family recipes, Connor taught me how to crush, peel, and chop a clove of garlic. While my mother and grandmother had cooked with mostly frozen and canned vegetables, Connor taught me how to sauté fresh greens. I ate organic spinach for the first time. I learned how to julienne an onion and sliver a shallot. I learned how to sear a steak and whisk a béchamel, how to fry a piece of fish in homemade batter, how to tie and bake a pork tenderloin and panfry potatoes. I learned about wine, what to pair with a white or a red.

For a while, one of my closest friends, Ash—who Connor and I had met in the BDSM scene, who was sometimes a lover but mostly a friend—came to live with us. She was in the middle of a divorce and had moved out of her place, so we invited her to stay with us. It was Connor's idea, one of many times he helped friends get back on their feet when they were struggling. Sometimes Ash and I shared a bed, and sometimes we didn't. She had a life of her own, a boyfriend, and a handful of other lovers, so she wasn't around much. But when she was, we cooked together. Ash was Connor's age, and she was something of a gourmand; she loved to feed people too. Like Connor, she taught me how to cook things I'd never had before: bone broth soup, pasta puttanesca with sardines, risotto with wild mushrooms or butternut squash. Risotto was something Ash and I made together often, a meal that became comfort food for both of us. In the tiny kitchen in our tiny apartment, cooking a family meal—sometimes with Ash, sometimes with Connor's daughter, and sometimes for friends—our strange little household felt like a family.

Food and community share an almost universal connection, across cultures and continents. In the American Midwest, in the early 1800s, when farmland was first being settled and developed by immigrants from northern Europe, barn raising became a community event. Farmers from several households would join together to build one another's barns, and each day of work would end with a big, communal supper. These meals typically meant a roast, a chicken, a turkey, or a ham; it meant baked potatoes, mashed potatoes, and whatever vegetable was in season and had been harvested that day by the women and girls, who prepared the food and tended the garden while the men built the barns. All the food they ate was grown on those farms, and the practice would carry from household to household as the barns were built.

In my immediate family, most of our meals were pretty quiet. We sat, the three of us, around our little kitchen table; we didn't often have people over, nor did we go to other people's houses. We didn't have Sunday-night extended-family dinner, like so many of my friends did. When we went to family gatherings, a few times a year, it was always a potluck: Everyone brought a dish to pass, carrying Crock-Pots and Saran-Wrapped casserole dishes, pies and cookies and pans of brownies. We'd set it all up in the basement of my grandmother's house, and rather than have a meal sitting around a table, the whole day was spent eating, working our way down an assembly line of food with paper plates and forks, soda and beer in coolers (or, in the winter, outside in the snow). We'd stand around in the basement talking, assembling sloppy joes and pulled pork sandwiches, piling deviled eggs, taco dip, pickles, chips, and cubes of cheese onto our plates, double stacked and sagging under the weight of the food. We'd gather around the TV to watch football, then trickle in and out of the food room, grazing for hours, until the pies and cookies and bars were laid out. Then we'd do it again.

Whenever we traveled to New Jersey to visit my father's family, we always sat around a table. Prepared and served by my grandmother and aunts and female cousins, meals were many-coursed dinners of lasagna ("lasagn"), manicotti ("manigott"), and antipasto ("antibast"). It was never a potluck; gathering around a table was an important part of the meal. When I left home, I discovered the concept of the "family meal" among nonbiological or chosen families too. Some queer communities I was part of hosted a weekly Sunday-night dinner, which rotated houses. When Ash got her own place, she hosted annual dinners at Thanksgiving and Christmas for people without families or who were alone on the holidays. In New York, a friend helped start a Sunday-night event called Queer Soup Night, for which various chefs cook multiple vats of soup to feed a community, an event that has since expanded to several other cities across the country. In each case, the food serves more than just to feed people; it becomes a symbol of community and family. It's a way for people, wherever their lives have taken them, to have a place to come home to for dinner.

~

Our safe word was "asparagus." It started out as a joke, the least sexy word we could think of. And then it stuck. We began using it the way many people in the scene use "red," or some similar unambiguous word, to communicate that they want to stop during play—if the pain got to be too much, if they got uncomfortable, if they just needed a break.

In the BDSM community, safe words are necessary; role-playing is about power and often involves playing out fantasies of power, where the words *no* or *stop* can mean the opposite. For anyone involved in the scene, the safe word thus becomes a prerequisite to play. For us, "asparagus" became a way to both say no and to lighten the mood. It shook us out of a moment of drama and made us laugh. And every time we ate asparagus, or saw it on the menu at a restaurant, we giggled. It was a little secret, an inside joke, and above all, it was safe. After a while, it even became kind of sexy.

Throughout our relationship, Connor slept with men, I slept with women. We slept with both, together and on our own. We dated other people, had brief romances with a few. Sometimes it worked, and sometimes it didn't. Sometimes we got jealous; sometimes we fought. We spent hours renegotiating our contract: whether we had to ask permission before sleeping with someone else, whether we wanted details of a new tryst, who was off-limits and who we might share. We made rules and broke them, established new ones, and started over. Like any relationship, sometimes our life together was ecstatic. Sometimes it was awful. It was usually hard.

But bucking a traditional system is never easy. And I wanted to try things even—and maybe especially—if they were hard. I wanted to be, as Dan Savage told me I should be, good, giving, and game. (No matter, of course, that Mr. Savage didn't believe my particular sexuality existed; he was the god of queer and kinky sex advice at the turn of the century, so I took it, and those of us in the scene returned to this mantra often.) But it wasn't just that I wanted to have new experiences; I wanted to break the mold of what I'd learned love should be, what sex and sexuality should be, what a woman should be.

What's also true is I wanted to please a man I loved, and there was part of me that thought if I was dark enough, subversive enough—and submissive enough—if I was willing to do everything he wanted, I would be able to keep him. Connor was the older, experienced, and educated man I'd always wanted, and in our first years together I was driven in no small part by the desire to serve him. I also liked relinquishing control—the kind I had been working for so much of my young life to attain. But sometimes I did things I didn't want to do.

It has taken me a long time to admit this. It has taken me a long time to wrestle with this truth, to peer closely into the murky spaces of consent—as well as those of desire, violence, sex, and power—that, at its best, BDSM forces one to confront. What I know is that Connor and I loved one another, deeply and genuinely, and over time I got better at communicating with him about what I wanted and what I didn't, which parts of our relationship made me happy and which ones didn't, to recognize when a situation made me uncomfortable and say so. But it took a long time for us to break through the power dynamic upon which our relationship was built, to get to a place that felt more equal.

It took me a long time to understand that equity might be something I wanted.

We started spending less time in the scene. We still went to theme nights, but we stopped going to play parties. We were still technically open, but we weren't dating anyone else. We spent our weekends scouting used bookstores, finding more pleasure in spotting a rare first edition tucked away on the dusty shelves of Half Price Books than being tied up and whipped. We saw more movies and spent more time writing rather than scouring Craigslist for people to play with. We hosted Dungeons & Dragons nights with Connor's daughter and our friends—Connor, of course, was the Dungeon Master. We invited our friends over for family dinners. We still traveled but didn't seek out as many kinky adventures in the cities we explored; we brought our friends along instead. And in our last years together, I think we were happy. I'm not sure if what I wanted with him was a balance of power, or if we ever made it there. I don't know if anyone ever does. I do know that we tried.

~

For the past decade, I've tried to be a vegetarian. Sometimes it holds, and sometimes it doesn't. In New York, my partner and I cook almost exclusively vegetarian food, meals made of tofu and tempeh, vegetables and grains; many of our family recipes, like chili and spaghetti, we make without meat. My motivations are both ethical and environmental, and as long as I stay in the city, I can usually stick to it. But when I go back to Wisconsin, I almost always end up eating meat. When this happens, two things are at play: First, I'm not comfortable telling anyone who's cooking for me that I don't eat meat or asking them to cook differently for me. But the other thing is that after living away from Wisconsin for so long, I want the food that tastes like home. I don't want tofu or tempeh or quinoa or kale. What I want is my mother's food. What I want, it turns out, is meat. I want scrambled eggs with sausage and cheese in the mornings. I want meatloaf or beef stew at night. I want a roast with potatoes and carrots in the oven. I want my mother's meaty lasagna. I want spaghetti and meatballs. When I go to Madison, I want Ash to take me out to her favorite new restaurants and tell me what to eat; I want her to order for me, to feed me liver and lamb and pork belly and roe, pierogi stuffed with meat and onions and cheese. When I go home, on a very basic level, I want to be fed by the people I call family.

In small-town Wisconsin in the late '80s and early '90s, there were no labels telling us where our food came from. This was long before Whole Foods and Trader Joe's made their way to the flyover states, before phrases like *organic, free-range, fair-trade, grass-fed,* and *cage-free* had entered the vernacular. Before anyone knew the acronyms BGH and GMO. It was a time when slogans like "Beef: It's What's for Dinner" and "Pork: The Other White Meat" were seen on every television commercial break. When the meat we ate didn't come from the family farm, it often came from factories—whatever was on sale for ninety-nine cents per pound, whatever could last us for days in the form of leftovers. This was what made its way to our kitchen, along with foods of convenience like Schwan's frozen pot pies, Hot Pockets, and prepackaged and preservative-rich lunch meats and cheeses from the deli aisle. For about a decade, my father had a cubicle at the Oscar Mayer plant in Madison, and he brought home armfuls of food from the assembly lines: vacuum-sealed cylinders of bologna; thin watery packages of turkey, ham, and salami; stacks of individually wrapped cheese-product singles; and, when I was lucky, that brand-new and most coveted culinary treasure of my childhood—the sodium-packed, heavily processed, gelatinous dream known as Lunchables.

For a long time, my mother was a supporter of PETA. A World Wildlife Fund sticker has been long pressed to the back bumper of her 1995 Saturn coupe, and there's one stuck to the kitchen window, too, to stop birds from flying into the glass. She volunteers at the Humane

Society, builds houses for stray cats, and feeds the birds, squirrels, and deer around her house, creating a veritable wildlife refuge in the backyard. For as long as I can remember, she has hated hunting, and recently, she told me that, when she was young, she shot and killed a squirrel and felt so terrible that she vowed to never kill an animal again. Her mother felt the same way about animals, and they both ate meat.

On a recent trip home, I asked my mother about eating animals. I told her that since I'd left I'd tried to be a vegetarian, or at the very least make an effort to know where what little meat I did eat came from—to be a so-called ethical omnivore. We'd never talked about it before, and I was afraid I might upset her just by bringing it up.

"You know," she said, chopping an onion on the counter, "I spent a very long time when I was younger trying to think about that." She paused for a beat, letting the knife hover above the pile of diced onions, which would be browned with meat for sauce later on. "But I just can't think about it anymore," she said. "If I think about it, then I have to look at my whole life."

When I was younger, I might have called my mother out on this disconnect. But instead, I was struck by her honesty. She didn't get defensive, as is our midwestern wont. She didn't make excuses, try to lay it on how she was brought up, on class, or on circumstance. Rather, she admitted something that a lot of people are unwilling to admit: That it's easier to exist within the structures we're given than to interrogate them or to do the work required to live outside them. That to ask questions of ourselves might mean having to face some hard truths, and maybe even dismantle our entire way of life. And so we choose not to ask those questions at all.

But the other thing that's true of my parents, and even more so of my late grandparents, is that they never had access to the kind of eating I have access to, especially in a city like Brooklyn. Today, there's an organic section in my hometown grocery store, and there are co-ops and a Whole Foods thirty minutes away. But people like my parents aren't going to spend six dollars on a half-gallon of milk, regardless of how happy those cows might be. My parents aren't poor, but they also aren't rich. They built a life that has been relatively comfortable, but they've also been imprinted with some indelible understandings about food: that its primary function is to feed as many people as possible at the lowest possible cost, and that food is a way to provide and care for the people you love—to ensure that they have enough of something, even or perhaps especially when they don't have enough of something else. That they are fed and full and never hungry. It takes a great deal of privilege—by way of money, education, and access—to live within one's ideals. It took me leaving home and moving to one of the most expensive cities in the country to understand this.

My parents and I ate junk food. In addition to their full-time jobs, they had an inventory business. It was meant to be a way to reach financial independence, but it never turned out that way. So we woke before dawn on weekends, the three of us traveling to roadside gas stations and country convenience stores across rural Wisconsin. I hated getting up early, having to spend the weekend working when I could be with my friends. But what I loved about the job was the food. Before we hit the road, we'd stop at a gas station in town to fuel up and grab breakfast. This meant coffee (drip for my parents, something sweet and frothy and fake-vanilla-flavored from a machine for me), orange juice, and a box of doughnuts. On the best days, we hit McDonald's for Egg McMuffins and hash browns. Then we'd drive an hour or so to our first store of the day. Crouched on our hands and knees, we counted everything in those small, dark stores—cramped places with cracked-tile floors and smoke-stained walls, in tiny, unincorporated towns or on the highway just outside them. My beat was nonperishables: I counted every dusty bag of chips, every stale loaf of bread, every end-cap of Little Debbie Swiss Rolls and cream-filled Hostess CupCakes. But the best part was the candy aisle, that hallowed row of sweet treasures that I had all to myself. I counted the Milky Ways and Butterfingers, the Whatchamacallits and Charleston Chews, each bag of peach rings and Circus Peanuts and Sour Patch Kids. As I counted, I imagined the chocolate on my tongue, the first pop of sugar hitting my jaw like a shot.

When we finished a store, we grabbed a snack for the road—something to fuel us through the next job, in some other rural town. I chose carefully, taking my time, as if I didn't know the entire aisle by heart. I almost always picked a candy bar and a bag of chips, maybe some Skittles or Gummy Worms, and always a bottle of pop—Dr Pepper or Mountain Dew or Cherry Coke.

I don't eat much junk food these days, but whenever I take a road trip, this is the food I crave. It's the food I sometimes allow myself to buy. I close my eyes on the first bite, and I can taste those back roads of Wisconsin. I can taste those dusty stores, out in the middle of nowhere. I recall how much better the sugar tasted after a particularly long day of work, when the knees of my jeans were stained with dirt from the floor, when my hands were covered in dark-gray dust, when the flickering fluorescent lights had given me a headache in my temples. How it hit my brain like an electric surge, like a bright spinning burst of joy. The melting chocolate and the fizz of the pop on my tongue, the pain in my head turned pleasant buzz as we drove toward home.

In my midwestern BDSM scene, play parties at people's houses always doubled as potlucks. Everyone brought a dish to pass, and in the kitchen of a suburban duplex or a farmhouse in the country, we'd gather around a table or a marble island counter filled with Crock-Pots and Pyrex casserole dishes and platters of food, just like my family gatherings—except surrounded by half-naked bodies, mottled and red under a harness or corset, eating crudité and Tater Tot casserole, Swedish meatballs and cocktail wieners in sauce, chips and dip, cheese and crackers and slices of summer sausage. My ass raw beneath a PVC skirt, I talked to people who had just tortured me and each other about the weather, about school, about summer plans as I piled my paper plate with pulled pork, pasta salad, and homemade chocolate chip cookies. Then, just like any midwestern family gathering, we stood around those tables, sagging paper plates in hand, and ate.

These days, my sex life is simpler than it used to be. I've been with one partner, a man, for nearly ten years. I don't go to play parties anymore, but I'm still interested in kink, and I'm still open to trying new things. I still like a little pain sometimes. I still have certain fantasies, and I know that I can ask my partner to act them out. I know I don't have to do anything I don't want to. But it turns out, stability is more important to me now than adventure. It turns out, I'd rather keep my sex life inside closed doors than on any kind of stage. It turns out, I'm more interested in culinary adventures than sexual ones. It turns out I actually kind of like monogamy. It took me a while to admit it, having thought for so long that to be monogamous would mean bowing to constructed expectations of love and intimacy. I still believe monogamy is a construct, and I don't necessarily think that humans are biologically cut out for it. Someday I might decide again that I'm not either. But for now, I like having one partner, and I like our life together. It feels safe here, and it feels like home. Maybe this makes me boring. Maybe this means I'm vanilla. Maybe, when Kacey called me meat and potatoes, she wasn't totally wrong.

There is a memory, and it happens in the kitchen of my youth: yellowed tiles and yellow wallpaper, yellow counters and a yellow fridge and yellowed paintings of farmhouses, their frames a dark wooden brown that match the cabinets. My mother stands at the counter in her work clothes, and I stand at her side. She's got her hands in a big metal bowl filled with raw meat. She works her hands in the pink of it, and I hear it squish between her fingers as she kneads. She has mixed into the meat two eggs, some milk, and bread crumbs. Some basil and oregano, salt and pepper and Parmesan. She works the meat until her fingers—which like mine, are long and narrow with big knuckles—turn pink. The sleeves of her blouse are rolled up above the elbow, and she is wrist-deep in the bowl. Her kneading is rhythmic, hypnotic. I stand on my toes to watch as she grasps and squeezes and massages the meat, as her hands work this mound of flesh, this ground-up body of an animal.

In years to come, I will mimic this process, repeat the ritual as she taught me. I will adopt and perfect this art, passed down among women for generations. Without children of my own, this recipe will die with me unless I pass it along to my friends. Maybe I will. Or maybe I'll keep it, this family secret, safe with me. And even though I'll keep trying my best not to eat meat, sometimes, particularly when I feel alone or far away, I'll put my hands in a cold metal bowl of raw beef or sweet Italian sausage. I'll feed the people I love, and I'll feel like I've come home.

GUN COUNTRY

The ground is solid beneath my boots, a crunch of frost on late-November earth. The morning is cold and clear. I breathe it in and keep it there, a quick sharp fire I haven't felt in a while. It's a comforting thing, this kind of air on the lungs—the real cold and real clean kind, the kind you can't find in a city.

There's a clearing here, just beyond a field of spruce and fir, where a few solitary oaks stand guard, their leaves gone and branches bare. A thin fog hangs over the cornfield, its rows of stalks chopped short to spikes, stiff and yellow and winter dead. Sparrows and finches perch there, then fly up to the trees. Their songs echo across the silence.

I breathe in again and hold it until the sharpness feels like it could shatter, then let it pour out of me like water, visible against the cold.

My shoulders relax, my pulse slows. My arms, stretched out before me as if in an offering, are still. My grip is loose but firm.

I am a statue. I am steady. I am a sea of calm.

I pull the trigger.

For the past several years, I've traveled with my partner, John, from New York to Ohio for Thanksgiving. His aunt and uncle have a tree farm not far from Dayton, a gorgeous stretch of land out in the country with over twenty acres of blue and Norway spruce, Canaan Fir, and farmland beyond it. It's a place that's quiet and calm, where the night is filled with stars. There's no smog, no pollution, no jackhammers or pile drivers or men screaming over the sounds of them. No trains, no taxis, no blaring horns, no rumbling of the ground beneath your feet. Just earth, solid and sturdy and sure, and row upon row of trees—towering, green, and alive.

We come here every year to escape the city and work on the farm. Thanksgiving is opening weekend for Christmas trees, and the busiest time of the season, so we spend a few days chopping wood, putting up lights, cutting down and baling trees, then hauling and tying them to pickup trucks. It was on the farm that, two years ago, I learned to use a maul—a rather wicked-looking, heavy-headed ax used for splitting wood. I chopped trunks of spruce and fir, throwing the weight of my whole body into it, hefting the heavy tool over my head, squaring my shoulders, finding my center—knees bent, core tight—and bringing it down. Driving the wedge into the wood, feeling it split beneath my hands neatly in two. It felt ecstatic, using my body to create fuel for the fire that would burn later that night, around which bodies would be gathered and warm.

The farm is also where I first shot a gun. I've done it twice now, over the past few years. On my first time out, I hit the target on nearly every shot. It was thrilling, to be good at something I'd never done before. It was also fun. But more than that, it made me feel powerful.

I grew up in a family of hunters. My parents didn't hunt, but my uncles and grandfather and second cousins did. In rural Wisconsin, deer season is holier than the holidays. For that brief stretch of weeks in late November, nothing else (except maybe football) matters. There are dozens of hunting seasons in the state, each species getting its own week or two: turkey and rabbit and bear; coyote and bobcat and fox;

woodchuck and pheasant and grouse; squirrels and ducks and mourning doves. But deer season is the most important. People take time off work; young boys are pulled out of school.

In my family, the hunters are men. They've been hunting since they were young, and it's a practice that's generations old. Much of it happens on seventy acres of wilderness surrounding the family farm, just over the border of Illinois and not far from where my mother and her seven siblings grew up. My mother was never a fan of hunting. A bleeding-heart liberal in a mostly conservative family, she called her brothers "Bambi killers." For a long time I echoed my mother's words, but when I was growing up, I secretly wanted to hunt. I loved to fish; we spent summers in the Northwoods, and I would go out in a fishing boat with my father and uncles every morning to catch blue gill and northern and perch. We gutted and ate what we caught, and even then, I got a thrill out of seeing something I'd snagged on my own line feed my family. Hunting felt like a bigger, more important version of fishing. But it was a part of our family history to which I never belonged.

I'm pretty sure if I had asked my uncles to take me hunting, they would have jumped at the chance. Neither of them had sons, and they might have loved to train me on a rifle or bow, to teach me how to skin a deer. They might have taken me to their tree stand and let me sip from a can of beer. (My uncle Lucky, after all, gave me my first swig of MGD when I was around seven.) But hunting was something I interpreted as being fundamentally male. It was something I didn't think I was allowed to have.

For people like my uncles, hunting is not just part of their lives but their very identity. It's as deeply rooted in the culture as farming, where to kill one's own food is tradition, a practice rooted in the necessity that bore it generations before. It's a place where hunting is considered not just a hobby or sport but an art, a ritual, one that some even consider holy: a way to participate in the cycle of life that God created, a way to stay connected to the earth and those who came before, to live in communion with the land.

It's also a place where you can buy a gun at Walmart with virtually no wait time. It's a place where gun shows and gun shops are as common as gas stations. It's a place where concealed carry is legal, where you can walk into a grocery store or a church or a bar with a semiautomatic handgun tucked inside the waistband of your jeans, where you can have a few beers while keeping a loaded weapon strapped to your body. It's a place where people say, *It's my God-given right* and *From my cold dead hands* and *How else are you going to protect yourself?*

If you had asked me a few years ago how I felt about guns, I would have said we should ban them all, confiscate those remaining, throw them in a massive fire, and watch them burn. And most of the time, I still feel this way. But in the past few years, something has shifted. It began after I moved to New York, and especially after the 2016 election, at which point people on the coasts began to talk about Midwesterners as if they were nothing more than uneducated, gun-toting rednecks. And I can't help but feel protective of my gun-toting midwestern family, and the scores of other Midwesterners I know who keep guns responsibly. As mass shootings in the United States become the cultural norm, as the NRA tightens its political stranglehold and gun worship is at its zenith, some people I know are getting rid of their guns. Others are holding on to them more tightly. But this question of guns is so often cast in black-and-white: You're either for guns or against them, and like so much of what divides this country, there's no room for the gray space. Some days—maybe most days—I still want to toss every gun into that fire. But other days, when I think of people close to me, that doesn't feel like the answer. It's a question, like so many, I'm still trying to figure out.

It's Mother's Day, and I'm home in Wisconsin. My family and I have driven out to the country to visit my grandparents' graves. We lay flowers there, and one of my aunts plants tulips. Afterward, we head to a roadside bar for lunch. It's in the middle of nowhere, the same place we went two years earlier when we buried my grandmother—a place with neon Miller and Leinenkugel's signs on the wall, that serves burgers and pitchers for cheap. My parents are here, along with three of my mother's five sisters and one of their two brothers, my uncle Lucky. I've always felt a kinship with Lucky. We were close when I was a kid, and though we live very different lives now, I still feel close to him. Lucky could be a poster child for the rural Wisconsinite: He hunts, drives a pickup truck, wears a baseball cap, drinks beer, chews tobacco, and carries a gun. He's handy, and for the past thirty years he has worked in maintenance for a nursing home in the small town where he lives. Like much of my family, he prefers the natural world to people.

At the bar, we order lunch—I get fried cheese curds, and Lucky gets a burger and gator balls (for the uninitiated, that's deep-fried alligator nuggets). We push a few sticky tables together, just a fraction of our big family gathered around red plastic baskets of bar food, Bloody Marys, and beer while my two young cousins, the sons of my mother's youngest sister, play darts and drop quarters in an ancient-looking gumball machine. Unlike my uncles, these boys are being raised in a suburb of Milwaukee, not far but somehow worlds away from the farmlands and small towns where my mother and her siblings grew up. Neither of them hunt or own guns. Lucky started hunting when he was twelve. He went with his older brother, Rick, and their father, Kenneth (for whom Lucky is named, though no one ever calls him that). My grandfather taught his boys how to hunt, and they learned first with a bow. Today, Lucky and Rick still hunt, and Lucky prefers his bow to a gun.

"And not a crossbow," he says. "A real bow and arrow."

Lucky has a quintessential Wisconsin accent—the "Sconnie," as we call it—with long, drawn-out vowel sounds, cutting off the *G* at the ends of most words. It's how most of my mom's family talks, and it's an accent I find myself slipping back into whenever I'm home.

Bow hunting is a practice that takes skill, patience, and thought. Lucky hunts with a rifle, too, but using a bow feels more natural to him, more like an art. On the walls at his house, he has a few mounted deer heads; Mary is his prize buck, a twelve-pointer named for his mother.

"It's exciting," Lucky says of hunting. He talks about "buck fever"— the thrill of being in range of a male deer. After a life of hunting, it's a feeling that hasn't gone away. "You're shaking, you're nervous, you're so excited," he says. "Once you start losing it, you might as well quit."

Lucky says it's probably easy to be antigun if you've never had this experience, that everyone should do it once.

"You've just gotta feel it," he says, and his giddiness is contagious. To Lucky, and many other hunters, the act of hunting is less about shooting an animal and more about being out in the wilderness. Lucky will sit in his tree stand for hours, setting up in the earliest hours of morning while it's still pitch black outside; he'll stay through sunrise, and sometimes all day. Sometimes he doesn't shoot anything at all. Sometimes it's too cold to even lift the bow or pull the trigger. The whole experience, for him, is about being alone in the silence of the woods.

"That's the best part about any of it," he says, chewing on a gator ball. "You know it's sunrise when the eagle lets loose, and all the baby coyotes start yipping."

Once, while turkey hunting—which, for the serious hunter like Lucky, often involves covering oneself in an elaborate disguise of leaves to blend in with the trees—two nuthatches landed on the bill of his camouflage hat. They stayed there, twittering to one another, while he sat stock-still, trying not to breathe.

"I'll share a granola bar with the squirrels and chipmunks," he says. "You sit there and you just take it all in."

Lucky believes in background checks. He thinks there should be a cool-down period to avoid so-called crimes of passion. He also places a good deal of onus on the medical industry when it comes to such crimes. He says more than once while we talk that there should be a way to know if a person has a history of mental illness before they're sold a gun, that perhaps medical records should be made available for gun sellers to review like a background check. I've heard this argument before, and it makes me uneasy; it's a way to say that guns aren't the problem, that mental illness is—and it feels like an easy way out, displacing blame and not confronting the fact that many people who commit violent crimes have no recorded history of mental illness.

When it comes to mass shootings, Lucky doesn't like to talk about it. But he believes that bump stocks and anything other than a ten-round clip should go.

"If I can't protect myself with five rounds," he says, "maybe I shouldn't be carrying."

Like many gun owners I've spoken to, Lucky is all for legislation—as long as it doesn't impinge upon his rights.

"If it doesn't affect me protecting myself, my family, putting food on the table, I'm happy," he says.

A few times during our conversation, my uncle emphasizes that to have a gun means being prepared to shoot one, and understanding the implications of that power—that you possess the capacity to end another human life. Unless he's hunting, he hopes to never have to use his gun. And a manual revolver is better than a semiautomatic, he says, because it's more deliberate.

"You have to think, 'Jesus, do I really want to do this?'"

Lucky doesn't know how much longer he'll be hunting—he's in his fifties now, and a lifelong lung disorder has been slowing him down. But he'll do it as long as he's able. As we finish our lunch, he mentions again the importance of respecting a weapon and understanding the harm it can cause. He carries this knowledge at all times, he says, when his revolver is strapped to his hip, when he walks into the woods with his rifle.

"I respect them," he says. "And if you don't, then maybe someone should think about taking the guns away."

My first time on the farm in Ohio, I find myself with a pistol in my hand. I don't particularly want to be here. I've always wanted to try new things, and for a long time I wanted to learn how to shoot a gun. The pistol in my hands is a .22 revolver—a small gun, an old gun, reminiscent of the kind in Spaghetti Westerns—and it feels surprisingly good in my hands. But it's just after the 2016 election, and I can't get my muscles to stop tensing.

John's father, Bob, is teaching me how to shoot. He tells me to breathe, and I do. He's calm, and breathes deeply and evenly, encouraging me to do the same. Even as I hold this deadly weapon, I trust him. I start to relax.

"For me, guns are a tool," he'll tell me later. This is something I hear from most gun owners I talk to. "Whether on the range in a rifle match or in the home for personal safety."

Bob is conservative. He grew up in a military family; his father was a master gunsmith for the army's Marksmanship Training Unit at Fort Benning, Georgia, where Bob grew up. As a kid, he would go with his dad to work on Saturdays and sweep up metal filings and brass. He started shooting in high school, when he joined the JROTC rifle team; and when he went to college at West Point, he kept it up. He was good too. A Georgia state champion and a New York state junior champion, he was also part of a team at West Point that won a national championship. During his second tour of duty in the army, Bob joined an international military rifle team and trained with top army shooters, including three Olympians. He spent as much time on the range as he did training other teams, including college, National Guard, and army reserve teams, and discovered he liked coaching at least as much as he did shooting. After the army he went on to coach a coed rifle team of middle and high school kids in Georgia.

He's a good coach. When he teaches me how to shoot, he makes me feel comfortable about something about which I'm inherently nervous. I tell him that in my family, girls didn't shoot guns, that this was something I'd internalized when I was young. As he coached both boys and girls, I ask him if he ever noticed differences in ability.

"You have to be cool," he says, and clarifies that cool for shooting isn't the same as for other sports. "Don't get your heart rate up, don't let your muscles tense, and don't get your adrenaline flowing. Testosterone is bad for this." Even though he says boys often have a physical advantage in terms of strength, girls tend to be more flexible and calmer with guns in their hands.

"Girls are cooler under pressure," he says. "All in all, girls have an edge."

Bob also competes in an annual shooting tournament, the Civilian Marksmanship Program (CMP) National Matches, held each year at Camp Perry, Ohio, on the banks of Lake Erie. The event, which draws thousands of people of all ages—many of them young people and former military veterans—includes a number of different competitions for both pistols and rifles. One event in which Bob participates specializes in the M1 Garand, a military rifle used in World War II. It's a large, heavy rifle made of metal and wood, antique looking among modern firearms, and shooting it requires strength, skill, focus, and an almost meditative state of mind.

"Shooting is more like chess than anything else," Bob says. "The ability to concentrate yet relax, to see each shot as a learning opportunity and to analyze, are key."

For the past several years, John has joined his father at the tournament, participating in the M1 match and a team competition nicknamed the "Rattle Battle," a prone rapid-fire match that, in 2018, featured the first all-girls junior team to participate—which beat a team of boys for the trophy. John, who like me lands pretty firmly in the antigun camp, had never shot competitively before deciding to join his father at the tournament. He saw it as a chance to spend time with his dad and to better understand his passion for shooting. Unlike the NRA, the CMP has no political affiliation; it doesn't lobby politicians and takes no funding from the government. It's a nonprofit organization whose mission is to train and educate people in responsible gun owner-ship and competitive shooting, offering safety classes, marksmanship training, and events around the country.

At the tournament, John wears a Pride flag and a Black Lives Matter pin on his hat. A few years ago, our friend Sean, a journalist from New York, joined John in Ohio for the tournament. Sean is black and an investigative reporter who writes about gun violence in the United States. He went to the tournament to write about it, which put some people on edge. Sean wasn't the only person of color at the event, but he was one of very few. For Sean, who's originally from Florida and lived in a fraternity house in college, being the only black man in the room wasn't anything new. Standing on a firing range in a sea of white conservative men with guns in their hands was perhaps a slightly newer experience.

"There was a tentativeness when people spoke with me," he says, "like it was their first time being around a person of color for an extended period, and they didn't want to say the wrong thing and offend me. But honestly, it's not that different from being around white liberals who try to show me how progressive they are. I was confident they'd warm up to me if I just gave them time."

They did, and Sean was soon palling around with Bob and his teammates, following them around and watching them shoot. At one point, the organization's general manager, who had admitted to being wary of talking to a liberal journalist writing about gun violence, told Sean that he wasn't what he had expected, and that Sean had changed his outlook on some things.

But Sean is also quick to note that despite how well he got along with everyone in Ohio, he was still aware of the possibility of violence—physical or otherwise, and directed toward him—that could exist in such a space. Like so many experiences as a black man subjected to stereotypes and the weight of others' baseless resentments or fears, he walked the grounds of Camp Perry and was never completely without worry.

In such situations, Sean says, "It's something that's always in the back of my mind."

When Bob was at West Point, he joined the NRA and was a member for ten years. He gave up his membership when he left the army, as he saw the organization as too political. But recently he rejoined.

"I now see their political work as necessary to protect my right to pursue my chosen sport," he says, "and to keep my ability to provide for my own home protection."

John and I are visiting his parents, who live just outside Dayton, where a shooting had just taken place days earlier. The president is in town, thanking responders, appeasing lobbyists, making no efforts to stop this from happening again. I'm angry and feel the tension lingering around us. I ask Bob what he thinks each time there's a mass shooting.

"I'm dismayed and saddened," he says, "but I see that as a problem with our culture and not with the prevalence of guns."

Bob believes in restrictions on gun ownership, but he says current legislation targets "honest and safe" gun owners like him and "not the criminals and mentally unstable people that make the headlines."

"Show me legislation that addresses the latter while protecting the former," he says, "and I'll support it."

On the Christmas tree farm, Bob tells me to loosen my grip and breathe, and I do. And in the moment after I fire, when I've hit the target and a slow snake of smoke rises up from the barrel into the cold air, my body is abuzz with adrenaline. It fills up my chest and makes a rush down my spine. I feel the anger and tension rush out of me with it, a bullet from the chamber.

Lately I've been thinking about rage. I've been thinking about the ways in which anger and rage intersect with gender and violence, and how the perpetrators of mass shootings in the United States are almost always white men. When I read stories about these men, they all seem to share one other thing in common: anger. Aimed at immigrants, at a religion or race, at queer people, at women—at a coworker or boss, an unrequited love interest. In one Wisconsin case, a young man rejected by his coworker at a grocery store buys a gun within an hour of being turned down, returns to work, and murders the woman in the parking lot. In Isla Vista, California, a young man declares war on the entire female population, who he believes has denied him his right to their bodies—he kills six people and injures fourteen others, and helps popularize the term *incel*. In their mug shots, you can see the anger in the eyes of these men: in their skin, mottled and ruddy in black and white. You can see their rage, just below the surface. Always cocked and ready, a finger on the trigger.

Lately I've been thinking about how rage is not just expected of men but excused in them. In women, it's surprising and alarming. Rage—like its counterpart, violence—is accepted as a part of our cultural definition of masculinity. Men are taught to fight, to kill, to defend, to protect: their family, their country, their honor, their ego. When women exhibit violence of any kind, it's shocking, unnatural, unearthly. A woman enraged is called crazy, hysterical, insane. She's told to calm down, that she needs help. She's gaslighted, made to feel like a freak, like she's out of control, like something is terribly wrong with her. And so she does her best to fight the anger that lives inside her. The anger that exists, perhaps, in every woman—because of fear, because of powerlessness, because of the sheer fact of being a woman. She presses it down in her guts and does her best to keep it there. But like most suppressed things, it will eventually find its way out.

I never wanted to own a gun. Bob has a .38 pistol that John would like some day, and he also gifted his son an M1 Garand rifle to use in the annual tournament. But neither of those guns is kept in our apartment, because neither of us wants a gun there. I'm not sure if I would ever want a gun in my home. Not just because I know what the statistics say—that a household is less safe with one inside it—or because I have no desire to contribute to America's obsession with them. But because I'm afraid that someday I'll use it.

My uncle Lucky owns three guns. Bob has six. On the farm in Ohio, John's uncle has more than fifty—many of which he built himself, others he's collected. I'm not afraid of any of these men. What I mean is I trust them and love them, and I know that they love me. I don't think they'd ever hurt anyone. But even so, there's a larger fear, a cultural one, and an ever-present one: Whether it's one gun or three or fifty, the bottom line is it's still a man with a gun. And *this* is what scares me.

I liked shooting. I was also afraid of it. On my first time out, I closed my eyes and leaned so far back, trying to create more distance between my body and the pistol than physically possible, that the tiny .22 was pointed toward the sky. Bob placed his hands over mine and moved them back down so the gun was aimed at the target. But when I took my first shot, it felt good. I took more shots, and those felt pretty good too. With each *ting!* of the bullet on the metal target, I felt the energy of it vibrate through my body. On my second time out, a year later, I tried my hand at a few more pistols: a .38 Special revolver, whose recoil I felt in my wrists; a .357 Magnum, a large, long-barreled pistol whose kick I felt more in my arms; and a semiautomatic .45. This one had no kick at all, and it frightened me the most. Simply knowing I was holding a semiautomatic weapon—a gun with an eight-round clip, that I didn't have to cock before each shot, with very little work separating me from eight bullets in my target—made me uneasy. I shot it once, and that was enough. The .22, I decided, was just right.

It took me a while to admit I liked shooting. But it also makes a certain amount of sense. When I'm out in the midwestern cold firing a gun, I feel connected to my family in a way I never did growing up. I've also historically taken great pleasure in sports and in learning new skills, and shooting felt like both. It brought out my competitive streak, which has always been mighty, and it made me feel strong. It also made me feel like I was channeling something I've been trying my entire life to channel.

My friend Nik was born in Brooklyn, a Jewish Italian daughter in a family of teachers. She's five two with short hair and a skin fade; she's a little androgynous like me, wears flannel and hiking shoes and glasses. Despite not being from the Midwest originally, she's lived in Wisconsin for most of her life, and she seems to fit in. This includes owning a couple of guns.

Nik has a husband and two daughters. We met in roller derby, more than a decade ago now and before she had kids. She's a rare kind of friend, and the kind you want to keep around you forever: fiercely loyal, supportive, generous, and takes no shit—qualities that extend to everyone she loves. And when she loves someone, she gives them everything she has.

I go to her house on a Tuesday night in May. It's unseasonably warm in Wisconsin, and the windows are open. Her two daughters are already in bed, and she asks if I mind if she works on a project while we talk. We walk down to her basement, through a perfectly appointed Sconnie barroom—complete with Badgers and Packers memorabilia, a neon beer sign, and a hand-lacquered bar top with concert and football ticket stubs mounted beneath it—and into an unfinished room she's turned into her workshop. Nik has a kinetic kind of energy. She loves projects and feels most comfortable when she's doing something. She works in IT at the University of Wisconsin; she's smart, capable, and the longtime breadwinner in her family. She's also an artist, a talented illustrator who loves taking on new forms. Her newest is stained glass, and tonight she's working on one of her first pieces, a geometrical pattern made of white and blue glass. We sit on metal stools in her workshop and she solders two pieces of glass together.

Having been raised for a good part of her childhood in Brooklyn, Nik didn't grow up around guns.

"Jewish city people do not hunt," she says. "They don't own firearms or seek out experiences which include those activities."

Nik is funny and makes regular reference to her Jewishness in a place where it's scarce. Like me, Nik sees herself as both an outsider in the Midwest and as midwestern as it gets. For her, getting into guns was about learning something new and embracing a culture in which she found herself entrenched.

"I like to take on a process I've never been exposed to before," she says. "Case in point," she adds, gesturing to the stained glass. "I like to know how to do things."

When she moved to Wisconsin as a teenager, Nik was amazed by the ubiquity of guns. "They were everywhere. Everybody had guns. Fourteen-year-old boys owned their own shotguns and rifles. It was so alien to me, but I was really curious about it."

Nik's husband was born and raised in Wisconsin. He grew up in a hunting family, and several of his guns were passed down to him. The first time Nik fired a gun was with him, and the first gun she owned—a small snub-nosed .38 revolver—was a gift from him.

"For me, a gun is a tool," she says, carefully tracing the tip of the soldering gun back and forth along the edge where the two pieces of glass meet.

I ask her about fear and about the concept of keeping guns for protection.

"I'm a tiny girl," she says. "I don't ever feel completely safe. But I also don't have any illusions about a gun making me safer. My logical brain comprehends the statistics related to safety and gun ownership, but my emotional brain knows that as a last line of defense, I have a tool, and I know how to use it."

I tell her that, when it comes to fear, a lot of gun owners I know—most of whom are men—seem to be most afraid of the government coming after their guns.

"I'm not afraid of the government," she says. "But there are people out there who will hurt you."

I ask her who she's afraid of.

"People who want something you have," she says. She stops soldering and looks at me when she says it, and I know immediately what she's talking about. When Nik was three years old, her mother was murdered. The crime was committed at home, in their Brooklyn apartment, at the hands of the man her mother was seeing. It happened while Nik and her brother were asleep in the next room.

"I have this really fierce protective instinct for my kids, for me, for our family," she says, "and I think it has a lot to do with the fact that my mother wasn't able to protect herself or her family."

Nik is tough. I've seen her cry only a handful of times in our many years of friendship, but she does when she says this. She sets her soldering gun down and wipes the tears from her face.

"I'm not saying if she had a gun on her that she could have saved herself," she says, "but the fact that she wasn't capable of protecting herself or her children—when she was that vulnerable, and when her kids were that vulnerable—that really has shaped my defense mechanisms."

She takes a breath. "I don't talk about it a whole lot," she says, picking up the soldering gun again. "I think, especially now that I have little girls, I don't want them ever to feel as unprotected as I felt growing up. Not that their knowing that I have a gun is going to make them feel protected, but I want to know that I did every fucking thing I could. That I took every step I could to make sure that they don't end up like I did. Part of that is not relying on someone else to take care of you or save you or rescue you."

She stresses again the warring parts of her brain: the logical and the lizard.

"The emotional brain needs what it needs," she says, and she shrugs when she says it, an acknowledgment of the fault in this thinking. "Being proficient with firearms and owning them as a tool for defending what I hold dear is not something I can logic my way out of."

Recently, Nik started hunting. Growing up, Nik spent her summers with her grandmother in the Adirondacks, camping and canoeing and fishing. She's always loved the wilderness. But hunting, she says, is a whole new way of being in the woods.

"The hairs on the back of your neck are standing up, and everything is heightened," she says. "You start to connect with all the things around you in a much more sensual way. It's like getting in touch with something more primal within yourself."

Her love of hunting is also connected to her desire for self-reliance.

"I get an immense amount of satisfaction from being able to catch a fish, clean it, cook it, eat it. Forage in the woods, bring home morels and ramps, find food not at a grocery store or a restaurant. Growing up in the city, nobody was connected to anything they were consuming." Hunting allows Nik to feel both connected to the land and capable of providing for her family should she ever need to.

"I'm not a doomsday prepper," she says, drawing the soldering gun over the same spot a few more times, leaving a fine silver line. "But there are certain life skills we don't learn anymore as modern humans. Civilization is fragile. And when shit falls apart, I want to protect my family."

As the climate crisis reaches new irrevocable heights and politics in the United States become increasingly polarized, this sense of impending doom seems to be more common. Behind us in the workshop, there's a box with targets in it: an empty can of beer and various hanging metal spoons. This is where Nik shoots target practice with a BB gun, and I tell her I've never shot a rifle before.

"You wanna learn?" she asks, and I do. She loads it, lines up a shot herself, then takes a quick shot to the target. Then she hands me the gun, and shows me how to hold it—butt to cheek, elbow tucked to my side, line up the target between the sights. She tells me to breathe in and out, and then again.

I'm still nervous, even though it's only a BB gun. But I like the feeling of metal against my cheek. I breathe. I pull the trigger. I hit the target.

"It feels good to be good at this," I say.

"Right?" she says.

Nik has been teaching her oldest daughter to shoot, and soon she'll teach her younger daughter.

"I want them to know how they work, how to use them, and how to be safe around them," Nik says. Ultimately, she wants them to be able to protect themselves. She takes me to a locker where she and her husband keep their guns. They also have a strongbox in their bedroom where they keep her .38 and ammunition. We close up the workshop and head upstairs, then step out onto her back porch. The night is cool but not cold; the stars are out and the crickets are chirping . We sit in camp chairs and look up at the sky, listen to the wind in the trees that surround her house. Nik lights a cigarette and smokes; I take a few drags like I usually do. We talk, keeping our voices low so as not to wake her family. She tells me that when she started hunting, she felt like she was being let into a secret world of men.

"It felt like being let into masculine culture," she says, noting that when she was growing up, she always hung out with boys and was never into feminine things. She always wanted to be let in, she says, and I tell her I was the same way—that I felt left out and angry that I couldn't be part of it. But we also discuss the dangers of that masculine culture, that men seem to be at the root of the gun problem in the United States. We talk about the practice of collecting guns—and in particular semiautomatic weapons—that has become such a fetish among so many men.

"It's an insecurity thing," Nik says. "It's a dick-measuring thing."

I agree with this, and we laugh.

"It's all about the dick," she adds, and we laugh some more. Sometimes it's easier to laugh about the things that frighten us most.

Nik describes her politics as "left of Mao," and I say I don't know many liberal women who own guns.

"I'm not a Second Amendment cultist," Nik says, "because at this point, it's a fucking cult. I don't have any insecure need to hold on to guns for some bullshit principle that was written by white slave owners two hundred–odd years ago. I think the NRA is evil and should not exist."

She says she gets shit sometimes from friends and family, particularly those in New York, who are shocked and sometimes horrified to learn she has guns.

"Everywhere outside your bubble people have guns," she tells them.

Nik believes in strict legislation and universal background checks, that no one with a history of violence should be able to own a firearm, and that no one outside the military should have an assault rifle. "Not even law enforcement," she adds. "They're killing machines. That is what they're made for, destroying human life. They're weapons of war."

She says something that my uncle Lucky said too: "If you need more than five shots, you shouldn't be shooting a gun."

And then she says something I've never heard a gun owner say: "I would give up every one of our guns if the mass shootings would stop. I would never touch another gun again if it meant that that would end."

"Really?" I ask.

"Fuck yeah," she says. "In a heartbeat. I don't have to have these. Just because it's my right doesn't mean it is right."

I have a history of violence. I've kicked holes in the wall, thrown and punched inanimate objects, and once, during college, after an argument with a roommate, dragged a large wicker chair off our porch into the middle of the street at night and thrashed it to death, much to the horror of my mild-mannered Madison neighbors. I've gotten into physical fights with some of the men I've dated. In most cases, I was the one who struck first: a shove, a slap, a palm to the face. More than once, the men struck back.

For a long time, I saw myself as the perpetrator. I felt a deep shame about my behavior, and I still do. None of these situations were rational; all of them involved heavy drinking, something ubiquitous in Wisconsin and something I know now can trigger rage in me. But it's no excuse: I got violent, and I'm ashamed of it. What took me a long time to recognize, however, is this: Those men were never afraid of me. They were never afraid I would seriously hurt them or worse. I was always afraid of them, though, which I think is part of what initiated my rage in the first place—the understanding that I was weaker, more vulnerable, more at risk than they would ever be.

In the physics of gunfire, dynamics—the study of forces and their effects on motion—is at work. Newton's third and most famous law of motion—for every action, there is an equal and opposite reaction—is key: the force on the bullet is equal to the force on the shooter. When a gun fires, there's a recoil, or "kick," which is the force pushing backward against the hand that restrains the gun as the bullet, or projectile, is fired. In terms of thermodynamics, a gun essentially operates as a piston engine in which the bullet functions as the piston. The bullet exists in a casing filled with gunpowder; when the trigger is pulled, the hammer presses against the casing and causes the powder to burn, filling the chamber with gas and propelling the bullet forward. There's a common misconception that what happens here is an explosion, and while it's true that the black powder used in the nineteenth century was a true explosive, what happens with modern gunpowder is, instead, a very rapid burn.

Ballistics is the field of mechanics that deals with the launching, flight, behavior, and effects of projectiles, in particular bombs, rockets, and bullets. In some circles, it's called a science, in others it's called an art: that of designing and accelerating projectiles so as to achieve a desired performance. A *ballistic body* is a body with momentum that is free to move, subject to forces, such as the pressure of gases in a firearm.

When I was a kid, whenever I threw a tantrum or flew into a rage, my mother would always say, "She went ballistic."

Growing up, I had a temper. This was what my parents, my teachers, my babysitters, my neighbors, my aunts and uncles called it. A better way to say it might be that I was a tiny ball of rage. I screamed, I fought, I pulled hair. I spat and kicked and clawed. I got pulled kicking and screaming from sandboxes and put in timeouts in Montessori school. And if you know anything about Montessori school, you'll know this is something of an accomplishment.

It was shocking, I'm sure, to encounter such aggression in a girl. Fighting, like all aggressive behavior and physical expressions of anger, was far more tolerated among boys. I got told to stop acting like a boy. Eventually I found outlets in sports—some of which, like roller derby, actively encouraged me to hit people, which was sublime. Today, when I start to feel tension coil up inside me, I do push-ups. I go for a run. I go to the gym and lift weights. Lately I've been thinking about taking up boxing. I don't know where my anger came from; all I know is that when I don't have an outlet, it can become dangerous.

The .22 is pretty. The handle is made of mother-of-pearl, the barrel a cold blue steel. Built by John's uncle, the gun is pleasing to hold. I feel its weight on my palm, wrap my fingers around the metal. The smoothness and sharpness of its lines, the scallops of the cylinder, the tautness of the action, its contours like a body. I can understand, holding this thing, how one might come to admire such an object, such a pretty and efficient piece of machinery: well designed, beautiful, powerful. How one might start to worship it. How one might start to collect others like it, as they might any object—like I do books, like some do pieces of art. I could imagine, in a different life maybe, carrying a gun like this one on my hip. I could imagine learning to take comfort in its weight against my body, feeling safer with it there. I could imagine starting to need it.

Very few women on my mother's side of the family own guns. My grandmother apparently had a pistol, though I never saw it; I'm told she kept it hidden—maybe in a purse at the bottom of her closet, along with a secret stash of stubbed-out cigarettes and ash. Within the past few years, two of my aunts have gotten handguns; in both cases, their husbands gifted them these weapons for protection. The rest of the women in my family don't own guns, and some have never shot them.

This is not to say that women in Wisconsin don't carry guns or hunt. Hunting and gun ownership in the state are, in fact, hugely popular among girls and women. Many girls grow up hunting like my uncles did and continue to hunt well into adulthood. Perhaps unsurprisingly, there's also an entire industry dedicated to feminizing hunting: pink rifles and pink camouflage, formfitting field jackets and pants. It's absurd, of course, to imagine girls traipsing around the woods in pink camo, their hair and makeup done up, before shooting and gutting a deer. But in a place like the rural Midwest, where traditional gender norms are still so often practiced, girls and women are taught to project their femininity at all times, even when doing the dirtiest kind of work. As if to say they are still girls under all that camo, all woman as they drag a bloody buck carcass back to the truck, rifle strapped to their back. A gun, after all, is historically a symbol of masculinity. Guns are inherently aggressive, violent, dangerous, and capable of damage—things women aren't supposed to be. They're instruments of power, weapons of rage—things women aren't supposed to have.

Lately I've been struggling to reconcile the way girls are taught to fear boys and women are taught to fear men, and yet so often we aren't believed when we speak of the violence that occurs at their hands. I've been struggling to reconcile the intersections between gender and rage: that so often rage is expressed externally by men through violence—physical, verbal, or otherwise—while among women it's so often self-directed.

I've been struggling to reconcile a problem in me: the fact that for so long I wanted to possess a specific kind of power, a masculine power, that was never fully available to me and has certainly never been accepted in me—and the increasing desire to separate myself from it. There are days when the more masculine parts of me—the way I walk sometimes, for instance, shoulders forward and swaggering, a walk that's been called *brolike*—make me feel stronger, more confident as I move through the world. Like so many people, I wear my masculinity like armor. But there are other days when these very qualities make me feel self-conscious. When I feel ashamed of that swagger. On those days I want to extract my masculinity from myself entirely, like separating the white from the yolk. Lately I've been wondering if there's a good kind of masculinity, a kind apart from that which struts around the gym like it's ready for a fight or carries a gun like it's ready to use it. Or if, instead, masculinity, at least as we know it, inherently carries with it a violence. And if I was born with this masculinity, what does that mean about me?

This is what it looks like: A darkening of the vision, a black curtain closing in on all sides. A dissociation, a body pulling apart from itself. A chemical reaction or physical force; for every action, an equal and opposite; bursts of movement, a blur. And then nothing but a ringing in the ears, the beat of blood behind the eyes.

They say "blind rage" and it's true: In moments of rage, I see nothing. And later, I remember very little, only scraps of memory like the remnants of a dream on waking—one you can feel, almost as if you could take hold of it, but as soon as you get a grip on an image it dissolves again, fading away into the darkness. There's a flash of an image: the heel of a boot smashing plaster, a palm connecting with a jaw. Fingernails sinking into the soft flesh of a neck. Surreal, disconnected, like watching a movie.

That's not me, the consciousness thinks. That's anyone but me.

Many years of therapy have helped me work through this rage, to recognize the patterns and behaviors that enable it, to channel it through productive things like physical work and exercise. I'm still not sure whether it was inherited or learned. Maybe I was born with it, maybe it's in my blood, the unlucky combination of Italian and Irish temperaments, like my parents always joked. Maybe it's the product of some event or situation, familial or cultural or socioeconomic, that I don't remember. Maybe it's hormonal, and I have more androgen than most girls, my boyishness rooted in my DNA. Or maybe I just learned it by observing the world around me—a world that, if you're looking closely enough, you begin to understand is built on violence.

One thing I know is my own rage—like most rage, maybe—is born, at least in part, of fear. I know my rage has something—maybe everything—to do with the fact that I was born a girl who was angry she was not a boy, who understood very early that being a girl meant having less power. Maybe I've always been angry at boys, and at men, for their power over me, for their ability to hurt me. Maybe I'm angry that several of them have.

The part of me that would like to see guns abolished is motivated by the hope of a future in which mass murders are no longer a part of the American identity. So that we can all feel less afraid in the streets, in our churches and offices and schools. So that fewer people die. But there's something else at work too. As a woman, I've spent most of my life learning that what strength or security I do have can be taken away at any second by a man. I think, on some level, I want to give this feeling to men. I want to take away what makes them feel powerful. I want to strip them of their security like they, for so long, have stripped women of ours. I want them to understand what it feels like to be vulnerable, to be powerless, to be afraid—to be left alone on this earth without armor.

I can't imagine what might have happened during the fights I've had if there had been a gun in the house. If there had been a pistol tucked beneath a pillow, kept in a nightstand or closet to protect us from intruders, to keep us safe. I'm terrified to think of it. In the rational light of day, I can tell you pretty confidently I could never shoot a human being. But rage does not exist in the light of day. It lives in darkness, in a split-second decision, in an impulse. Rage, in the end, is not rational.

Sometimes I think of it as a living thing, a monster trapped inside us all, just waiting to get out.

I t's not rage," my friend Jude says. We're talking about guns, white men, and mass shootings. "It's fear and anger. You don't go to a church and methodically execute the people who welcomed you in because of rage. Rage is much more immediate. You don't plan rage."

We're sitting outside at Mickey's Tavern, my favorite bar in my old neighborhood in Madison. It's happy hour on a Wednesday, the sun is out, and the patio is packed. Around us, Madisonians drink like Madisonians do, but I sip my beer slowly. I couldn't drink like I used to even if I wanted to. Sometimes I forget what the drinking culture was like here—where, during the eight years I lived in Madison, "going out to the bars" meant a dozen drinks or more; where "college night" meant tap pours for a nickel; where wastedness was worn like a badge and so often became a fight. And this was before concealed carry was legal, before people came out to the bars with handguns secretly holstered to their hips, tucked out of sight beneath their belts. Sometimes it seems like a miracle I survived that time of my life, and I can't imagine living that way now, knowing that any drunk guy bellied up to the bar and belligerent could be armed.

Jude and I have been friends for more than a decade. We met in this city, to which he was a transplant. Originally from Mississippi, Jude was in the navy and spent a good part of his life in a submarine. He's lived all over the country, including New York, and eventually settled in Madison. Now he works for the state, doesn't own a car, and finds himself at home with the crunchie liberal denizens of Madison's near-east side. For a long time, Jude owned a handgun.

During a training command stint in North Charleston, South Carolina, he lived in a neighborhood with a lot of drugs, a lot of robberies, and a lot of shootings.

"So I bought a pistol to keep by my bed while I slept," he says. "And I knew what I was getting—a tool that I would explicitly use to murder another human if my person were threatened."

He pauses while the waitress runs by, carrying a tray of pints filled to the rim with golden ale, sloshing over and glowing in the sun.

"But here's the thing," he says, taking a sip of his own beer. "I held on to that fucker long after I moved out of that neighborhood, long after I left the military, and through at least eight moves." He still went target shooting sometimes, and then he just took the gun out of its case once a month, cleaned and oiled it, changed the magazines, and put it away.

"And then that maniac went and wasted two dozen six-year-olds."

After the shooting in Newtown, Connecticut, in 2012, something changed in Jude. Even so, he didn't get rid of his gun immediately. But then he read an article in the *New York Review of Books* about the United States' collective fetishization of firearms. The piece was titled "Our Moloch"—a reference to the Canaanite god associated with child sacrifice.

"And I wept for shame," Jude says. Then he destroyed his gun.

He wrote about it himself too. In his essay titled "Making America Safer," Jude writes of holding on to his gun: "The data says: get rid of it," he writes. "And I didn't. I held on to it because we're trained to have an irrational adoration of firearms; in a way, we're told it's our duty to own them." He continues:

> I have come to realize that there are no "bad guys" who exist outside of us. The people who use firearms to harm other people aren't monsters from another dimension. They are us. We are all good and bad, and some of us just have bad days—maybe you're at the end of your rope financially, or maybe you're inconsolably heartbroken, or maybe you're dealing with an improperly treated mental

illness, or maybe you're dealing with any one of the other thousand ways the world can collapse on you. When this happens, some of us might see reckless use of a firearm as an answer to what's bothering us. That means that, if you have access to a firearm, your very bad day may give other people unimaginably bad days. That's never an answer, and I'm removing that possibility from my life and the lives of people who enter my house.

At Mickey's, we order another round and close the tab. Growing up in the southeastern United States, Jude says he wasn't exposed to guns for most of his youth.

"But for three years I lived out in the sticks and *fuck* those people love their guns," he says. His father bought a .22 rifle, and Jude would take it out with him on walks in the woods, mostly to fend off snakes.

"Wildlife in the southeastern U.S. will fuckin' kill you," he says, laughing.

Despite his military background Jude is not what you would call a joiner, and he didn't come from a family of hunters. I ask if he ever felt like he was part of a gun culture, either during those days in the snake-swarmed South or later when he was in the navy.

"I never really felt like part of a gun culture anywhere," he says. "I never connected with anyone over them. I don't have a familial connection to them, either."

He pauses, takes a pull from his new pint. "They're tools to me," he says.

"They're also kind of fun," I say.

"Shooting firearms can be wicked fun," he says. "I mean, they're serious weapons that are meant solely to maim and kill living things, but goddamn if going to the range isn't a blast."

Jude hates the phrase "accidental shooting" and says there are no accidents when it comes to firearms; there is only negligence.

"That's the training I got from my pop and from Uncle Sam," he says. "Unless a weapon is disassembled in pieces in front of you, it's loaded."

He says he won't touch a gun if he's had even the slightest bit of alcohol or any intoxicant.

"And you never, ever point one at a person or thing unless you are 100 percent prepared to kill that person or thing. This includes yourself."

We talk about the correlation between gender and violent crime, and in particular, mass shootings. Jude is funny, and something of a cynic—while we talk, he repeatedly refers to people who fetishize firearms as "gun humpers" and wagers that the majority of such people are men.

"Further, white men," he says. "Even further, cisgendered straight white men."

Jude is a pretty rare kind of man. He's the first to call out other men, toxic masculinity, and their intersections with gun violence. And he does it loudly. So often it feels like the ones speaking the loudest about such things are the marginalized, those who are more often the victims of it. Jude identifies as bisexual, but it's refreshing to hear a cisgendered white man—and in particular a military veteran who used to own a gun—say these things aloud. To acknowledge that women's fears are not crazy, that men are committing the worst crimes in America, and are most concerned about their historical possession of power—and that someone might try to take it away. It always comes back, he says, to fear and anger.

"Fear that more rights for others mean fewer for them," Jude says, "and anger that they have to learn something new or share their perquisites with those people."

All the midwestern gun owners I talked to are white. Everyone I know who owns guns, including one woman I know in New York, is white. This isn't much of a surprise.

Recently, I was talking to a friend in Brooklyn, a black woman originally from the South named Amina. She told me that her dad, who lives in the South, has recently been thinking about buying a gun.

"I had to call him and be like, 'Dad, are you crazy? Please don't do that,'" she said.

She'll never own a gun, she told me, and hopes her father never will either. Because the truth is that people of color who own firearms are far less safe than those who don't. When it comes to the rhetoric of guns, my friend said, a lot of people talk about freedom.

"But when they talk about freedom," she said, "whose freedom are they talking about?"

I try to keep this question in mind. As I write this, I'm alone in the remote woods of northern Wisconsin. I'm here for five weeks, on my own. And though I've never wanted to own a gun, as I prepared for this trip I thought about bringing one with me. "What if a bear tears through the screen door?" I found myself thinking. And while such an encounter is not uncommon here, it's not really what I'm afraid of.

What I'm afraid of is a man. He looks like all the men up here, and like most of my Wisconsin family: He's white, maybe bearded, wears a baseball cap and jeans. He probably drives a pickup truck, because all men drive pickup trucks here. He probably carries a rifle or a handgun or both, because most men up here hunt and keep pistols in their belts or glove compartments. He's not afraid of a cop pulling him over and shooting him when he reaches for his wallet or when he says he has a concealed carry license. He's not afraid at all.

And he could be anyone.

It's true that I've seen way too many horror movies. In my first few days here, I played out dozens of scenarios leading to my grizzly death—each of which, I realized, was the plot to some slasher film I've seen. But it's also true that men harm women. And up here, in the remote Wisconsin woods, men have stalked, kidnapped, raped, and killed women, even recently. It happens, and for the first week I was here, I was afraid it would happen to me. It's a similar fear to the one I feel walking down a dark street in Brooklyn at night. The difference is that here, no one would hear me scream.

I thought it might be a good idea to bring a pistol or a rifle with me, to keep it next to my bed at night. Lucky or Nik might have lent me one of theirs, and I almost asked.

But I didn't. And the truth is, at night, I do get scared. But I also know having a gun here wouldn't make me, or anyone else, any safer. So I'm living in the woods like I live in New York, like I lived in Wisconsin: unarmed and sometimes afraid. When I do get scared, when I hear a twig snap outside my window or a rustle in the leaves, I take a deep breath. I listen to the wind. I listen to the crickets and the peepers and the loons and the owls singing their night songs in the trees all around me, and eventually the fear subsides.

There's a version of me, the midwestern me, who might someday like to live in the woods like this for good. She would be self-sufficient and independent and consume nothing more than what she can fish or forage or grow. She might learn to hunt, and she might have a gun. She might even learn to love that gun. But the other version of me—this me—sees a country collectively obsessed with weapons made to kill people. She sees a country that places the individual right to own those weapons above the lives of others, the safety of themselves and their own over the safety of a nation. She sees headlines about people being killed every day. She's sees a culture that's toxic, that's broken, and that's fueled, in the end, by fear. And she has no desire to be part of it.

It's complicated for me to love people who love guns. I think about the fact that the majority of gun owners I know and love are straight white men. I think about what a privilege it is to own those guns without being hassled, without being assaulted, without being shot and killed simply for possessing them. I think about how those men don't mention this privilege when they talk about their right to bear arms. I think about the things they don't mention—race, mass shootings, children and black men dead at the hands of cops. I think about how they focus on other things, like mental health, in an attempt to displace blame. I think about how the problem of mass shootings in America has pretty much everything to do with white men with guns. But I also think about the way so many people on the left—including many other people I love—talk about this problem: that guns are bad and the people who own them are bad too. It would be easier to think about it this way, but I can't—even if I've tried to. Because, like Jude says, there are no good guys or bad guys. There is only us.

It's Thanksgiving again, and we're back on the farm in Ohio. I don't shoot a gun this year. It's opening weekend for Christmas trees, and there's too much work to do. I don't use the maul this time, either, but I do learn how to use a hydraulic log splitter, a much more efficient tool for cutting firewood. All afternoon I haul logs from an eight-foot pile and place them on the splitter. With the engine chugging, I throw the crank and a mechanized steel press pushes the log forward onto a steel wedge. A sharp crack echoes over the sound of the engine, and then, with one fast fissure, the log splits in two. Each half falls to the ground. I pick them up one at a time and do it again, then throw each quartered piece onto a pile. Lift, pull, press, split, toss. It's a slow, methodical process. I get into a groove. There's something meditative in the rhythm of it.

John's aunt walks over to the woodpile. She reminds me not to put my hand on the log, not to snatch it away from the line before it's fallen.

"That's how hands get crushed," she says as she walks away. She wants me to stop, I know. She's afraid I'll get hurt. But I revel in the physicality of this work, in the danger of it, and not least in the brutality of it.

I take a breath, fill my lungs with clean, cold air. I stretch my arms and back and keep at it. By dusk, I'll have split most of the pile, and along with two high school boys we'll have stacked a cord of wood, which will help fuel the family's fire through winter.

It feels good, this work. It's satisfying to learn a new skill, to understand the mechanics of this tool, to use my body to make something useful. It's something I used to feel in Wisconsin, shoveling snow or raking a yard, working in a garden or building a fire, and it's something I rarely feel in New York. The work is hard and it hurts, and a week later the muscles in my back and arms and shoulders will still be sore. But as I stand outside in this cold midwestern November, the sun low in the afternoon sky, I feel good. As I lift each log, throw the press, and watch the wood split in half, I am calm. I am strong. I am unafraid.

MOTHERLAND

What if, instead of carrying / a child, I am supposed to carry grief?

—Ada Limón, *The Carrying*

*O*nce, there was a vegetable garden. I helped my mother till and mulch and plant and harvest. We grew tomatoes and carrots and cucumbers, green beans and radishes and bell peppers. It was a small plot, our little garden, up the hill from our house and past a rusted-out swing set, lined with chicken wire to keep the rabbits out. We weeded and raked the earth, dug holes in the dirt, and laid in seeds and bulbs. We worked with spades, filling the holes with soil and patting it down with our hands. We watered with a hose snaked up the grass from the garage, showering the seeds like rain. I loved the smell of wet soil, the dirt that got stuck under my nails, that pressed into the fibers of my jeans and stained my knees. Little mementos I carried with me, reminders of the things we had grown.

At harvesttime, we plucked the vegetables from their vines, pulled them up from the earth. I learned the singular smell of a ripe tomato, the grit of its skin and the red of its flesh. We cut them into thick slices and salted them, then ate them just like that, standing at the kitchen counter. We ate the green beans right in the garden, snapping into their skin with our teeth and sweating in the sun.

My friends are having kids. This is nothing new. I'm thirty-six, and where I come from people start having kids in their early twenties. But lately, each time another friend decides to have kids—especially if that friend is among my closest community—I feel a wave of grief pitch up inside me. It's sudden and squall-like and rocks through me like a storm.

It isn't necessarily about my friends' decision to have children, this grief. If anything, I'm excited about the humans these people I love will bring into the world, to see who they will become. And it isn't necessarily about my own decision not to have children. It's the feeling, instead, that I've lost something. Sometimes it's more tangible, as those friends move away to start new families. But the loss is more nebulous, too, a distance that can't be measured in miles. As more of my friends become parents, like the majority of the people in my life eventually will, I'm reminded that it's an experience I'll likely never share. And when it's someone with whom I've always felt a deep kinship—a fellow writer or musician; a person dedicated to their career; a queer person who once said they'd never have kids and who I felt, in this way, would forever be part of my childless tribe—there's a feeling that I've lost someone like me. And in this country and on this planet, where girls and women are expected to become mothers and most of them do, I'm already among the minority. Each time another friend has children, I feel a little more alone.

My mother taught me how to make things grow. When I was six or seven, we planted maple trees in our yard. They were saplings then, only a few feet tall.

"This one's for you," she said of the Japanese red.

"This one's for your dad," she said of the silver.

We planted several trees over the years, and I don't recall if she ever named one for herself.

Today, the maples are massive, the silver especially: fifty feet high, casting a wide canopy of shade over the lawn. Every time I go home, I'm shocked by the size of these trees. I can't believe how much they've grown. I suppose part of that shock has something to do with the passage of time made so tangible: I can see the thirty years that have passed since we planted them, the small saplings we put into the earth ourselves having become great living things that have thrived on their own, that have histories and lives of their own.

~

I've lived in New York for more than a decade, but I still call Wisconsin home. Things have changed since I left. The stretch of space between my hometown and the city of Madison—both places I think of as home—was once only farmland. There were red barns, silver silos, and faded white farmhouses, hills and prairies and crops and trees for miles. Now, much of it has been bought and developed—farmers forced into early retirement, their land razed and turned into condos, prefab siding painted the same three shades of beige. On a recent trip, as I drove the back roads between my two hometowns—a route I know by heart—I was struck by how much had changed. The trees were gone. The cornfields were gone. The houses and silos and barns were gone. For Sale signs dotted the roadside, too, the few remaining farms along that stretch of road having held on as long as they could.

Once or twice a year, I go back to Wisconsin to visit my family. When I say family, I mean both biological and chosen: the former, my parents and a collection of aunts and uncles and cousins on my mother's side, several generations of family scattered around the state;

the latter, a group of people who raised me in another way. On my last trip home, I went out with my friend Elle. Like most of my friends in Madison, I met Elle in roller derby, which we played together more than a decade ago. Like most of the women I met through that community, Elle is strong, smart, and driven. She's a queer Latina with a large, colorful quetzal—the national bird of her late father's native Guatemala—tattooed across her shoulder and chest. Elle is also a scientist, having worked for many years in biotech research, and the guitarist in a surf-punk band composed of queer women, one of whom is her wife. Ten years ago, their band was playing shows at Madison bars, jumping off stages to dance with the crowd. Today, they still do it. But now all of the women in the band, including Elle and her wife, are mothers.

When Elle and I get together, we usually talk about navigating the world as queer women—specifically within our careers and the music scene, these straight- and male-dominated spaces. But this time, we talk about motherhood. It's a Friday afternoon in May, and we meet at a dive bar in Madison. We order bottles of Spotted Cow and a basket of cheese curds. It being a Friday in Wisconsin, Elle plans to order some fish fry to bring home to her wife and their two-year-old daughter, Remy. We sit at a small, sticky table near a jukebox as people filter in for happy hour.

"For the longest time, I thought I was not going to have kids," Elle says, "because I'm an environmentalist. And when you add people to the population of the earth, you deplete resources and make waste. I thought if I ever had kids, it would be through adoption."

But when she got married, Elle found herself wondering about having children of her own.

"The scientist in me was curious," she says. "I thought, 'This is an experience my body can have. I want to understand it and know what that's like.'"

Elle carried their daughter. This is a decision that often has to be made in queer relationships, and it isn't always an easy one. Even though Elle was the one who wanted to carry, it was a decision that still came with struggle.

"I think my expectation, being with a woman, was that things were going to be more equal," Elle says. But she tells me about oxytocin, the hormone that kicks in when a biological mother is nursing. "You're flooded with all these love hormones; there's this bond. You have this relationship that's like, 'This baby needs *me*.'" Her wife didn't feel the same connection, at least at first, which caused some tension. There were other hardships too. Elle had a difficult labor that required two blood transfusions; she nearly died giving birth. After maternity leave, she went back to work for three months but found the separation from her daughter unbearable.

"I was miserable," she says. "I was so sad. I missed her so much, and just wanted to be with her." She realized she had to make a choice—she couldn't maintain her career and be home with her daughter, so she decided to leave her job.

When I met Elle, being a scientist was an important part of her identity. She was accomplished and had built an impressive career. I ask if she still feels this way.

"No," she says quickly. But then she takes a pull from her beer and thinks about it. "Yes and no. I did feel like I was throwing away my career, that I'd spent all this time building up to this point, and I had this education, and I was making good money. Is it stupid to throw away this job that's secure, that brings home health insurance for my family?"

Ultimately, Elle says, her priorities shifted when she had Remy.

"I really wanted that relationship with her," she says.

Lately Elle has been thinking of getting into teaching when Remy goes to preschool. Maybe, she says, she'll volunteer with a biotech program for high school students.

"I still want to exercise that part of my mind," she says.

I ask about music. Their band has been playing shows, and I say it seems like they're able to keep it up somehow. But Elle laughs and says they're not writing any new music.

"We're just barely getting by," she says. "You have to work really hard if you want to continue doing the things you did before."

It took Elle's wife a long time to come around to the idea of having kids, in large part because she wanted to build her business and pursue music.

"Maybe I should have listened to her more," Elle says.

Growing up, Elle had a difficult relationship with her parents. When she got pregnant she found herself thinking, *What if I'm like them?*

"I was really afraid," she says. "I worried about falling into some automatic behavior I learned from my parents. And I think sometimes I do. I disengage." She pauses for a beat; we pick at our cheese curds and sip our beer. Then she nods.

"We keep trying," she says. "I think we keep trying."

It can be hard to talk about kids, especially with people who have them. A built-in readiness to defend my choices always rises up in me, regardless of how much I love the person I'm talking to. I expect them to tell me—because they usually do—how great parenthood is, how life-changing it is, how they didn't know real love until they had a child. How nothing else really matters. Things that, while not necessarily meant to be condescending or hurtful, always end up feeling that way.

When I tell people why I don't want children, because I'm almost always expected to explain myself, I offer a litany of reasons. I say it's because I want to write, to dedicate myself to my work. I also say I just don't want children, that I'm happy with my life, that I'm pretty sure I wouldn't be a great parent anyway. But lately, I've admitted to a few people that the decision has caused me some grief. This is when they tell me all the ways I could have it all.

"You can still write," they say. "You can still have a career."

"You'll make it work," said one person.

"You should just do it!" said another.

"You'd be a great mother," they pretty much all say.

It's as if they don't hear the part about not wanting a child or being happy with my life as it is. It's as if they don't believe this is the life I would choose. Maybe they don't want to hear it. Maybe they're unable to fathom it. Either way, they seem only to hear the part about grief, and they interpret it as the grief of childlessness.

Elle has never said any of this to me. When she talks about motherhood, she talks about the wonder of biology, about the sheer audacity of science, of her body's ability to create and sustain life. And when I mention grief, she doesn't hear what she wants to hear or conflate my experience with her own. Instead, like a good scientist, she asks me questions with a desire to understand. She listens. It's one of the many reasons I count her among my family.

The concept of chosen family isn't limited to queer communities, but it's where the idea took root. According to a 2013 study by the Pew Research Center, 39 percent of LGBTQ-identified adults report that they have been rejected by their families because of their sexual orientation or gender identity. Forty percent of homeless youth identify as queer. Even if they're not forced out of their biological families, queer people often seek refuge among people like themselves—people who have had similar experiences, who are radically accepting and exist outside traditional, heteronormative family structures. In a country where same-sex marriage has until very recently been illegal (and where, if many people had their way, it would be again), queer people have developed other ways to create bonds with partners, to parent, to reimagine those structures that have cast them aside. Whatever shape it takes, they build a home and a family of their own.

I use the term *chosen family* to refer to my people, my partner and closest friends, a community that knows me better than most. But I also hold the knowledge that many people don't get to have both—to maintain connections with their biological family and build families of their own. There are people for whom chosen family is the only family.

There are countless shapes a family can take. And what looks like a traditional family to one person can seem unimaginable to another. Even among my own maternal family, that shape looks drastically different across generations—my great-grandmother's nine children, my grandmother's eight, my mother's one, my none. That side of the family is so massive I don't know everyone in it. There are husbands, wives, children, and grandchildren I've never met; great-aunts and great-uncles, second and third cousins, cousins once and twice removed who I couldn't list if I tried. When that side of the family gathers, the houses in which we meet are packed, bodies filling up couches and folding chairs and barstools, spilling out onto lawns, huddled around tables of food in garages, crowded around a basement television to watch the football game, playing horseshoes or cornhole in the backyard.

My grandmother died a few years ago, and in her absence we've been gathering less frequently. With the passing of each generation, our family gets a little smaller; more resources, more education, and more options tend to lead to fewer children. What's interesting is that queer communities often function in ways that mimic my grandmother's generation, or my great-grandmother's before it: with a group of people, not always related by blood, working together communally to take care of one another. For those generations, it meant people who didn't have a lot giving what they could. It was collective more than it was insular, everyone helping to raise one another's children. And when, at home, those children didn't always get what they needed—their people too tired, too desperate, too pained—they got it from each other, from neighbors, from friends. In the world of how we make families, nothing has changed much. We find family with those who take care of us, who love us and accept us as we are, who push us to become better versions of ourselves.

And yet, that most traditional model of family—husband and wife and 2.5 kids—is still placed above all others. For so many people, heterosexuality and having kids is still what makes the word *family* hold any meaning.

Once, when I told a coworker—a straight man with kids—that I spend a lot of time with family, he looked at me incredulously.

"Really?" he said. "You mean, like your parents? Or your extended family?"

I said yes, fumbling to find the right answer, struck by the particular brand of anger and shame that comes with having the legitimacy of one's life called into question. But what I meant was all of it—including my partner and my community, in New York and Wisconsin and scattered around the country, all of whom I call family. It's a family that functions much like one bound by blood, but is composed of people who in many cases are more tightly connected than the families they were born into. In my coworker's mind, the only kind of family one might possibly dedicate time to was one born of a ceremony, a legal certificate, and, ultimately, reproduction.

"Don't you want to have a family?" I've been asked, when I say I'm not married and don't plan to have children. What people don't seem to get is that I already do.

Alice is originally from Detroit, the youngest of five girls. She's in her late forties, moved to Madison for college, and has stayed ever since. She was one of the founding members of Madison's roller derby league, and she introduced me to the sport—where I would meet many of the other women I would eventually call family. Many of them were queer; all of them were strong, transgressive, and pushed against traditional expectations of femininity, love, and womanhood. Some of them chose not to have children, and some of them did. Some had children with other women or they parented alone or they parented in polyamorous families. Some were the breadwinners while their husbands stayed home and took care of the kids. In one way or another, they all broke the mold.

But Alice—whose close friends call her Al—came first. With glasses and sharp features and dark hair that's sometimes dyed pink, she looks a little like me. We sometimes tell people we're sisters, and she's always felt like the older sister I never had. Whenever I go back to Madison, I stay with her.

Al lives alone and has long been nonmonogamous, dating both women and men. There was a time when she considered adopting kids. She tells me this as we sit together one morning in May, drinking coffee in her living room. It comes as a surprise. For as long as I've known Al, one of the things I've understood most fundamentally about her—and what everyone close to her knows too—is that she doesn't like kids.

"I didn't want to have children biologically," she says, "because I didn't want to wreck my body."

Alice says her sisters, all of whom have children and are built like her—with small frames and narrow hips—had to have cesarean sections. And while for some people, carrying a baby or having to be cut open doesn't necessarily mean their body's wrecked, for others it does. This is also one of the reasons I've never wanted to have kids: I don't want to carry a child, and I don't want to give birth. And so often, when I've said this to people, they've laughed it off, as if it's not a serious consideration. They've said something dismissive like, "Oh, you'd get over that." But for me, carrying a child and giving birth is a notion that's not just terrifying—it's one I'm fairly certain would feel like violence against my body.

Al clarifies that she didn't really ever *want* children; she just thought that if she did, she would consider adopting. For a time, I considered this too. And I find it curious that, while neither of us actually wanted children, it's so ingrained that a woman should have them—that we should *want* them—that we consider our options anyway.

"But when I was married, I thought, 'If we ever fucking have a kid, I'm going to be doing all the goddamn work,'" she says. Al divorced her husband and got her tubes tied.

"No regrets," she says. Al's career is important to her, and so, too, is her lifestyle; she proudly calls herself a hedonist and spends much of her time and money going out to restaurants; cooking elaborate meals for friends and lovers with fresh foods from the local butcher, co-op, and farmers' market; and making cocktails at her professionally stocked bar, garnished with herbs she grows in her garden. On any given night, particularly in the summer, Al's front porch is filled with friends.

If she had children, she says, "I would not have any of what makes me the happiest in my life."

Al also doesn't like babies. This is something that seems to baffle people at best and anger them at worst.

"Babies smell, they're fragile—they just gross me out," she says, and we laugh. "No, I don't want to hold your baby, and I don't get people who are like, 'I want to cuddle babies.'"

My feelings about babies aren't quite as vehement, but in many respects I feel the same. Among the countless ways I've been told I'm less of a woman or some kind of monster, I've been called a freak for not loving "baby smell," which one person helpfully corrected me by saying: "You're wrong—it's objectively the best smell in the world."

While I'm happy to hold and play with the children of my friends and family, I've received some of the worst looks in my life when I've declined to hold a stranger's infant—an act, and a request, I find as strange as it is terrifying—or when, as something of a germophobe, I've been caught surreptitiously washing my hands after touching a child. So I rarely talk about these things. And this is one of the reasons Alice and I have always been such good friends: Much of what we share in common is well beyond the scope of normal or what can be acceptably said.

Al used to wear a pin that said, "Babies Creep Me Out." Most people thought it was a joke, but she meant it.

"I've had to overblow my disdain for children in order to get people to get it," she says.

We talk about the ways that people always try to tell us we're wrong for not wanting kids, that we would feel differently if it was our own.

"When it's my own, I could get arrested," Al says, and we laugh again.

We talk about the fact that so many people call not having children selfish. I say that I think bringing children into the world is just as selfish an act, if not more so.

"People want to see themselves in another being," Al says. "And I don't deny it's absolutely self-serving that I don't want to change my life, and I don't want to have to care for something."

Al's father, who is in his seventies and lives outside Detroit, worries about his youngest daughter and asks her who will take care of her when she's old.

"I've got a basket full of pills," Al says with a grin, one eyebrow raised above her glasses. "That's who's gonna take care of me when I'm old."

We laugh because it's funny, but I've thought about this too. I would never want someone to feel obligated to take care of me when I can no longer take care of myself, and that this is among the motivations to have children seems the most selfish of all.

As we sit in Alice's living room, her two kittens, Beurre and Onion, jump onto our laps. They curl up and start to purr. A self-described cat person, she recently adopted these two; when she brought them home, she remembered how much she loves taking care of cats—not least because they do such a good job of taking care of themselves.

"I walk around with Beurre like a baby," Al says. "And I'm like, 'You are so much fucking better than a baby.'"

~

My mother was born of the land, like her mother before her. My grandmother grew up on a farm and was in the 4-H Club, that hallowed organization ubiquitous to rural America. Her specialties were chickens and rabbits, which she raised herself. She was also known for her pickles, which she canned from the vegetables she grew. She won blue ribbons at the county fair, and in photos she holds a baby chick in one hand and a jar of pickles in the other. She looks proud.

My mother's mother was the last of my grandparents to go. Whenever I visited her, driving the country roads connecting my small town to hers, we fed the stray cats that lived in her yard. We fed the birds, too, and sat at her kitchen table for hours, watching the finches and sparrows and robins, an occasional pileated woodpecker, gather at the feeders. My mother feeds stray cats, too, and keeps a veritable bird sanctuary on her back patio; she treks out on even the coldest winter mornings to sprinkle seed in the snow, to refill her feeders with suet and peanuts and jam. She taught me about birds: how to distinguish between the female cardinal and the male, the thrush from the wren, the grackle from the starling; to spot red-winged blackbirds and dark-eyed juncos, chickadees and orioles and jays. We filled feeders with sugar water for the hummingbirds, then waited for their hum. We mastered the call of the mourning dove and tried to get them to talk to us.

There's a joke in my family that we love animals and plants more than people. In the Midwest, affection is not our strong suit. We're not big on physical contact; a quick hug, a few pats on the back are the extent of our physical displays of love. (When I moved to New York and people started greeting me with kisses on the face, I was horrified; I still don't deal with it well.) My mother, meanwhile, greets her cats every day with an elaborate routine of hugs and scratches and sweet-voiced song. She tends to her birds and plants with a gentle fastidiousness I've never seen her give to humans. And sometimes, as I coo unintelligibly to my own cat, as I prune and water and talk to my plants, sometimes with a more tender touch than I give to my partner, I worry that I'm the same way.

But when I was young, our family took summer vacations to the Northwoods. The whole huge clan went, my mother and her seven siblings, their children, my grandparents, all of us descending upon the northern Wisconsin wilderness. We fished and swam and dove off docks into cold lakes, tubed down the Wisconsin River, built bonfires and told stories around it. And sometimes, my mother and grandmother and I would go for a walk in the woods. We stopped to watch the warblers as they hopped from branch to branch. We hiked through forests of birch and pine. During these walks, we communed with nature; and in our own way, we communed with each other too.

My friend Rivka is divorced and in her forties. She grew up in Madison and still lives there. I've known Rivka for a long time: When I was a barista in college, she was a regular—she's a black belt and owned a karate school across the street. A few years later, we found ourselves on the same roller derby team, and she's still one of my closest friends. Rivka grew up believing she would follow the path she'd learned was the script for success: Go to college, get married, buy a house, have children. She did go to college and got married to a man when she was young, but she didn't have children. Fourteen years since her divorce, there's still part of her that wants kids, but she has uncoupled the desire for motherhood with the need for a partner.

"I've become more open to other kinds of relationships," she says, "and shifted the definition of what it means to be a mother and 'have children.'"

Rivka is an aunt in both blood and friendship to several children, including her niece and the daughter of her good friend, with whom she currently lives. She loves kids, worked for many years in an elementary school, and says she finds kids easier to connect with than adults.

"I would be a great mom," she says. And she's had some chances to be one—when she was married, when she had an abortion. These days, she considers adoption as a single parent not only a viable but a preferable option—one she can make on her own terms, if and when she's ready. She might also choose not to have kids. But despite her changing ideas about the shape that motherhood can take, she still feels some conflict about being a fortysomething woman without children. She still feels some grief.

"There's a societal expectation and blatant disdain for childless women that, despite being raised in a progressive family by a single mother half the time, wove its way into my personal expectations and definition of womanhood," Rivka says. "I can't help but worry about being a lonely lady with a cat in old age with no one to be there at the end of my life."

Rivka still believes, on some level, that as a human born with ovaries, motherhood is her duty. It's part of the script from which she's still uncoupling herself.

"At the end of the day," she says, "I often feel a sense of peace knowing that I am the only one I need to take care of. I have a freedom that my friends and family with children do not have." But she still feels doubt, which she calls both crippling and absurd.

"I'm still working to be fully confident in being whatever kind of woman I want to be," she says, "the woman I am at the core."

Where I grew up, girls learn one primary lesson: that their role in life—their Christian duty, their very reason for being—is to marry a man and breed, and to serve those men and children. Blessedly, I have parents who never pressured me to do either. But it was a lesson I learned nonetheless. It was all around me, impossible to escape: I learned it from the women in my family, even those who never married or had kids, who still performed the duties that were expected of women—at family gatherings, they cooked and cleaned up and did the dishes while the men watched football. I learned it from church, where in sermons the pastors (who were always men) spoke of the purity of the virgin mother, the importance of family. I learned it, of course, from TV and movies—from those perfect quartets of mother-father-daughter-son, whose husbands worked and whose wives took care of the kids.

Like my own mother, most of the women I knew growing up had full-time jobs and did most or all the caretaking too: They packed lunches and did laundry, got groceries and shopped for clothes, drove the kids to dentist appointments and softball practice and band concerts. They clipped coupons and made scrapbooks, planned holiday meals and bought all the gifts, stayed home when kids were sick. No one had help, because no one could afford it. So this work, too, was their job, even if it was never spoken aloud. Even if it was met with frustration and resentment and silent anger, which worked its way into their fingers as they cooked, curled into their damp hair in the heat of the stove. They did it anyway, because it was what women did.

When I was in my early twenties, I attended the wedding of a high school friend. We sat in a small Catholic church in the country, just outside our hometown, as the priest spoke of my friend's new role as wife: that she could now fulfill the duty that God had bestowed upon her, to serve her husband and breed, then serve the children she would have. He warned too of the dangers of "zoologists"—those trickster scientists who would tell you that humans evolved from monkeys, who would have you believe that we were not the children of God, who might suggest that women had other possibilities before them than marriage and motherhood.

I looked at my friend in her white dress—a girl who knew how to operate a tractor, who liked to drive fast on country roads with the windows down, who I loved for her strength and her independence—and I couldn't believe she bought this message. Maybe she didn't. Maybe she just nodded along and rolled her eyes internally, because she was raised Catholic and this old message was what was expected of her. Or maybe she did believe it. Where we come from, even the strongest and smartest women still so often believe in their God-given duty to be mother and wife. Even if they have other plans, other ambitions or dreams, marriage and family is the only certainty. It's the ultimate goal, the picture of success. Motherhood is not just what girls are expected to do—it's what they're trained to want.

Devon and I grew up in the same small town. We didn't get to know one another until we'd left, though, and were both living in Madison. We worked for the same publisher, had mutual friends in the BDSM scene, and were both in nonmonogamous relationships. We also inhabited similarly murky spaces of sexuality and gender identity.

I was surprised and delighted to reencounter Devon, a queer feminist kinkster and book nerd, who came from the same place I did. Today, Devon identifies as genderqueer, uses they/them pronouns, and is the co-owner of a feminist bookstore in Madison that I frequented in college. Devon is also in a queer polyamorous triad.

We meet at a coffee shop on State Street, a block from the bookstore, where I used to study in college. Devon and I drink coffee and share a muffin. Devon is androgynous like me, with short curly hair and glasses. They and their partners have a three-year-old son, and another baby on the way, both of them carried by the same partner. I ask Devon about growing up where we did, and how that informed the way they understand love, family, and parenthood now.

"I feel like there was a certain sense of cognitive dissonance," Devon says, and I know immediately what they mean. We talk about how, in a small, mostly Christian, midwestern town, we learn about love through the lens of the nuclear family. But up close, physical evidence of love can be hard to find. Love looks a lot like service. It looks a lot like sacrifice and duty. It can look like genuine care and devotion, but it rarely looks like affection, and certainly not desire. Like so many midwestern couples I've known, including most in my own family, Devon's parents, who eventually divorced, were not affectionate with one another. And so, Devon says, it took a long time to learn what a loving, emotionally intelligent relationship looked like. I tell Devon it's something I'm still learning.

"I never wanted children and I never wanted to be married because I had seen how shitty marriage is," Devon says. "Even if it were legal for me to be married to my partners, I would not choose it."

When Devon joined the triad, they knew their partners wanted children. At first, Devon wasn't sure what role they would play.

"I was like, 'I'm going to be the cool aunt that lives upstairs. I'm not going to parent.'"

But then Devon decided they wanted to help raise the child. I ask whether Devon's parents, and their partners' parents, were accepting of this family structure.

"In some respects, the Midwest nice culture worked in my favor," Devon says. I laugh, because again I know exactly what they mean. In the Midwest, or at least in our Midwest, people avoid talking about the uncomfortable things at all costs.

"And when you say, 'My partners and I are raising a child together,' they're like, 'What? Three parents? That's genius!'"

We talk at length about this, the fact that having a baby seems to legitimize relationships and families that might otherwise be considered strange or somehow deviant.

"Whenever I tell people about being poly," Devon says, "I'm really talking about parenting my kid."

Devon's partner struggled to conceive, and for a while Devon considered the possibility of carrying a child.

"I'm just grateful that I did not have to use my body to carry a baby," Devon says. "Would I have to go off my antidepressant? And in a situation that stressful, would that be good? If my breasts grew, would I feel more dysphoria than I generally do? Probably. I have a lot of control issues over my body, and pregnancy is such an out-of-control thing. And in so many instances, it's also a very dehumanizing experience culturally."

I've always had similar concerns. And it hits me, as Devon and I talk, that when you already feel at odds with your body, when perhaps you've spent your whole life trying to find a way to live inside it, it makes sense that you might be afraid of it changing more, and in a way that's beyond your control—for another being to take it over, and to be forced, in my and Devon's case, into a body more female.

Devon's partners—one of whom is a cisgender woman, who carried their son, and the other who is trans—are married. Before their son was born, Devon spent a long time considering what they would be called. In the end, they settled on *Mom*.

"I really wanted to access the legitimacy of motherhood," Devon says. "And I still do. Now we've got him in preschool, and he's got three moms. I think we all feel like his mom."

Devon does prefer the term *parent* over *mother*, but also understands that we live in a culture in which *mother* carries more weight.

"I'll use *mother* in positions where I feel the need to be more legitimized," Devon says. "Like at school, it's definitely *mother* and not just *parent*. And partly to normalize our family in situations like that."

For Devon, identity as a parent is closely tied to queerness, and it's a terrain that can be complicated to navigate, especially when it comes to how they might present on a given day.

"Although I do identify with the term *mother*, I don't identify with everything that means," Devon says. "But I also think that that's true of the term *woman*. There's no one thing that woman means. I feel like my nonbinary identity is just about giving myself enough space to be who I need to be in a particular moment, more than it is about finding a fixed point that works."

It's refreshing to talk to someone who came from the same place I did, who has had similar struggles with concepts of gender, sexuality, and family, who exists somewhere beyond the categories into which society prefers us to fit. I've felt disconnected from my hometown for so long, and knowing that Devon and I come from the same small place, that we made it out and into the world in this way, feels like a small miracle. It feels almost like a homecoming.

A week after we meet, Devon's family have their second baby, a girl. Their son, meanwhile, is three; he's starting to understand pronouns, the differences between gender and sex, and is playing with a lot of trains.

"He just really likes trains!" Devon says, laughing. "For all the dolls we've given him. And that's kind of our parenting philosophy: It's the kid's choice, and even if the kid is choosing the stereotypical thing, as long as we are choosing to instill empathy and open-mindedness in him, to push back against any received erroneous information he's getting from the world—that's just part of raising a conscientious probably-boy."

For a while, Devon and their partners tried using gender-neutral pronouns with their son, but decided that this in itself could be an imposition.

"He's already in this kind of weird family structure. We don't want him to have to correct people about his pronouns when he hasn't even had the opportunity to become cognitive enough about what that means," Devon says. "I mean, obviously if he chooses to change his pronouns, we'll be real chill about it and remarkably suited."

My mother doesn't grow vegetables anymore, but she still has flower gardens. They run along all sides of the house, lush landscapes of ferns and lilies, marigolds and sunflowers, handmade trellises and stone paths leading to bubbling ponds. Barrels of perennials dot the deck; smaller pots trail the stairs. Inside the house, she keeps a veritable greenhouse. In my New York apartment, this is what I do too.

It started out small, my indoor garden, just a spider plant and a corn plant from friends who moved away. Then more friends left, and I inherited their plants too: a peace lily and a jade and a mother-in-law's tongue; aloe and pothos and peperomia, croton and schefflera, a variegated Moses-in-the-cradle. I have dozens of plants now, and I take them on with a sense of duty: In my friends' absence, it's my job to keep these creatures alive. And for the most part, it's working. The mother-in-law's tongue contracted blight and died, the peace lily struggles, the nerve plant may not survive the winter. But I water and mist and prune; I rotate and repot and refresh the soil; I make sure my plants have the right kind of light. And most of them are thriving. Some are growing at alarming rates, propagating faster than I can prune or repot them. It's stressful sometimes, to keep them going. Sometimes I think about letting the struggling ones slip away, but I can never bring myself to let go. In a city made of concrete, with no trees or grass or gardens, sometimes it feels like my plants are the only connection I have left to the land. Sometimes they feel like the only connection I have left to the people I love who have gone, who have new lives and families of their own in places far away.

I don't want kids because I'm pretty sure I wouldn't like being a mother. Because I'm finally starting to feel at home in my life, in my work, and in my body. And because, thankfully, I live in a time—one that mothers fought for their daughters to have—in which I can choose who and what my body carries.

Because, in the end, my biological clock has simply never gone off. I just don't want children, and that should be enough. But it's never enough. And it's not the whole story. The rest of the story is that I have a history of undesirable afflictions, addictions, illnesses, and behaviors—some of which were inherited, and none of which I want to pass on. Sometimes I get angry, and in the past I've gotten violent. I struggle to talk about my feelings, to be affectionate and present, and sometimes I can be passive-aggressive—behaviors I'm still trying to unlearn. At the root of these behaviors and afflictions, I think, there is an old, heavy grief—one that so many women in my family seem to carry. I don't know where it came from, or in which generation its roots took hold. All I know is that it's in us, and has been for a long time. Even if I wanted a child, I wouldn't want to give her this grief. I wouldn't want her to carry it, like we all carry the grief of our mothers, maybe, and the generations of women who came before us.

So I'll sever the vein of inheritance, and end this line with me. I'll carry the grief alone instead, the last of my name, and one day I'll be buried with it. But buried alongside it will be all the good that might have lived too: the trees and flowers and gardens we might have planted; the tomatoes we might have popped off the vine in the sun; the birds and cats and people we might have fed; the family that might have gathered around us. And this—this life that will never be lived, this good that might have been carried on—I'll grieve this too.

M y spider plant is a problem. Also known as spider ivy, ribbon plant, airplane plant, and hen and chickens, *Chlorophytum comosum* is known for its canopy of long, narrow leaves, which fan out like an umbrella or a spider's legs. It's also known for its wild propagation. I have four in large pots, all from the same original plant: the mother and three of her children, one of which recently sprang children of her own. The mother, now a grandmother, who sits atop an eight-foot bookshelf by the window, has been growing new babies for over a year now. Not long ago, her many vines of children hanging to the floor, tangled together in a thick jumbled mass for my cat to tackle and pounce on and eat, I decided it was time to prune them. I cut off all the vines—there were about ten of them, each roughly eight feet long—and realized as I trimmed that many of the babies had had babies too. I snipped somewhere around fifty children from those vines—dark-green bundles of leaves, long and thick and bursting from milk-white roots. I gathered the children in mason jars filled with water, and for the next several months I will watch their roots grow.

The mother, meanwhile, is not doing well. Her children, it seems, have used up all her resources. Her leaves, once thick and green, are cracked and yellowed, burned at the edges. Where once they were buoyant, now they are bent. I give her new soil, trim away her dead leaves, and give her a good soaking, hoping to wake in the morning to find her revived. But the next day, her leaves are still sagging. And I can't help but think I have failed her. That I should have freed her sooner. One day, as I prune her, out of nowhere I start weeping. I don't cry often, and this is the kind that makes my whole body shake. And I realize that maybe the grief I'm feeling is about more than this plant. Maybe I'm grieving my friends who have left. Maybe I'm grieving my grandmother: for the loss of her, which maybe hasn't hit me yet, and for her losses too—the people she loved that passed on before her, the things she never got to do. Maybe I grieve for my mother, who lives with her own grief over the loss of her mother, and all the other secret losses a woman keeps and carries alone.

I no longer believe in God, at least not in the way I used to. But as I put my mother spider plant back on her shelf, I say a prayer anyway. I ask that, somehow, she might find new life. I ask that she forgive me.

When I moved to New York, my grandmother and I started exchanging letters. She was always supportive of my writing and music, and never once asked if I was going to get married or when I'd start thinking about kids. Her life was filled with children and grandchildren, and she didn't seem to expect any of them, who were mostly girls and women, to follow the same path.

"You can do whatever you want to do," she wrote to me once. I'd been told this before, but for some reason, when she said it, I believed it. I'm sure she told her own kids this too. But I wonder if she was ever able to believe it about herself.

I'm an only child. This was a rare thing where I came from, where most families had at least two or three children, sometimes several more.

"Didn't she want more kids?" people would ask me about my mother.

"Why only one?"

As if I should know. As if they had any right to ask. Usually I made a joke out of it.

"Well, look at me," I'd say, already a midwestern master of self-deprecation at eight years old. "You'd only want one too!"

But beneath the jokes grew a small flame. People asked my mother these questions, too, like they feel they have the right to. Maybe she wanted only one child. Maybe she wanted more and couldn't have them. Maybe, as was my suspicion when I was young, she never wanted any at all.

My mother was the oldest of eight, and she spent much of her childhood taking care of her siblings. She helped get them fed in the mornings before school, did laundry and chores while her parents were at work, helped her mother with dinner, and helped her brothers and sisters with their homework before she did her own. She was more a mother by the time she was a teenager than some people will ever be. For these reasons, maybe she only wanted one child of her own. And maybe she wanted to give that one the kind of life she never had.

My mother also wanted to be an artist. She got into college to study art but dropped out after a year, lived in a commune, then hopped on the back of her boyfriend's motorcycle and moved to Florida. She worked double shifts at a gas station, lived in a trailer, drew in her sketchbook, and painted. Then she met my father, got married, and moved back to Wisconsin to be closer to her family. A few years later, she had me.

My mother worked full-time for most of my childhood, on her feet all day as the manager of a Marshall's in Madison. She left early in the mornings, her pumps clicking down the hall and waking me up before school, and sometimes worked until late at night. As a kid, I played in her closet, running my fingers along the fabrics of her blouses and skirts, organizing the pumps into neat rows and trying them on, staggering around the house. She brought me home stonewashed Jordache Jeans and Esprit T-shirts bought on steep discount, and sometimes she took me to work with her on the weekends, if my father was out of town. She still drew sometimes, on her days off. Sometimes we'd spend a Sunday together, sprawled out on our stomachs on the yellow shag carpet in a slant of afternoon sun, Jackson Browne or Bob Seger or the Temptations on the stereo, drawing in our sketchbooks. But she was never able to become the artist she wanted to be. For a long time, I blamed myself for this. Maybe there's a part of me that still does. But as I got older, I began to understand that my mother made a choice. And with that choice came certain joys but also grief—for the life that could have been, for all the lives that preceded her life as a mother. It took me a long time to understand that all choices are a sacrifice.

When I tell people one of the main reasons I don't want kids is because I want to write, to dedicate my life to this path I've known I've wanted to take since I was a kid, it's strange to me that they don't seem to understand. Because when I say that what I want to do with my life is create something that maybe, if I'm lucky, will carry on after me, it seems to stem from a desire not dissimilar to wanting children.

In both cases, I think, creating something that exists beyond us, that lives on when we are gone, is a fundamentally human desire. Some might even say it's our purpose, this biological imperative to survive.

What I'm saying is that we're all just trying to fend off death however we can.

She is Mother Nature. She is Mother Earth. In ancient Greece, she was Gaia; in ancient Rome, she was Tellus, or Terra. The Norse have the goddess Jord, or "Earth." The Incas had Pachamama, Mother Universe. The Algonquians have Nokomis, the Grandmother. Odudua is the Yoruba Earth Goddess, a deity who protects women and children. The personification of the Earth as a mother is one of the first stories ever told. In some mythologies she is a goddess; in others she is the planet itself, or the universe that holds it—the source from which all life is born.

I like to think of a mother's body on a slightly smaller scale—as the lands upon which we are born, the small towns and farmlands and cities that make us. She maps the geography of our bodies, our identities, our idea of home. We come from her, are composed of her, are raised by her and defined by her. She is rich and fertile; she shelters us and keeps us safe. But she can also be volatile and unpredictable, sometimes brutal. Eventually we leave her, to find new lands upon which to build families and homes. And yet when we are gone, we might long for her. We might remember the days of our youth when the trees were full and the hills were lush and rolling, when we were children in the sun. And sometimes, we go home. We return to our motherland. And if we are good, we give back to her. We tend to her, care for her, in the way she once did us—because we know that someday she will be gone.

We seem to be making more room for conversations about motherhood and grief. More books about postpartum depression, narratives that bring to light a dark reality that many mothers have historically faced in silence. We also seem to be having more conversations about grief surrounding not having children; specifically, about the struggle or inability to conceive, about the traumatic process of in vitro fertilization, about freezing eggs, about adoption, about age and the cultural and internalized implications of not being able to have children.

What I've yet to see is a conversation about the grief that accompanies choosing not to have children. To some, of course, this choice is still an affront. It's sacrilegious, hedonistic, an injury to God, a denial of duty, a waste of womanhood. It's selfish, strange, and inconceivable. But even for those who support a woman's right to choose her own path, we still don't seem capable of understanding that this choice, like the others, is a complex one, that it comes with its own kind of loss.

People often think of us nonbreeders as so made up in our minds, so settled in our conviction to not have kids, that the decision couldn't possibly be complicated. And maybe for some people it's not. But just as choosing to have a child is sacrifice, so too is choosing not to.

"Must be nice," so many people have said to me, wistfully or sarcastically or both, when I say I'm leaving for a week or a month to write, to record an album with my band. "What a luxury," said one woman. The people who say such things are always parents, and what they mean is that they could never get away from their lives or their families to do such a thing. If they're bitter about this fact, their response seems a direct attempt to make me feel guilty.

And you know what? It is nice. I love it. But it's not a luxury. It's not some opulent accident, some frivolous narcissistic lifestyle. It's work, and it's the product of a choice I've made, that I'm making every day. It's a choice that, like most choices, can be difficult.

Sometimes I see my friends and family with their kids, and I watch those kids grow up, and I think: *My partner would be such a good parent.* Sometimes I think: *Who knows? Maybe I'd be a good parent too.* Sometimes I think it would be interesting to see what kind of human we would make, to watch that life grow, to raise kids alongside our friends. Sometimes I think of my parents, who will never be grandparents, even though I think they'd like to be. Sometimes I wonder what my life would look like if I made different choices. Sometimes, just as I celebrate my choices, I carry the grief of them.

But none of this means I would choose differently. None of this means I'm asking to be told all the ways I'm wrong, all the other choices I could make, all the ways my life could be different.

I t seems like our job is to figure out what to do with our grief," my friend Jules says. "Like, do you just drag it behind you? Do you figure out a different way to relate to it? Do you use it to fuel something? Do you make it your own?"

Jules was the first person who ever talked to me about grief. We met in roller derby, when I was in my midtwenties and she was a few years older, and we quickly became close. She was queer and loud and funny, had a sleeve of tattoos and prematurely gray hair, a short curly shock of it in the front and shaved in the back. We rode our bikes around town and went out dancing; when she tore her ACL, I took care of her through her recovery, driving her to physical therapy and changing her icepacks. One summer, we traveled together to France. We slept together once but realized we were better off as friends. When I met her, she had a long-term girlfriend, and then another one, but had loved both women and men. A few years before we met, she had been diagnosed with leukemia; by the time we became friends, she had been in remission for a few years.

No one I knew had ever used the word *grief* like Jules did. I'd only ever heard the word within the context of death. Jules, instead, talked about grief as if it was just a part of life, that it was something we carried.

Today, Jules is in her early forties. She's married to a man and they have two daughters, one who Jules gave birth to and one stepdaughter. Jules's marriage has historically been nonmonogamous; for a while she and her husband had a third, a woman who lived with them, but they're not currently seeing anyone else. Their daughters are five and nine, and after a few years of working as a full-time mom, Jules now has a second-shift job three nights a week. I tell her, over beers at a sports bar, this thing about grief; that she was the first person I ever heard talk about it so openly.

"Well you know where that came from, right?" she says. "It came from confronting my mortality. And I think mourning the person I was who didn't have any idea about it."

We're in a place called the Blue Moon, which I used to frequent when I lived on this side of town. We meet up when she gets off work one night and drink a couple of pints while college kids watch the Bucks game and play pinball.

"The only time you're allowed to use that word is if it's associated with losing a loved one," Jules says. "But you can mourn the loss of your younger self, or your oblivious self, or your innocence. In the last year, I think in particular I mourned the loss of my idealism."

In life, Jules says, we get prepared for so many things. We get an education, we get training, we get how-to instructions from the internet. But what we really need to learn is how to deal with the grief we possess. It was Jules's battle with leukemia that allowed her to see the greater role that grief plays in one's life.

"How do I carry it with me?" she says. "Because you can't cut it off and you can't leave it behind. I think that might actually become a defining feature of a person—how to relate to your grief and what you do with it."

I tell her about my own grief—for friends whose lives have diverged from mine, for my grandmother and her children. And I realize as we talk that so much of the grief I carry is not actually my own—that it belongs to the women and the family who came before me.

"I think we need to expand the definitions of grief," Jules says. "Sometimes you get angry, and sometimes you get sad, and sometimes you profoundly mourn something. And I wish it was more a conversation in general, so it would be seen as a normal part of living, as opposed to the way you're broken."

I talk to her about my thoughts on grief as inheritance, and tell her that one of my reasons for not having children is not wanting to pass that grief along.

"Honestly the reasons I didn't want to have kids were all purely selfish," she says. I've heard this before, but what she says next is surprising. "I didn't want to watch their hearts break, and I didn't want to watch them struggle, and I didn't want my heart to be broken by watching them go through the same things I went through or things I don't even know about now—I didn't want to feel the pain."

Jules grew up in Iowa and has lived in Wisconsin for many years. We talk about midwestern parents, about trying to raise kids differently than we were raised, than our parents were raised.

"She had such a picture in her mind of what a good mom was, and she tried to do it," Jules says of her own mother. "But she didn't really have the ability because no one fucking does." I think about my own mother, and my grandmother, and the resources that were available to them. I think about the access and information and choices Jules has, and what her daughters will have.

For a long time, Jules said she never wanted kids. And then one day, something shifted inside her.

"And I had to come out to you guys, remember?" she says, laughing. "I was like, 'Hey everybody. I think—I think I want to be a mom.'"

I do remember. Jules was one of my first queer friends to become a parent. I had moved to New York by the time she got married and had her daughter, and it took me a while to realize that I felt grief around it: that I wasn't home to be part of her daughter's life and that our lives had changed so radically. Jules and I have always shared similar struggles when it comes to identity; we often talk about bisexuality and the ways our identity gets erased when we're in relationships with men. When she married a man and had children, Jules says, she felt like she had to let go of the only community to which she had ever belonged, the identity that defined her for more than twenty-five years.

"I really don't know how to bring all the parts of me to all the places," she says.

"Is there anywhere that you feel like you can be your full self?" I ask.

"No!" she yells, slapping the table and laughing. It's a huge, contagious laugh, and it cuts through the noise of the bar. A few college kids look over at us. "Never! I don't think I've ever been my full self anywhere. I don't even think that's a thing."

We laugh, because it is kind of funny, and because we both understand on some level that the idea of a whole self seems like the dream of a much younger person, who has yet to make the hardest decisions—the kind that thrust a person down one path instead of another; the kind that are immutable. We laugh because we both know now it's not possible. But as we part ways that night, and I watch the blinking taillight of her bike disappear into the darkness, I grieve the person who used to think it was.

My partner wants kids more than I do. There's part of him that would like to experience being a father, and in particular to parent with me. He tells me he's fine with not having kids, but he has grief around it too. It's a grief that's different from mine. He, like me, watches our friends have kids, watches them bond over being parents, watches their kids grow up together and their families expand in a way that ours won't. He, like me, grieves his parents not being able to be grandparents. He, like me, understands that without children, we face a different kind of mortality than so many of the people we love.

The fear I carry alone is this: that someday he'll change his mind. He assures me he won't, that he'd rather choose a life with me than one with children—which feels like its own separate weight for me to bear. But when we talk about kids, I feel defensive. I feel guilty—like I'm disappointing him, like there's another person who might be able to make him happier, who might make his life feel more complete. I fear that someday he'll wake up and regret this decision, that he'll realize I'm not enough. And I feel angry—that he doesn't have to feel this fear. He assures me he won't change his mind, and I believe him. Or at least I believe he believes it now. How he'll feel in the future—when it's far too late for me but not necessarily for him—is something I can never know. It's a conversation we continue to have, a question that has no conclusion.

A few years before my grandmother died, I helped her plant flowers. She was alone by then, and my mother and I drove to her house in the spring. We planted annuals—yellow-and-purple marigolds, pink-and-white impatiens; and we planted perennials—daffodils and daisies, black-eyed Susans—that would come back every year. We did it together, dirt under our fingernails, our hands in the earth. Years later, my grandmother still called them "Melissa's flowers."

I have a picture of my grandmother above my desk. It's my favorite shot of her, one I picked out after she died, when my mother and I went through old photos to display at her funeral. There are a lot of good photos of her: on the farm when she was young, with her prizewinning pickles and chicks; on a blanket in the grass with my grandfather. In one she's smoking a cigarette, but she's pinching it like a joint. She wears dark shades, holds up two fingers in a peace sign, and she's laughing.

But this one is special: It was taken in the Northwoods, during one of our family vacations. She sits in a lawn chair, the cheap wicker-and-metal kind, with one leg folded beneath her and the other stretched out in front of her. One arm rests along her leg. My grandmother struggled with weight for most of her life, but in this photo she looks healthy, boyish and lean. She was always strong, and you can see the line of her triceps on that outstretched arm, a contour of muscle in which you can see the farm girl, the factory worker, the nurse's assistant lifting the weight of bodies. You can see the mother, holding her children.

She looks about sixty. She wears shorts and a T-shirt and glasses; her skin is freckled and tan, as she always got in the summer—the same skin my mom has, the skin I increasingly share as I get older. Her dark hair is cut short, like she always wore it, and it's going gray. I see my mother in her, and I see myself. That outstretched arm could be my arm. She's not looking at the camera but past it, maybe at one of her kids or grandkids. She's smiling, and it's a tight-lipped smile—a little impish, a little wry, a furrow at the brow. But it's a tender look, too, a midwestern kind of affection: tempered, a little removed, but love nonetheless.

There's a can below her chair, and I can't tell what was in it, but I'll bet it was either a Coke or a beer. My grandmother, like so many people in my family, was a drinker. It's something so many of us do: a preferred way of dealing or not dealing—both inherited and learned—with the things we carry.

But behind her is the forest, deep and dark and green, a whole wilderness that together we might have explored. I'm not sure what's in front of her, but I'll bet it's a lake, where she liked to sit with a book and watch the birds and wait for the fish to jump. Or maybe it's the firepit, around which the family will gather that night to tell stories. I'm not sure who took the picture, who or what she's looking at with that sly and knowing smile. I'm not sure if she's alone out there or if her whole family is gathered around her. I like to think we are.

Last year, my parents had to cut down one of their trees. They've had to cut down a few over the years—the mountain ash that got a bore, the spruce that went to rot. The birch tree in the front yard isn't doing well, and I'm sure it will eventually go too. But this loss was harder. It was a sugar maple, the only one of its kind in the yard. It stood alone on the front lawn, just outside what was once my bedroom window. It was a beautiful tree, with a perfect canopy of leaves—dark green in the summer and fire-engine red in the fall.

Its root system became tangled. No longer able to receive nutrients from the soil, its leaves started to fall. Its branches turned brittle and began to crack. Rot worked its way up from the roots. My parents waited a long time to cut it down, their hearts too broken to do it. And then, the last time I went home, it was gone.

The sugar maple is the state tree of Wisconsin. It's also the state tree of New York. I decided that, before I leave this city, I'll get a new tattoo. It will be a sugar maple tree—maybe just a branch and a few leaves, some falling samaras, or seed pods, those little propellers we called whirligigs when we were kids—that will fall down my arm. I met with a tattoo artist, and she asked me what the concept means. There were a lot of things I could have told her: about my mother and the maples, about my grandmother; about loss, transience, and the ever-shifting idea of home. What I told her, instead, is that it will serve as a reminder—that wherever we go, whatever shape our lives and loves and families may take, we carry our grief along with us. But whatever it is we've lost, we carry the potential for new growth too.

~

A waitress brings two carry-out bags of fish fry to the table, and Elle picks up the check. As we leave the bar, she asks me to tell her more about the grief I've been feeling about not having kids. I tell her as best I can, about my feelings of isolation and loss, of slipping farther away from the people I love.

"You know," she says, a bit of motherly chiding in her voice, "if you want to be a part of Remy's life, you can be." She's telling me I have a choice in this, that I don't need to let conventional confines of family keep me out of hers; that I'm still family if I want to be. She invites me over to her house for dinner and I go, and she brings the fish home for her family. We sit down at the table, and I help Remy butter a roll. After dinner, she and Elle and I run around outside in their backyard with their dog. Remy chases me with a toy lawn mower that blows bubbles. Elle calls me "Aunt Lou" and Remy repeats it, with a big bright laugh that sounds a lot like my friend's.

I might not want kids of my own, but it feels good to be here, to hang out with this kid that's part of my friend—to be some small part of her life, to wonder who she'll become, and to know I'll be around to find out.

My spider plant mother is coming back. Not long ago, I went into the living room on a Sunday morning to water my plants, and there she was, perched atop the bookshelf, her leaves once again tall and buoyant and green. The other day, I saw she'd sprung a new vine. It reached toward the window, in the direction of the sun, and it was blooming. A small spray of white flowers sprang from the vine, delicate and tiny and new. And soon, from those flowers, a new tiny spider plant will grow. But this time, I promised, and I said it aloud, I wouldn't leave the mother on her own for so long. I'd take better care of her children, and I'd take better care of her.

Last fall, I went home for another wedding. This one was for two women I also met through roller derby, who I also think of as family. They live in Chicago now but chose to have their wedding in Madison, the place they still call home. They decided they won't have children, but they've developed close relationships with their friends' kids, serving as godparents, aunts, and role models—women who lead interesting, successful lives, women those children might look up to.

They got married in a park and chose a venue with a playground. On the day of the wedding, their friends' kids—ten girls in all—carried flowers along the grass, sprinkling a path of petals to where the two women were standing. Then they were told to go play.

During the ceremony, I stood up next to several of the women I love most, and watched their kids run and jump and climb. They took their shoes off and ran in the grass, swooped across monkey bars and flew down slides, while two women they loved got married. I thought about myself at those girls' age—six and ten and twelve, small and strong, a tomboy in torn jeans and a grass-stained T-shirt, hiking with my mother and grandmother in the woods. And I thought about these children, who will grow up with more options. Who will make decisions about their bodies and lives with fewer boundaries, without as much expectation as we had, as our parents and grandparents had before us. Who will have more women and people in their lives who did things differently.

O n my last trip home, I worked in two gardens. The first was the vegetable garden of a woman named Paige, a woman I once loved in the way I once thought of as family, but who has since become family in a different kind of way. She, like me, has chosen not to have children. We met, of course, playing roller derby in Madison, but she lives outside Milwaukee now, where she works as a veterinarian. She has a little house, a dog, and lives near Lake Michigan. It's late spring, and Paige shows me the produce she's planted: the green beans and radishes, the onions and peppers, the tomatoes and strawberries, the lettuce and kale we'll later pick for dinner. On the morning I leave, my friend takes me to the front of her house.

"I forgot to show you these!" she says with a thrill, and leads me to a short row of echinops that line the garden. Also known as globe thistle, the plants are hard to grow, but Paige's are thriving. Soon they'll bloom spiky, spherical flowers of violet and white, but for now, they just look like thistles. Paige beams as she shows them to me, rubbing their spiny leaves.

"Only a mother would be proud," she says.

She sends me off as she usually does, with a miniature bouquet of herbs from her garden—a small bundle of rosemary and mint, whose leaves I'll keep in my pocket to carry with me long after I've left her. I drive home then, to the house where I grew up, and I'll help my mother in her garden. It's the garden that once grew vegetables but now houses tulips and irises and ferns, black-eyed Susans and purple Johnny Jump Ups. There are gravestones in this garden, for all our long-dead pets. (Lifelong Stephen King fans, we still call it the Pet Sematary, convinced our old cats come back on occasion to haunt us.) The stones are pressed into the earth next to the compost pile we built when I was small, and we spend a while looking for the grave of my hamster, but he seems to have been lost among the ferns. Above us, the massive silver maple shades the garden, fifty feet high and nearly as wide.

"I can't believe how huge this has grown," I say to my mother.

"Do you remember when we planted it?" she says to me.

"Of course I do," I say. "How could I forget?"

We spend the afternoon in the garden, under this great maple, raking leaves and pulling up weeds, preparing the ground to be turned, planted, and mulched. We sweat together in the sun, and for a moment, it feels like no time has passed. And I feel gratitude for my mother, for teaching me how to make things grow; for my grandmother, who taught us both. I feel gratitude for my family, both biological and chosen, for the mothers and nonmothers alike, for the various lives and homes and families they have built—who have grieved the choices they've made and lived in the joy of them. As I pull up weeds, I hold with them the knowledge that, regardless of what we make or raise or choose in this life, we'll all disappear in the end, seed pods spinning away on the wind. But maybe, if we're lucky, we'll land somewhere again and take root. And in the meantime, while we're still here, we'll press our fingers into the earth and leave something of ourselves behind.

DRIFTLESS

Now by the path I climbed, I journey back. / The oaks have grown; I have been long away.

—Edna St. Vincent Millay

In the summer of '89, it barely rained. More than fifty days passed without a drop. The corn dried up. The crops didn't yield. Acres of farmland turned brown in the sun. Neighbors and livestock died in the heat; wildfires tore across the plains. But we were too young to worry, to know what the word *drought* could mean to a small midwestern town like ours, or the miles of farmland that surrounded it.

We spent our days in the fields and woods, the sun high and bright through the leaves. We traveled in packs; we wandered alone. We were great in number; we were two at a time. We scuffed up our jeans, scraped up our knees, tore holes in shirts that got snagged on branches. We climbed the trees and yelled into the wind, and no one heard but us. We ran for miles, the dry summer grasses nicking our shins, trying to find the place where land met sky. We hiked through the goldenrod, up to our waists, our eyes swelling and legs itching, and laid down to watch the clouds move east. And then we walked back the way we came, outlines of our bodies on the ground behind us, bright-yellow dust on our skin.

We were people of the prairie. We were people of the trees. We were the maple and birch, the oak and elm. We were corn and wheat and soy, we were the black earth that grew it. We were bluestem and switchgrass, we were rivers and lakes. And out past the horizon of hardwood and pine, we were mountains.

We were girls. We were boys. We were neither and both.

We were small. We were nothing. We were taller than the trees.

In southwestern Wisconsin, where I grew up, there exists a geological phenomenon. It's called the Driftless Area, a narrow stretch of land that, somewhat miraculously, was bypassed by the last continental glacier. What results is a strange, rare terrain that extends some twenty thousand square miles, composed primarily of that small corner of the state and edging over the borders of Iowa, Minnesota, and Illinois. Its name refers to *drift*—rocks and gravel, silt and clay and sand—the sediment left in the wake of retreating glaciers. It's the stuff that exists beneath the surface of most terrain. But here in the Driftless Area, such elemental makeup is scarce, when it exists at all.

The Upper Midwest owes much of its landscape to the movement of the glaciers: Minnesota's ten thousand lakes, carved from the earth by walls of ice and filled with water; the long rolling prairies of south-central Wisconsin and northern Illinois. But the Driftless Area, also known as the Paleozoic Plateau, is marked instead by a landscape wholly unlike the rest of the region: that of rolling hills and steep, forested hillsides that stretch down to valleys, sharp limestone cliffs and bedrock outcroppings with lakes and quarries below them, paths cut by winding rivers and cold-water streams. If you look to the horizon, you'll see the most striking part of the region: small mountains, or mounds, and among them monadnocks—strange, solitary peaks that seem to rise up, out of nowhere, from the middle of a plain.

These are the tops of ancient mountains, whole ranges long buried beneath the surface of the earth. After generations of erosion, when layers of softer rock have been washed away in the formation of the surrounding valleys, the harder rock is all that remains, emerging from the earth as isolated mountains.

The mountains shouldn't be here. They're incongruous, out of place. They're an anomaly, an abnormality, a glitch in the system. They're also beautiful. The landscape of Wisconsin is both forest and farm, lands both flat and rolling. It is endless prairie and deep, untouched woods. It is a place of lakes both great and small, of rivers, creeks, and streams. It is a place whose lands are neither one thing nor the other, a whole containing multitudes. But the mountains, they're not quite right. Amid the rest of the landscape, it would seem clear to someone first encountering them that they just don't belong.

This is the landscape that made me.

I n the summer of '98, we drank pilfered beer in unfinished basements. We stayed up late and cut our fingers with scissors, pressing them together until our pulses beat in time. We snuck out to the softball field just before sunrise, the sky a blaze of black and blue. We ran the bases, our legs wobbly, the sand and rock beneath the mud, our bare feet slapping against the cold slick of it. We passed a bottle between us, taking long pulls like old pros, like we watched so many people do before us. We rolled our bodies like barrels down the hill to center field, where cleat marks were carved in cold earth, where the ghosts of mosquitoes still buzzed. We breathed hard, our backs on the ground, our knees and elbows slick with sand; our bodies close but not touching. Silent as the sky before a storm.

We were girls but not yet women. We were something in between. We were fifteen; we were on fire. Our skin was hot all the time, buzzing and open and raw, like it could be peeled off entirely—a whole girl-shaped shell, like the thin shedding vellum of a sunburn. To quiet the constant itch of it, we did everything we could to feel something else, to feel anything or nothing at all. We drank, we fought, we went without sleep. We lay on our backs on bedroom floors and turned the music up loud, longing to be the subjects of love songs. We talked on the phone late into the night, the long pink coil of cords wrapped around fingers and wrists. Breasts smashed into sports bras, dirt beneath black-painted nails, we were starting to think about the power our bodies might hold. We did not yet know of the power they lacked, or that which could be taken. We tried on skirts, and our shirts got tighter. We shaved our legs and hair-sprayed our bangs and painted our eyes. We rode with boys in pickup trucks out into the country, the summer wind in our hair. We started kissing those boys, and sometimes let them go further. We might have dreamed of kissing girls, though none of us had the words for it yet.

We ached for everything, and for anything other than this: the slow, quiet life of our small hometown, its stillness and silence, the feeling we were stuck. We knew that somewhere, beyond this place, the whole huge world was waiting.

The word *monadnock* means "isolated hill." It comes, most likely, from the language of the Abenaki, a First Nation tribe from the northern United States—some of whom made their way into Wisconsin in the 1600s, during colonial oppression in the eastern Great Lakes States, and would later be forced out again. It's a word that's assumed to share a root with *menonadenak* ("smooth mountain") and *menadena* ("isolated mountain"). In German, the colonial language of much of Wisconsin and the Upper Midwest, the word is *inselberg*, meaning "island mountain."

One such stretch of monadnocks, beginning about thirty miles north of my hometown on the eastern edge of the Driftless Area, is the

Baraboo Range. It stretches for twenty-five miles in length and varies from five to ten miles in width, reaching elevations of up to seventeen hundred feet. Their very shape is a juxtaposition: edges both sharp and rolling, steep angles cut through rock, climbing and reaching and dropping smoothly away, their surfaces draped in a thick green blanket of trees. At the base of the range, the Wisconsin River—which otherwise travels north to south, splitting the state in half—takes a sharp and sudden turn west, wending its way to the Mississippi. Along this same stretch of land is the Mississippi Flyway—the migratory path along which birds migrate north in the springtime and south in the fall, along that great mystic waterway that eventually leads to the sea.

Once, I met a man and fell in love. He came from the flattest plains of Illinois but had come to Wisconsin to study the trees. By then I lived in Madison, the capital city—an isthmus, a narrow strip of land between lakes. We spent our days walking the streets of our small island city, along the banks of Monona and Mendota, Waubesa and Wingra, those bodies of water that gave this place its first name, long before it was a city: Four Lakes, a name given by the Ho-Chunk, the earliest inhabitants of southern Wisconsin. We walked along the Yahara River, which connected the two largest lakes and led us toward home. We walked in the woods north of town, through forests of white pine and balsam fir, through cedar, hemlock, and tamarack. Through bur oak and poplar, basswood and chestnut, box elder and beech. Through trees with more dangerous names, like buckthorn and chokecherry. He knew the Latin and taught me their forgotten names. Quizzed me beneath the fat heart-shaped leaves of the catalpa, beneath the long trailing strands of the weeping willow, beneath the maple and birch. *Acer Rubrum. Pinus Strobus. Betulaceae.* Under the Dutch elms, he told me of the disease that had almost wiped them from the earth. He held the buds in his fingers, ran his hands over the bark. *If you hold your hand here long enough,* he said, *you can feel the life of it hum inside your skin.* And I wanted him to touch me like he touched the trees.

Together we explored the Driftless Area—the stretch of land that reached north to Winona, south to Galena, and west to Dubuque, where the stuff that lived beneath the surface in all the surrounding land simply did not exist. A place where, in the wake of something missing, there existed something far greater.

We hiked through tall pines to the edge of the woods, where the land broke beneath us and fell sharply away, revealing a slow rolling valley below and a seemingly infinite horizon beyond. Out there were the peaks of the Baraboo Range, and the rivers named—like so many bodies of both water and land, like so many cities and towns—for the native tribes from whom the land was taken: the Chippewa, the Kickapoo, the Pecatonica, where my mother and her seven siblings fished for perch when they were kids. Somewhere not far west was the Mississippi. The wind tossed the grasses at our feet, made them bend and blow and buckle like knees. Out there, he said, in the land of Amish farmers—in the land before them of the Ho-Chunk—he had once built a cabin. He'd take me there, he said, one day.

The man and I liked to hop trains. We lived near the tracks, on the east side of town, where freight trains carried coal into the city. He taught me how to do it, gave me a lesson one summer day. When we heard the horn, and felt the humming in our feet, he said: *Grab on to a rung as it passes—it won't be going fast—and hold on. Run alongside till you catch your footing, then swing your legs up. Let it carry you.* And so we hopped the train that ran through the trees, like we would for years to come—when we were bored, when we wanted to kill the time. We rode the rails, our fingers wrapped tight around the rusted ladder. We tried to yell, our faces to the sky, the wind keeping our voices stuck in our throats.

We went north one summer, to where the deciduous trees of the south give way to evergreens. We went to a place I'd spent summers as a kid, to a lake surrounded on all sides by dense forests of cedar and pine. It was August, and hot—hotter, we'd heard, than the drought of '89. But the high trees gave us shade, and the wind that breathed through the branches was cool on our skin. We swam in the lake and the water was cold, and for a moment or two I let my arms and legs go limp, let my body fall beneath the surface. I opened my eyes in the murky brown water, and in the darkness felt the sand and silt and tiny rocks between my toes. I saw schools of small fish, bluegill maybe, like my father taught me to catch so many summers before, on a lake just like this one. Standing on the dock, he'd shown me how to bait the hook myself, how to stab a nightcrawler through its chest with the sharp metal hook and tie its body in a knot. I'd wanted to run, the slick thing writhing in my hands, blood and dirt on my fingers, but I refused to stop until the worm was tied, knotted tight in my hand and still wriggling.

That night, the man and I lay on our backs on the ground, surrounded by forest. Above us, a small opening of stars broke through the canopy of trees. I ran a finger down the length of his forearms and across his wrists, tracing the paths of his scars and comparing them with my own, drawing routes on a map and searching for patterns, finding two matching sets of parallel lines on our shoulders. The scars were still red then, but eventually they would fade to pink, then white, so pale over time they were barely visible at all.

There was a red-haired girl who lived in our house, who was ours but never mine. Her skin, like his, was the color of paper birch, her hair like the leaves of sugar maples in the fall. We stepped lightly around each other, careful and guarded, wanting always to make contact but never knowing quite how to take hold. Each day she looked more and more like him.

In the springtime when she was seven, we walked together through the park, along the lake by our house. We touched the trunks of ancient oaks and stopped at a newly planted maple, young and thin, still held up by posts and wire, small buds beginning to bloom.

I said: *One day this tree will be taller than you.*

And she said: *I will grow tall as the sky.*

And I was her age in a heartbeat, planting trees with my mother. A red maple in the front yard and a silver maple in the back, near the mountain ash with the bright-orange berries that would wither and rot after I left home, and would eventually be cut down. In the spring, we planted perennials: the burning bush, the bleeding heart. And I cried that first September, when the flowers—small and thick and pink, whose petals had just a few weeks before been bursting—shriveled and fell to the ground.

Once, I kicked a hole in the wall. Once I threw books from their shelves, pounded my fists against his chest. I screamed as he held my wrists: *I never wanted this.*

I didn't choose to have children of my own. I didn't choose to share my life with a child, to help take care of a child, and certainly not then, when I was something of a child myself—angry and sad and still so young, often drunk and filled with a rage I could not yet name. I had no idea how to share my home, or my life, with this small girl.

But then there she was: six and on my shoulders, running down the sidewalk and laughing; eight and curled up beside me on a red couch, her small toes kneading my shins. Eleven and across from me in our favorite booth at the diner.

"Your hair," she said one night, over vegan sloppy joes. We'd walked to dinner as we always had, in our neighborhood by the lake, the sun hanging low as the waves lapped against the shore.

It was a game we played, the three of us, our sudden little family, while we ate. What physical trait about me do you like best?

"Your eyes," I said, "but it's too hard to pick just one."

And she smiled, and her teeth were crooked, and she was missing one toward the back. Two straws in a milkshake, whipped cream on her nose, our faces so close as we drank.

Once, I met a woman and fell in love. She had a body like the earth, both hard and soft, the slope and curve of muscle under golden skin, her hair the color of a wheat field in summer. She smelled like the earth too; a musky scent of dirt and sweat she wore like perfume. She had come to Wisconsin from the East Coast to study the earth: rocks and sediment and sand, the stuff beneath the surface. On a T-shirt she wore in the summer, layers of earth were cut open like a cake, a fork next to the slice on a plate. With her I wanted to eat the earth, too, put whole pieces of it in my mouth, taste the dirt and sand on my tongue, fill my body with it. I wanted to be buried in it, to smell it always on my skin. I stopped showering every day like her, so we could smell like the earth together.

It was surprising, this love. It came on like a quake. It was consuming and sudden, the way such loves are when you are young and are never quite the same as you get older. She was the first woman I loved in this way, and beneath my feet I felt the ground start to shift, exposing a new layer of earth sliced and plated before me. A fast crack, a fissure, and then an opening, and the world around us seemed to fall away. We stood alone atop an island mountain of our own making.

We worked together in her garden, her backyard in the summer blooming with life. Tomatoes and green beans, peppers and kale, carrots and onions and mint. Dirt on our skin and grass stains on our knees, we dug our fingers into the soil, and I could swear I felt the pulse of the earth beating in time with our own. We planted and harvested, ate vegetables all summer long, standing at her kitchen counter on Sunday mornings, the smell of fresh herbs in the window. Together we were part of the earth, connected to the land, even if our bodies were connected for only a brief time.

I wanted to give her everything. I told her this, or tried to, as best as any Midwesterner could, my palms open. I thought we, too, might hop a train one day—that we might grab the rungs and go somewhere far away. That we might let the tracks lead us. That we might hold on. She held my hand in a car late at night, and we watched the train pass on the tracks across the street from her house. A rumble of ground beneath us, a horn in the darkness, canceling out the sound. After it passed her fingers slipped from mine, and I was alone again in the silence of the night. And I knew then that we all, eventually, let go.

The word *driftless* is so curious. It's a paradox, the word *drift* suggesting movement and *less* without. It's a word that at once recalls motion while implying stasis. A word that refers inherently to lack, whose identity is defined by what it doesn't possess. It's a word that suggests stagnancy, stillness, something that remains, but at the same time feels like something moving. A simultaneous leaving and staying.

For years I've returned to this word, turning it over on my tongue. I try to crack it open, inspect its incongruities, make sense of its contradictions. I try to solve the puzzle of it. I try to hold it, keep it still in my hands, but every time I think I've grasped it, held it tight in my fist, it slips through my fingers like sand.

Just south of Baraboo, on the eastern edge of the Driftless Area, there is a place called Devil's Lake. It's an anomaly within an anomaly, the only natural upland lake in the region, with no discernable entrance or exit waterways. It's also one of the most geologically interesting locations in the state, with five-hundred-foot quartzite bluffs and uncanny rock formations, and the most stunning view of the Driftless Area. Wisconsin's Ho-Chunk Nation once made their winter head-quarters on the north shore of the lake. One of two First Nations of Wisconsin, the Ho-Chunk are one of several indigenous tribes that likely descended from ancient mound-building cultures, and if you go to Devil's Lake and look hard enough, you can still find the effigy mounds that were built more than a thousand years ago—there's one in the shape of a winged man, one in the shape of a lynx. The lake's origi-nal name, "Day-wa-kun-chunk," meant "sacred lake" or "holy lake." In his 1930 account of the area, Ulysses S. White of the Ho-Chunk Nation wrote, "But the white people call it Devils Lake."

Devil's Lake is now a state park. Much of the Ho-Chunk, also formerly known as the Wisconsin Winnebago, were forcibly displaced to Nebraska in the 1800s. Today, only approximately eight thousand Ho-Chunk Nation citizens remain, predominantly in Wisconsin. When I was young, I rarely thought of the Ho-Chunk. I heard their name in passing, in radio advertisements for the casino, on a small sign as we drove past the reservations of the Wisconsin Northwoods, where my family had a small cabin. I rarely thought of any of the state's indig-enous tribes, even when I swam in lakes that were named for them, when I played softball in towns with names like Wausau and Waukesha, Menominee and Mazomanie, Minocqua and Mosinee.

But I think about them now, every time I go home and every time I leave. I think about leaving as choice, and leaving as violence, as a forc-ing out. I think about how the places that bear us, the lands upon which we make our lives and our homes, are so often what shape our sense of self. I think of how easily that self can fracture, can become multiple and more complex, can be completely destroyed, when the body leaves a place it once called home. I think about displacement—whether by the forced removal from a family or a land or by the willing desire to leave—to escape, to build a new life in exile, and sometimes take a new name in other lands. To start again in a new place that might someday, too, become your home.

It took me a long time to understand that the lands that bore me—those that made me, that I still call my home—were stolen. That the people who called this land home first were slaughtered, so that white colonists could claim it. That these prairies and valleys and bluffs and lakes and trees I grew up thinking were mine never were at all. That no one can ever claim a land as their own. It's a truth about our bodies and the land that those who lived here first knew most of all. It's a truth that people like me are never taught, a story we don't want to tell.

O nce, in the summer, the man and I drove to Devil's Lake. We hiked to the highest point and stood on the edge of a steep out-cropping, looking over the dark-blue lake below.

What if I jumped? he said. And I said, *I'd catch you. I'm stronger than you think.*

We dropped rocks into the wide, dark mouth of the water but never heard them fall. I thought of rock quarries near my hometown where, as a teenager, I had come with the kids in my class to drink beer around bonfires, where we wore sneakers to run should the cops come. Where I made out with boys in pickup trucks, let them put their hands on my body, run their fingers along borders that had never been crossed.

We're made of sturdy stuff, I said, dropping a pebble into the dark. *We have a thicker skin.* A tough constitution, hardy stock. Rough and tumble. Skinned knees and charley horses, goose eggs and black eyes, but never a broken bone. Stoic like the farmers who came before us. Harder than the earth in a drought.

These were the words that had been passed down for generations, the stories we grew up hearing, that we were told until we believed them. Until the mythology of the place we had come from—what it meant to be *midwestern*—had become so deeply ingrained, so much a part of our histories and mythologies, the stories we told about ourselves, that we believed it.

O f all the states in the union, none has had more names, more spellings, or more interpretations, than Wisconsin. Attributed at various points to the languages of the Menominee, Ojibwa, Potawatomi, Sauk-Fox, Winnebago, and French, it has been called, among several other names, Mesconsin, Meskousing, Mishkonsing, Ouisconsin, Owisconsing, Quisconsing, Weeskonsan, Wishkonsing, and Wiskonsin. Among several interpretations, the word has been said to mean "Gathering of the Waters" and "Stream of a Thousand Isles."

T hey say things grow differently in the Midwest. That the crops grow stronger to survive the elements, which are volatile and unpredictable. That the heat is heavier, the air is drier; the winters are colder, the droughts harsher, and that the rains can be unrelenting but that the soil beneath the surface is more fertile. That life, somehow, sustains. As a child of the farmlands, they say your body grows differently too. They say your back and shoulders are broader, your hands are harder. They say *big-boned* and *built like a boy* and *built like a barn*, that a body is born to work. They say the fields and the plains make your body grow stronger.

What they don't say is this: As you grow you will slowly erode, the impenetrable rock walls of your body ground down over time to softer stone, until all that has been cultivated, all that once was lush and verdant, will be washed away by rain. That the high sun will eventually drop from the sky and the air will turn cold, and you will run through sudden darkened fields, and you will try with no fortune to find the trees. And all that is left around you will be prairie, dried up and dusky and fallow with drought, its reaches vaster than you can see. And the shadows of those who once ran alongside you will fade with the last of the light, their voices disappearing on the wind.

The Driftless Area, like the natural world, is in trouble. As I write this, developers threaten to build power lines that would cut through the Driftless land of Wisconsin, a project that would fell trees and kill plant life and pollute rivers. The area, too, like so many in the state and around the country, is being developed: stretches of land being torn up and turned into condos and cheaply built houses, software companies and tech firms where once there was farmland; blacktop and cement and prefab siding where there once was only earth and trees. The economy, they say, is in better shape than it was, but at what cost to the land? Each time I go home, a little more of the landscape has changed. A little more of the land that made me, a little more of the place I love, is gone. I worry, sometimes, that the next time I come home there will be nothing left at all.

Just a few miles west of the house where I grew up, and visible from the windows of my childhood bedroom, is a stretch of small mountains called the Blue Mounds. It's a small, sloping range that appears dark blue in the distance. The row of hills, which reaches the highest elevation in the region, houses caves beneath the ground, tunnels of limestones and graphite and quartz. It's a place I explored as a kid, hiking steep trails and climbing up to the top of a fire tower on the eastern end of the park, the highest point in southern Wisconsin, with an impossibly vast view of the Driftless Area, its peaks and hills and valleys and bluffs. On class field trips, we explored the caves below the mounds, where I first learned of erosion—of stalactites, stalagmites, and the way that water, almost magically it seemed to me then, possessed the ability to form both. Brushing hands in the dark, the *drip drip* of water against rock, we saw cave drawings from some of the area's earliest inhabitants: a deer head, or maybe an elk, with a straight line running from its mouth to its center. This, we were told, was the heartline.

On summer nights when I was young—the kind of nights that seemed to catch hold of the sun and refuse to let go, when the big smoldering ball of it hovers for hours just above the horizon—I'd lie on my bedroom floor and look out the window that faced west, watching the sky settle over the Blue Mounds. To the south and east, and just across the street, there was prairie, forest, and farm. But out there in the west there were mountains—the kind that seem small to me now that I've seen the Rockies, the Alps, and the Pyrenees. But back then, these mountains loomed even larger in the closeness of dusk, in the enveloping darkness of night—the blues and reds above them growing darker, the colors like a bruise, the swelling sphere of the sun eventually slipping behind the peaks, the last ribbons of orange and yellow swallowed into blue.

And what was left in the twilight were the silhouettes of those strange, small mountains: crouching, towering, standing vigil, I imagined, keeping me safe through the night. The mountains, I thought, were mine.

I didn't realize until I was much older, long after I left Wisconsin, that the land I came from was different. I didn't appreciate the miracle of it. When a girl is very young, especially in a place where to be different is suspect, she sees such difference as a curse, as a cage, as a blight on the terrain, a topography of rocks to struggle across and eventually escape. It isn't until she leaves that she is able to see the beauty of the land that made her.

J ust before I left home and moved to New York, more than a decade ago now, the man I loved and the woman I loved moved in together in the little house by the railroad tracks. They lived not as lovers but as friends. The red-haired girl lived there, too, like she once had lived with me—coming and going on nights and weekends, a backpack stuffed with books and clothes, getting taller every day. Over time, the three of them became a little family, too, planting and harvesting the garden, three sets of hands in the dirt, making meals and eating together, curling up to watch movies on the couch. They would call me, sometimes, on a video screen, a thousand miles between us and the connection bad. The images of their faces flickered and swam, a picture that looked something like the sea. I sat alone in New York and they sat together in Wisconsin, waving at me through the pixelated distance. On the kitchen counter, I saw the carrots they had plucked from the garden, the basil and mint they had pulled. And this, I realized, was what it meant to be homesick. To long for both people and place, for family and the land upon which it was built.

And that night, as I watched the digitized faces of my loves halfway across the country, I knew that I would never stay in one place long. That I would remove myself from each place I went, maybe right as it started to feel like home. That I might plant myself in a plot of land just long enough for roots to take hold, then pull myself up from the earth and keep moving. Despite the pain of each new beginning, and maybe also because of it.

M y last summer in Wisconsin, I go with the man I love to the cabin he built, near a town called Sugar Grove, in the heart of the Driftless Area. The red-haired girl is with us, too, and we build a bonfire one last time; we run and we dance and we sing in the woods. It is late August, and a few days later I will pack up some boxes, toss them into a truck, and drive a thousand miles east. I will leave behind the fields and farmland, the rivers and lakes named for slaughtered Native tribes, the trees and the mountains and the endless prairie—the only place I've ever called home—and I will start again, alone. When I get there, I'll take a train to the ocean. I'll stand in salt water and sit in the sand, a great glittering city behind me, my home in a past life just out of view, a reminder that we are driftless too. We are mountains, small and solitary, rising bare among the plains. And the rocks and silt and sand and clay—the stuff that should be inside us, right here below the skin—just doesn't exist in us. But there is fertile soil somewhere too; we just have to search to find it.

I'll take the train back from the beach at sunrise, toward the city I will someday call home too. It will be strange and massive, this new city, looming and close; it will be loud and hard, a great forest of metal and concrete, a horizon built entirely by man, buildings of brick and cement and glass. There will be no hills or forest here, no prairie or farm, no mounds and no mountains, no walking barefoot in the grass. I will miss the land that made me, sometimes so much the pain will be unbearable. I will grow harder here in this city, but I will grow.

And the people I knew and loved will grow too. Some of them will leave our homeland behind, moving on to new cities and continents, new prairies and farms, new lakes and oceans and trees. Some of them will stay. And there will be other girls like me, like the red-haired girl, and those I'll never know, girls I'll never watch grow but whose bodies will be small mountains, too. And we will all remain suspended in the glow of a fire, on a late-August Wisconsin night, somewhere out in the Driftless Area—out in the land of the Ho-Chunk Nation, out in the land that made us. And we will run until we find the trees, and we will yell into the wind. And our voices will rise from our lungs and up through the leaves, will climb quarry walls and sail over the high peaks of mountains, along the big winding river that leads to the sea. And the sound will surge and pitch and swell until it shakes the branches, although no one will hear but us. And we will fall together when we reach the river, the level low and the banks dry from another summer without rain, and we will throw our bodies into the water. And when the shock of the cold hits our skin, bare feet digging into the rock and silt and sand, we will feel the blood beat louder inside us. It will thrum beneath our skin. It will rush with the current and we will let go, let it carry us out to sea, and we will know we are alive.

ACKNOWLEDGMENTS

In some respects this book has been a decade in the making, but in reality it's been a lifetime. It was a long and often lonely road to get here, and there were stretches of time when I was sure I wouldn't make it. But there were people at every turn who kept me going, who pushed me forward, and for whom I am eternally grateful.

Thank you first to my teachers, in particular at the University of Wisconsin: John Tiedemann, who helped me fall in love with literature when I thought I already had, and Rob Nixon and Martin Nystrand, who introduced me to the essay; and those at Sarah Lawrence College: Vijay Seshadri, Stephen O'Connor, Nick Flynn, Suzanne Gardinier, and Rachel Cohen, who helped me take that form further than I knew it could go; and Jo Ann Beard—thesis advisor, magnetic north, mentor, and friend—who listened, who helped me listen, who told me what I had to say was worth saying.

To the greater Sarah Lawrence community, for giving me such a rich and lasting literary life; to Brian Morton, Paige Ackerson-Kiely, Amparo Rios, Patricia Dunn, and Sweet Orifice for inviting me back so often and making me feel so at home.

To my students, and to the many writers who have trusted me with their stories over the years, who teach me to be a better writer, editor, reader, listener, and human.

To my first editors, Marc Eisen and Kenneth Burns at *Isthmus*, who took a chance on a twenty-one-year-old kid, let her pitch her own stories (some of which inspired material in this book), and gave her the cover; who not only published my first work, but helped me believe that "writer" was a job, and that it was one I could do. To the editors who published some of the essays in this book in their earliest forms: Ander Monson and Nicole Walker at *DIAGRAM*, who dug my weird little moths; Robert James Russell and Jeff Pfaller at *Midwestern Gothic*, and Robert Atwan at *Best American Essays*, who understood what "Driftless" meant; Ashley Strosnider and Kwame Dawes at *Prairie Schooner*, for giving "The Finger of God" its first home, and Esmé Weijun Wang for choosing it to live there.

To Calliope Nicholas and Monika Burczyk at the Millay Colony for the Arts, for giving me a room of my own in the barn that Vincent built, where these essays began to become a book and my path to finishing it became clear. To Cara Benson for getting me there.

To the hardworking librarians at the Barneveld Public Library, for their back-room archives, and at the Boulder Junction Public Library in the Wisconsin Northwoods for their help (and internet connection) as I researched and finished the first draft. To Orin Greb for checking in on me while I was alone in those woods, and for the old-fashioneds and fish fry. To Ann Mawicke for giving me something to weed.

To the sweet folks at Sweetleaf Coffee Roasters in Greenpoint, Brooklyn, for keeping me well fueled and allowing me to set up camp for so many days on end.

To my Poets & Writers crew: I miss you.

To my *Paris Review* softball team: Thanks for letting me be a ringer.

To my roller derby family: Harlot Brontë ain't got shit on you.

To my agent, the brilliant and badass Adriann Ranta Zurhellen, for believing in this book, for being a pillar of support and a sea of calm. To my editor, Hafizah Geter, for understanding it from the beginning, when not many people did, and helping to make it so much better;

and to Jill Soloway, Carmen Johnson, Emma Reh, Jennifer Blanksteen, Robin O'Dell, Lucy Silag, and the whole TOPPLE/Little A team for their hard work in bringing this book to life. To Micaela Alcaino for creating a gorgeous cover and Beth Parker for her publicity brilliance.

To an army of friends, family, and fellow writers—far too many to name—who have carried me, and to those whose help has been critical in creating this book: Melissa Febos, first reader, confidante, and extraordinarily generous friend, who has kept me afloat; Beth Aplin, Amy Beth Wright, and Stephanie Mankins, who read the earliest drafts of these essays and offered invaluable feedback; Ben LeRoy, partner in adventure and tornado chasing, who put the wheels in motion; Elena Passarello, Alex Marzano-Lesnevich, Megan Stielstra, and Lacy Johnson, who took the time to read this book and write some truly humbling words about it; Michael Taeckens, Kimberly Burns, and Whitney Peeling for the amazing support, advice, and friendship; Kat Van Hampler, Rachel Weinberg, Victoria Echeverría, Beth Wendt, Jennie Matthews, Gretchen Treu, Rae Kyritsi, Kerri Poulson, Karen Hinz, Jude Toche, Victoria Cooper, Amy Gall, Katherine Hurley, Lucky Neuenschwander, Sean Campbell, Beth Binhammer, Amber Janssen, Stephanie Schneider, Kristin Cerling Niemann, Sarah Erickson, Scott and Lauren Graves, Tabea Vohmann, and all the Madison girls, whose lives are in these pages; Jessica Ankeny, Rachel Lieff Axelbank, Davi Marra, Briana Parker, Kelly Forsythe, Joni Tevis, Jimin Han, Christie Taylor, Kima Jones, Kristen Radtke, and Jeanna Kadlec, for advice, phone calls, postcards, texts, dinners, and many drinks. To my bandmates David Schneider, Michael Myers, Angela Savvas, Alex Lezburg, and Alex Picca, for the music.

To Paul Houseman and Paige Wilder, without whom this book would not be.

To Al Wright, Jerry Wright, Sue Clerkin, and Joyce Aschliman, for telling a stranger some of your hardest stories. And to all those affected by the Barneveld tornado, whose stories are in these pages too.

To Mount Horeb, my first hometown; and to Madison, where my heart still lives.

To my extended family, on both sides, for not disowning me yet.

To Bob, Sue, and Maggie Walsh, for being a second and surrogate family.

To my parents, earliest champions and number one fans, for encouraging me to be what I wanted to be, for helping me believe I could, for giving me everything you had to help me get there, and for always saying *Do it*—even when it meant moving a thousand miles away. Thank you.

Finally, to Jonathan Walsh, my partner, challenger, creative collaborator, and closest reader, for gifting me that first at-home writing retreat; for being so supportive every time I disappeared to work on this thing; for your unwavering belief in me, even and especially when I lack it; for loving me better than I ever thought possible.

ABOUT THE AUTHOR

Photo © 2019 Maggie Walsh

Melissa Faliveno is a writer, editor, and teacher. The former senior editor of *Poets & Writers Magazine*, she has also had essays and interviews appear in *Bitch* magazine, the *Millions*, *Prairie Schooner*, *Isthmus*, *DIAGRAM*, and *Midwestern Gothic*, among others, and received a notable selection in *The Best American Essays 2016*. Born and raised in small-town Wisconsin, she currently lives in Brooklyn, New York, and teaches writing at Sarah Lawrence College. *Tomboyland* is her first book. Learn more at www.melissafaliveno.com.